BEN SHAHN

NEW DEAL ARTIST IN A COLD WAR CLIMATE, 1947–1954

AMERICAN STUDIES SERIES

William H. Goetzmann, Editor

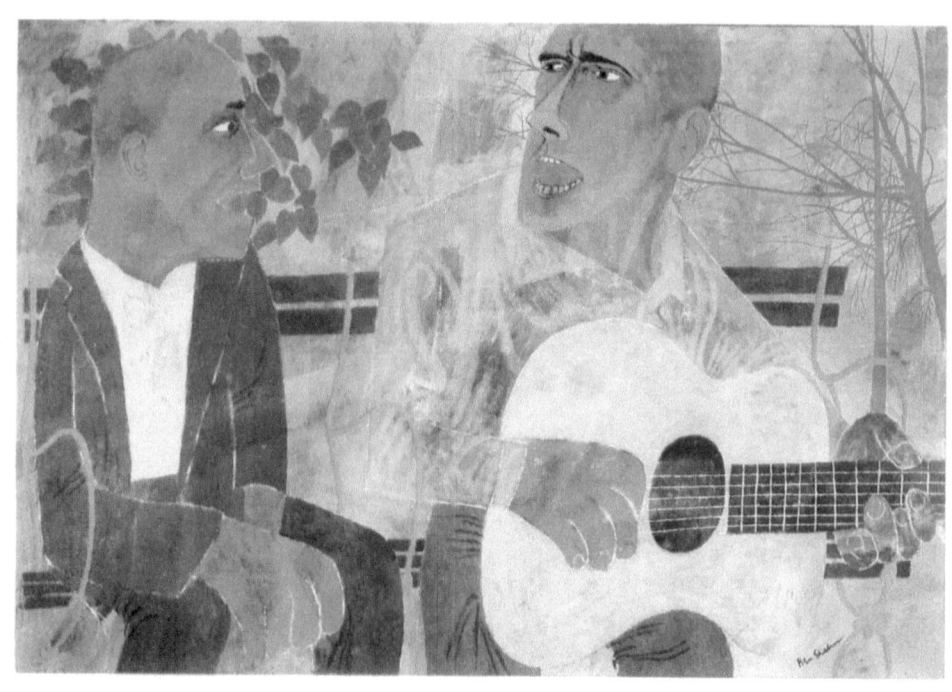

Ben Shahn, *Nocturne*, 1949
Tempera
26¾ × 40″
Collection: Willard Straight Hall,
Student Union, Cornell University

BEN SHAHN

NEW DEAL ARTIST IN A COLD WAR CLIMATE, 1947–1954

FRANCES K. POHL

UNIVERSITY OF TEXAS PRESS, AUSTIN

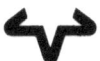

First edition, 1989

Requests for permission to reproduce material from this
work should be sent to: Permissions, University of Texas Press,
Box 7819, Austin, Texas 78713-7819.

LIBRARY OF CONGRESS CATALOGING-IN-PUBLICATION DATA
Pohl, Frances K. (Frances Kathryn), 1952–
    Ben Shahn : New Deal artist in a cold war climate, 1947–1954
Frances K. Pohl.—1st ed.
        p.   cm.—(American studies series)
    Bibliography: p.
    Includes index.

    ISBN: 978-0-292-75538-3

    1. Shahn, Ben, 1898–1969—Criticism and interpretation.   2. Social
problems in art.   3. Politics in art.   I. Title.   II. Series.
N6537.S5P64   1989
760'.092'4—dc19   88-39304
[B]   CIP

Cover illustration: *Composition with Clarinets and Tin Horn*, 1951.
© The Detroit Institute of Arts. Full documentation on page 114.

See page 238 for acknowledgments of permission to use archival and
previously published materials.

To my parents, sisters, and brother

CONTENTS

ACKNOWLEDGMENTS

This book was many years in the making. It began with my master's thesis at the University of British Columbia and continued through my years as a doctoral student at the University of California, Los Angeles, and into my tenure at Pomona College. All three institutions have been stimulating environments within which to work. At UBC I was fortunate enough to have as my M.A. advisor Serge Guilbaut, who encouraged me to pursue my interest in Shahn. Albert Boime, David Kunzle, and Jonathan Wiener helped guide the next stage of my research through to completion at UCLA. It was here, also, that Blanche Wiesen Cook alerted me to the importance of the Freedom of Information Act (FOIA) for historical research. My colleagues at Pomona College—Gerald Ackerman, Judson Emerick, and George Gorse—provided me with much-needed support and friendship during the final revisions of the manuscript.

My work has been made even more rewarding by the people I have met during the course of my research who knew Shahn or knew of him and who held him in the highest esteem. Even if they did not totally agree with his political or aesthetic views, they regarded him as a man of integrity and commitment.

I would like to extend special thanks to Bernarda Bryson Shahn and Jonathan Shahn for their hospitality and willingness to share information and time with me, and to Ezra Shahn for the many hours spent in the estate warehouse in New York. Special thanks are also due to Mirella Bentivoglio; Garnett McCoy, former director of the Archives of American Art in Washington, D.C., and his staff; the staff of the Venice Biennial Archives in Venice; and Stephen L. Taller, whose collection of published material on and by Shahn is undoubtedly the most complete in existence, and whose enthusiasm for Shahn and his work seems to know no bounds.

My work on Shahn would not have been possible without financial support, and I would like to thank, in this regard, the Social Sciences and Humanities Research Council of Canada, the Edward A. Dickson Art History Doctoral Fellowship Fund at UCLA, and the Faculty Research Fund at Pomona College. An earlier version of Chapter 5 appeared in the March 1981 issue of the British journal *Art History*.

Historians often experience moments of *déjà vu* in the course of their investigations, and this has certainly been true with my work on Shahn. Reading about the 1988 Contragate hearings in the *Los Angeles Times* immediately brought to mind a 1952 article by Carey McWilliams in the *Nation* on J. Edgar Hoover's network of FBI informers in the White House in the early 1950s. President Reagan's "Project Truth," begun in November 1981 to counter Soviet "disinformation," parallels President Truman's "campaign of truth," begun in April 1950 to combat Soviet "propaganda." Mikhail Gorbachev's current "peace offensive" brings to mind a similar effort by Nikita Khrushchev in the mid-1950s to open up dialogue, including cultural exchanges, between the United States and the Soviet Union. This does not mean that history repeats itself. The 1980s are not the 1950s. Yet the events of the 1980s do have a history, and understanding this history will help us understand, and hopefully respond to, what is happening today. It is this realization, more than anything else, that has sustained me throughout my work on Shahn.

INTRODUCTION

> It was pretty easy to march with the liberals and the
> progressives in the years of Roosevelt. We knew he
> wouldn't let us go wrong. Until another leader we can
> trust, as we trusted him, takes up the fight we like to
> think of as ours—the fight for tolerance, which is the
> basis of any fight for peace—it's going to be tough to
> be a liberal. —FRANK SINATRA
> "Letter to the Editor,"
> *New Republic*, January 6, 1947

> "All art," wrote Roger Fry in *Vision and Design*, "gives
> us an experience freed from the disturbing conditions
> of actual life." If we accept this definition, then we
> must reject much of Ben Shahn's painting, as Fry
> rejected Bruegel's, for it does more than remind
> us of the living world; it takes strong issue with
> contemporary reality, and urges us to sympathetic
> choice. —JAMES THRALL SOBY
> *Ben Shahn*, 1947

The late 1940s and early 1950s were difficult times for liberals in
the United States. The Cold War had begun and the New Deal of
Franklin D. Roosevelt had lost much of its aura of respectability.
Those who had reveled in the political optimism of Roosevelt's administration were brought up short by the suspicions and political purges
that marked Harry S. Truman's presidency and the early years of
Dwight D. Eisenhower's reign. From the pronouncement of the Truman Doctrine in March 1947 to the Army-McCarthy hearings in the
summer of 1954, American domestic and foreign policies were dominated as never before by anti-communist rhetoric. While the Cold
War did not end in 1954, the hysteria with which it had been conducted since 1947 was greatly reduced by the censoring of Senator
Joseph McCarthy by the Senate in the fall and the meeting of Soviet
leader Nikita Khrushchev and President Eisenhower in Geneva the
following year.

The period 1947 to 1954 was also a difficult time for artists who attempted to maintain the political commitment and artistic ideals of the
New Deal era. One such artist was Ben Shahn. A stalwart New Dealer,
he found himself enmeshed in the Cold War battles of the late forties

and early fifties. His work was included in international campaigns sponsored by both public and private organizations to improve the image of the United States abroad. At the same time, his paintings and posters were cited as communistic by right-wing politicians and artists in the United States. He was investigated by the Federal Bureau of Investigation (FBI) and blacklisted by the Columbia Broadcasting System (CBS). In 1947 he joined the Progressive Citizens of America (PCA) and the following year became a key member of Henry Wallace's graphic arts team during the 1948 Progressive Party presidential campaign.

Shahn was also caught in a split within the art community, characterized at the time as a "struggle between the modernist and the realist tradition, expressed in other terms as an opposition between the 'pure' and the social artist."[1] Robert Motherwell and Harold Rosenberg, members of the former group, argued in 1947 that "political commitment in our times means logically no art, no literature." In order to create works of contemporary relevance free of the limitations imposed by prior outmoded art forms and by a repressive political climate, artists had to find a way to inhabit "the space between art and political action."[2] That space would function as the arena in which artists could act out their search for personal liberation through art, utilizing a new abstract visual language.

While sensitive to the need for a new visual language to articulate changing political and artistic concerns, Shahn was unwilling to abandon his faith in the compatibility of art and political action. As the Cold War progressed, however, the connection between the two became increasingly fraught with problems. The following pages are an effort to understand the nature of these problems, to examine in more detail, through a study of Shahn's work from 1947 to 1954, the options open to artists who identified themselves as New Deal liberals and humanists and who wanted their work to be an expression of their political beliefs.[3]

On September 30, 1947, the Museum of Modern Art in New York (MOMA) opened its first retrospective exhibition of Shahn's work.[4] In the introduction to the Penguin publication *Ben Shahn*, issued in conjunction with the show, curator James Thrall Soby attempted to locate Shahn within the highly complex and changing art world of the late 1940s.[5] Shahn was an artist outside the mainstream of the modernist, abstract tradition, "the opposite of the 'pure' painter nourished in his studio by esthetic faith." Instead, he worked for labor unions and government bureaus in order to maintain contact with social activity. According to Soby, Honoré Daumier and George Grosz were Shahn's precursors, and, like them, he was able to effect a direct translation of his art into social instrument. "As a propagandist," stated Soby, "he is involved in mass appeal on the far-flung scale peculiar to our times." Yet Shahn had also benefited from cubism and other modern movements and his work was "as inspired in structure as in humanistic content."[6]

Soby also emphasized Shahn's Americanness, his unique personal style and vision, and his international artistic standing, ending his essay with the observation that Shahn's current success was of great reassurance for artists and non-artists alike:

> No one has told Shahn what or how to paint. He has worked from personal conviction, under no imposed directive or compulsion. So doing, he has earned an acclaim which, though in no sense popular as yet, is in diversity something of a tribute to this country's critical resilience, its willingness to treasure the artist who speaks with sincere authority, in whatever idiom he alone prefers.[7]

Soby's essay has been quoted extensively in the subsequent literature on Shahn, yet few have attempted to answer the numerous questions raised by this text. What did it mean to be contrasted to the "pure" painters of his day, to be lauded as a propagandist on a far-flung scale, to be defended as absolutely American and as representative of a country's critical resilience?

The significance of such descriptive phrases can be better understood by situating them within the broader political and artistic debates and events of 1947. For example, in 1933 the Mexican muralist Diego Rivera had used similar words to describe Shahn. Shahn was "a man absorbed in the interests of his own class and in its defense," a man whose work contained "all the technical assets of French bourgeois art as well as naïveté of the 'American Folk Art' style." "Ben Shahn," claimed Rivera, "has humanized the technical methods of the Paris painters." In addition, his work appealed to "the most sophisticated connoisseurs of art as well as . . . the masses of workers."[8] Though similar in many ways, the words of Rivera and Soby carried significantly different meanings for their respective art world audiences. The early 1930s was a time when millions of Americans were out of work; when the newly elected president inaugurated a New Deal era that promised a solution to the country's problems through federally funded programs, including the Federal Art Project; when widespread radical political consciousness and activism were beginning to take root. Shahn was deeply involved in a social and political movement that engaged art and artists in a particularly active way. He participated in many of the debates concerning the proper form for politically radical art. In the mid-1930s he joined the Artists' Union and worked on its publication *Art Front*. He demonstrated against the destruction of Rivera's Rockefeller mural in 1933 and, a few years later, made photographic records for the Resettlement Administration/Farm Security Administration (RA/FSA) of the poverty and destitution of millions of Americans. The early thirties was also a time of strong nationalist and isolationist sentiment, a time when pride in things American was widespread and independence from European culture deemed desirable. To have benefited from the artistic lessons of Paris but to have combined them with a truly American tradition to form a distinctively American art was thus an admirable achievement.

By the late 1940s, the political climate had shifted decisively to the right. Shortly after proclaiming the Truman Doctrine in March 1947, the president instituted a loyalty program requiring the purging of all communists or suspected communists from government employment. A similar purge was carried out within American labor unions. The political arena was polarized: one was either a communist (i.e., a traitor) or an anti-communist (i.e., an American). For many, an atomic third world war seemed a catastrophic possibility and yet, at the same time, unimaginable.

The antagonism between European and American artistic traditions also took on a new significance as the United States became the number one world power after the Second World War. With political and economic supremacy assured, certain American critics began claiming cultural supremacy as well, championing an art characterized by alienation and introspection rather than political engagement and mass appeal. While Shahn's work was being honored at MOMA, Jackson Pollock was executing his first drip paintings and the art critic Clement Greenberg was pronouncing the death of the School of Paris and the rise of American painting, with Pollock as its most advanced practitioner.

Apprehensive about the uncritical adoption of abstraction and the celebration of political isolation by increasing numbers of artists, Shahn voiced his concerns in articles and public lectures. He defended both recognizable content in art and social reform principles in politics. He also rejected the idea that political, or even recognizable, imagery had to be purged from art in the name of artistic, if not political, progressiveness. He believed, along with many New Deal liberals, that open political commitment on the part of artists need not be abandoned. To be labeled a humanist and a social critic in 1947 and the years immediately after, and to produce an art lauded for its broad social acceptance, thus meant something very different in 1947 than it had in 1933.

Nineteen forty-seven was, in fact, a crucial year in which battle lines were drawn: between the social liberals of the New Deal era and the new, stridently anti-communist liberals who accompanied and contributed to the intensification of the Cold War; between the defenders of a modern art with recognizable, often politically explicit subject matter and a modern art devoid of such subject matter, whose creators argued in favor of an avant-garde strategy of isolation from organized politics. Of overriding importance to all groups was the defense of their positions or their art as "American," a defense made necessary by the constant use of Red-baiting to suppress both political and artistic dissent.

Seven years later, in 1954, MOMA organized another extensive exhibition of Shahn's work that was sent to Venice to represent American painting at the 27th Venice Biennial. Again, the artist emerged as the defender of socially relevant content and as the champion of the poor and oppressed. The presence of an exhibition of Willem de Kooning's work alongside Shahn's in the American pavilion reinforced Shahn's status as the opposite of the "pure" painter. In the seven years that had passed since his 1947 show, however, Shahn's work had changed. In his desire to achieve a broader, more universal understanding of human aspirations and human suffering he had abandoned depictions of the specific, the historical, for a more generalized, symbolic—though always recognizable—language. At the same time he searched for new avenues through which to present his political concerns to a mass audience after his departure from the Congress of Industrial Organizations' Political Action Committee (CIO-PAC) in 1947 and the failure of the Wallace campaign in 1948. One such avenue was the illustration of articles in magazines such as *Fortune, The New Republic, Harper's Weekly,* and *The Nation.* Political and moral issues—racism, poverty, child welfare—were the focus of the articles he illustrated and ultimately marked the paintings he executed during this period, many of which grew out of these illustrations.

Political and moral issues were also the focus of both the promotional literature for the Venice Biennial exhibition and the press reaction to it. In particular, Shahn's role as a vocal critic of the repressive activities of the American right gained him great favor among Europeans who saw McCarthy as a greater threat to European security than either Stalin or Khrushchev because of the senator's potential influence on American foreign policy. It was, in part, to counter this concern that both government and private agencies in the United States undertook a campaign to improve the country's image abroad as a free and democratic nation, an undertaking that was a vital part of the political warfare between Soviet Russia and the United States and that drew heavily upon the arts for its ammunition. A study of Shahn's work from 1947 to 1954 thus leads inevitably into an investigation of the cultural ramifications of McCarthyism and the Cold War.

My examination of Shahn's life and work focuses on a number of key questions. Who was Shahn's public? How did he reach this public? Why did people like his work? Where did they display it? How did Shahn respond to the changing political climate as both an artist and a political activist? The answers to these questions are found not only in the writings of artists, critics, and historians, but also in the letters sent to Shahn by labor organizers, art directors, friends, and admirers of his works. They are found by examining, among other things, the materials Shahn worked with; the way he divided his time between writing, painting, and lecturing; where he chose to live and with whom he chose to associate; the sources of his visual imagery and practical artistic and political knowledge; how he derived his income and what he did with it. For example, the small town of Roosevelt, New Jersey (formerly Jersey Homesteads), in which Shahn lived and worked for thirty years, provided him with a strong sense of community. He actively socialized with the garment workers who had originally settled there, artists from the area and New York City, and scholars from the nearby town of Princeton. He was married to Bernarda Bryson, an artist and a political activist with whom he often collaborated on art projects for labor unions or political groups.[9] Shahn's writings, opinions, and art developed, therefore, within the context of discussions and debates with those employed in a variety of occupations and within a coherent community.

A consideration of parts of Shahn's life prior to 1947 is also necessary in order to make sense of the events between 1947 and 1954. This material appears at various points in the following chapters, but it will be helpful to include here a brief biography of Shahn's early years. He was born in Kovno, Lithuania, on September 12, 1898, and moved with his family to Vilkomir, a small town forty miles east of Kovno, at the age of four. Both Kovno and Vilkomir were located in the Pale of Settlement on the western edge of Russia, where most of Russia's Jews were forced to settle. Shahn's father, Hessel, like his grandfather, was a woodcarver, who instilled in Shahn a respect for the skilled mastery of a craft (the craftspeople on his mother's side of the family were potters). Shahn's father was also an intellectual and an active socialist, who published philosophical pieces in the Yiddish press and organized resistance to the Czar.[10] This latter activity was particularly dangerous after March 1, 1881, when the moderate Czar Alexander II was assassinated. The subsequent regime instituted a wave of extreme persecution and violence against Jews, forcing many families to flee to Western Europe and the United States. While Shahn and his family escaped the pogroms that swept through the area at this time, his father's anti-Czar activities ultimately led to his departure from Lithuania for South Africa, where he worked as a carpenter before continuing on to the United States. The rest of the family joined him there in 1906.[11]

The family settled in the Bronx, which, along with the Lower East Side of Manhattan, formed the crowded center of Eastern European Jewish life in New York City. After completing an apprenticeship in lithography and brief stays at the Art Students' League, New York University, City College of New York, and the National Academy of Design, Shahn made two trips to Europe, joining the numerous expatriate artists in search of first-hand knowledge of European art, both old and new. Upon his return to the United States, he chose to reject the more abstract of the formal experiments he had undertaken in favor of a style more able to clearly convey the stories he wanted to tell.

During most of the thirties, these stories dealt with highly publicized instances of social and political injustice—e.g., the trials of Nicola Sacco and Bartolomeo Vanzetti and of the labor leader Tom Mooney. By the end of the decade, however, Shahn had begun to shift the focus of his easel and mural work from such publicized incidents to the more private, daily experiences of working-class Americans. In his graphic work, however—posters, drawings, prints—he continued to produce images connected to specific political causes, particularly the attempts of the Office of War Information (OWI) to publicize the war effort and of labor unions to organize workers behind President Roosevelt and the Democratic Party.

The Democratic Party was backed, in fact, by a strong left/liberal alliance during the presidential and congressional campaigns of the early forties. But this alliance was short-lived, for as World War II drew to an end, so too did the Democratic Party's tolerance of political radicalism. This growing intolerance transformed the organizations within which Shahn worked—first the OWI, then the CIO—and forced him to begin to re-evaluate both his position along the left/liberal continuum and the artistic language he would utilize to articulate this position.

In his 1947 essay on Shahn, Soby noted that the artist's current success presented something of a paradox:

> For Shahn, who belongs to the Left, is appreciated by both Left and Right; his work has been published in conservative magazines as often as in liberal; he has fulfilled commissions for labor unions and for industrial corporations; his paintings are bought on completion by collectors of every political hue.[12]

By exploring in detail Shahn's life and work from 1947 to 1954 I hope to show which left Shahn actually belonged to and which elements of the right appreciated him; whether he was really able to achieve a balance between these two ends of the political spectrum in 1947; and, if so, whether he was able to maintain this balance in the subsequent seven-year period. What emerges in the process is a clearer understanding of Shahn the artist and political activist, of the nature of the debates and tensions between figurative and abstract artists, and of the mechanics of trying to remain politically progressive in one of the most repressive periods in American history.

THE BATTLE LINES ARE DRAWN

Again we are faced with this recurrent counterpoint
which has dominated American art since 1913—the
struggle between the modernist and the realist
tradition, expressed in other terms as an opposition
between the "pure" and the social artist. The abstract
and surrealist contingent has gained new strength and
a host of young followers. The small though strong
social group seems to be fighting for its life. But
prediction for the future is dangerous, for the course
of art is not determined by inherent factors. The
future of American painting, the cultural issues which
it will be forced to face, will depend on economic,
social, and political events.   —MILTON BROWN
          "The Forces behind Modern U.S. Painting,"
                                    Art News, 1947

The CIO-PAC

Any understanding of Shahn's political and artistic activities in 1947
must begin with a review of his prior involvement with organized labor. In 1946 Shahn commented to Walter Abell, a faculty member at
Michigan State College, that while commercial and industrial projects
provided financial benefits to the artist, they could not "hold out the
spiritual comfort that work with labor gives."[1] For most of his tenure
with the CIO, Shahn was imbued with a sense of feeling "useful," of
communicating with not thousands, but millions.[2]

Shahn's work for labor unions began at least as early as the latter half
of the 1930s, when he executed a series of three poster designs for the
Steel Workers Organizing Committee of the newly founded CIO. The
posters were never printed, however, because, according to Bernarda
Bryson Shahn, a high union leader decided the faces and figures were
"too ugly to appeal to workers."[3] This early rejection did not prevent
Shahn, however, from accepting, in the summer of 1944, the position
of chief artist of the graphics division of the CIO's Political Action Committee. The PAC had been founded in July 1943 in direct response to
the passage of the anti-labor Smith-Connally Act. The act was designed
to eliminate wartime strikes and the amount of financial support unions
could contribute to political campaigns. The CIO set up its Political
Action Committee in order to sidestep this latter restriction.

The PAC subsequently emerged "as the spearhead of the liberal-labor alliance, becoming for most liberal observers the last great hope of the New Deal."[4] The organization was headed by CIO leader Sidney Hillman, and its staff included a number of members of the American Communist Party (CPUSA).[5] Many Republicans made a major issue of this CPUSA support for Roosevelt, singling out the PAC and claiming that it was "buying" the election. Others claimed that Sidney Hillman, who, like Shahn, was Jewish and had been born in Lithuania, "was motivated by these two circumstances to destroy the American way of life."[6]

The main function of the CIO-PAC, as stated by Philip Murray, president of the CIO, in November 1943, was "to conduct a broad and intensive program of education for the purpose of mobilizing the five million members of CIO and enlisting the active support of all other trade unions, AFL, Railroad Brotherhoods and unaffiliated, for effective labor action on the political front."[7] In addition, alliances with farmers and liberal and progressive elements in both parties would be cultivated in order to bring about a Democratic Party victory in the fall. Early in 1944 a national office was set up in New York City, and the atmosphere was, in the words of one observer, like that of a crusade:

> While the furniture was being moved in, people were already telephoning printers, telephoning artists and writers and radio script makers, . . . Men were at work preparing publications, posters, stickers, buttons, songs and slogans. Each division head worked late into the night devising plans . . . plans that had to be discussed, co-ordinated, sifted, and developed into what ultimately evolved as a unified program of activities.
>
> Anyone entering the national offices at that time, and up to November 7, was struck by the earnest exuberance with which the people worked day and night, as if it were an emergency, as if it were a matter of life and death.[8]

As head of the national office's graphics division, Shahn was assigned three assistants, James Grunbaum, David Stone Martin, and Mary Collier. Between the four of them they met the daily needs of a continually expanding organization for posters, drawings, layouts, and lettering. Shahn's work appeared, therefore, in union halls, newsletters, and magazines across the country. One of the most widely reproduced posters executed by Shahn during the 1944 presidential campaign was *For Full Employment after the War: Register/Vote* (1944), an image of two welders, one black and one white (Figure 1).

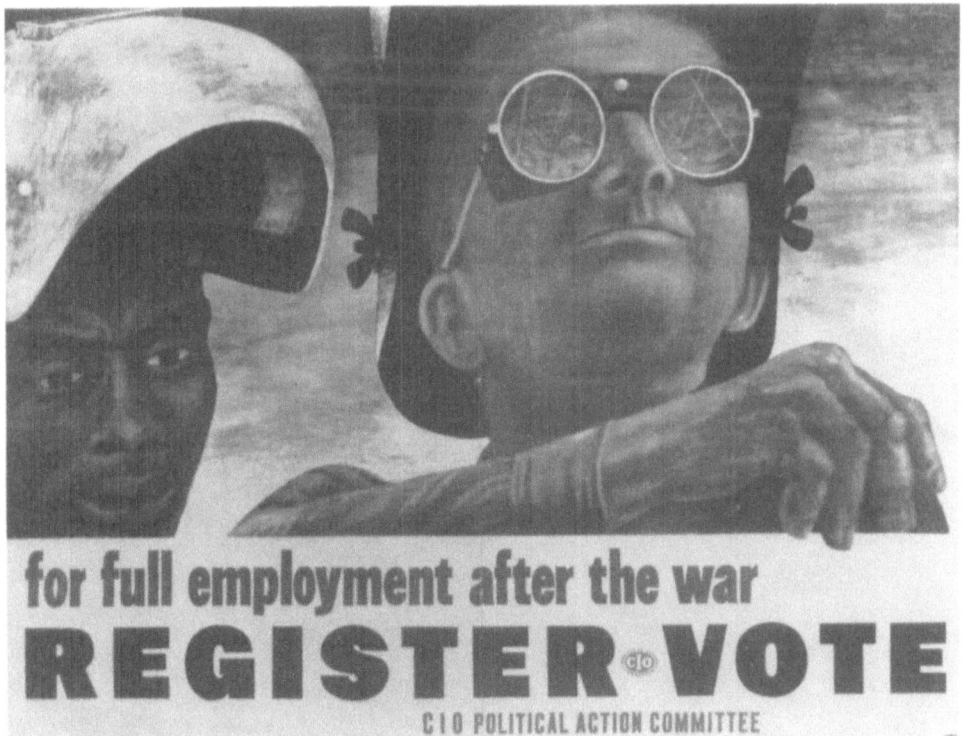

for full employment after the war
REGISTER•VOTE
C I O POLITICAL ACTION COMMITTEE

FIGURE 1
Ben Shahn, *For Full Employment after
the War: Register/Vote,* 1944
Lithograph in colors
29¾ × 39⅜″
New Jersey State Museum Collection,
Trenton; Gift of Circle F
Photographer: Elton Pope-Lance

The poster had, in fact, originally been designed as a war production poster for the OWI during Shahn's tenure there in 1942–1943,
with the caption "A Need for All in Time of War, a Place for All in
Time of Peace." Its rejection by Hank Brennan, head of the OWI
graphics bureau, was indicative of an ongoing battle Shahn often had
to wage with both government and union officials over the suitability
of his images for posters. Only two of the posters Shahn designed for
the OWI were actually printed, both in the latter part of 1942—*This
Is Nazi Brutality* (Figure 2) and *We French Workers Warn You . . .
Defeat Means Slavery, Starvation, Death* (Figure 3).

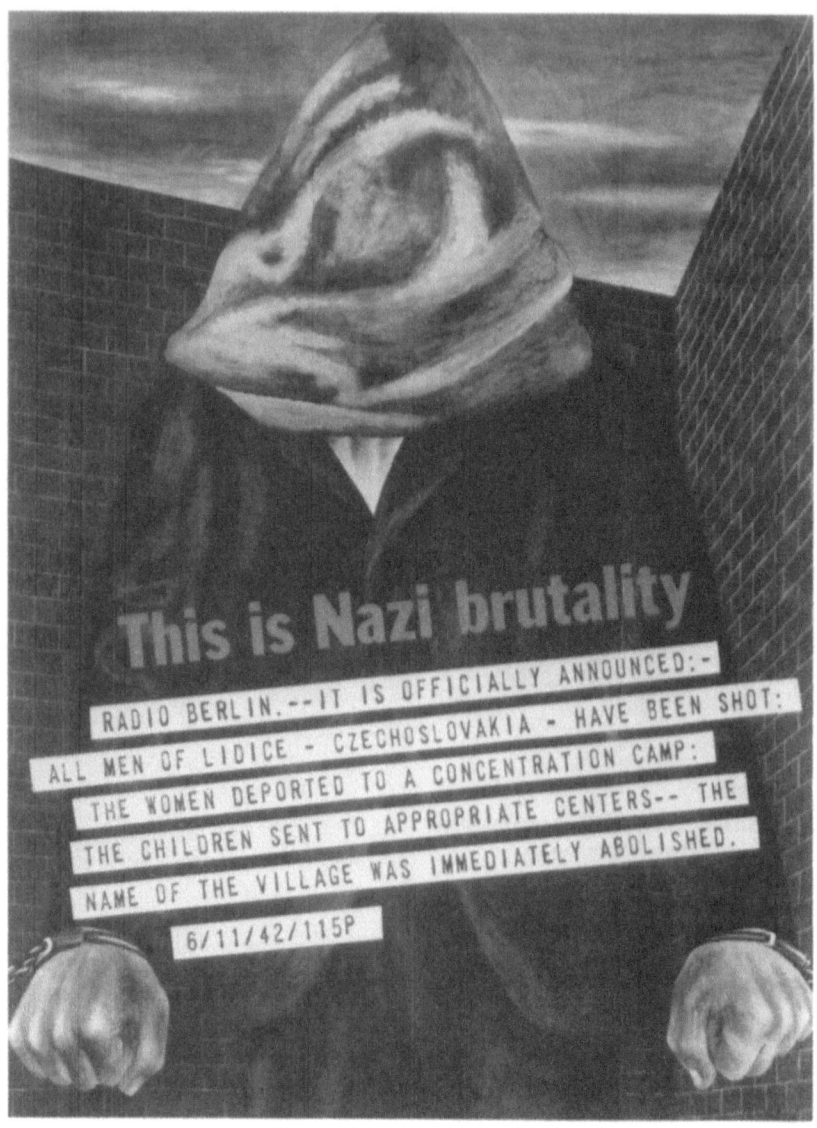

FIGURE 2

Ben Shahn, *This Is Nazi Brutality*, 1942
Photo-offset in colors
37⅞ × 28¼″
New Jersey State Museum Collection,
Trenton; Gift of *The Record*, Hacken-
sack, N.J.
Photographer: Dan Dragan

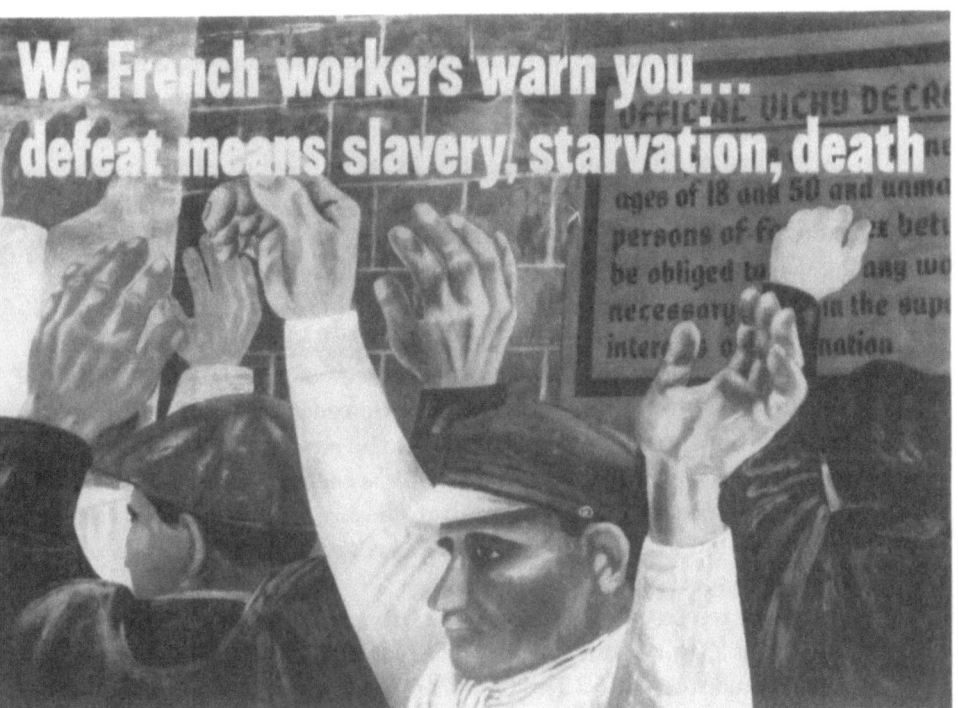

FIGURE 3
Ben Shahn, *We French Workers Warn
You . . . Defeat Means Slavery, Starva-
tion, Death,* 1942
Photo-offset in colors
28¼ × 39¾"
New Jersey State Museum Collection,
Trenton; Gift of Circle F
Photographer: Dan Dragan

This Is Nazi Brutality was inspired by the destruction of the village
of Lidice, Czechoslovakia, by the Germans, who claimed that some of
the inhabitants had been involved in the killing of the German Police
General and Reichsprotektor for Bohemia and Moravia. Printed as if
on ticker tape across the front of a large hooded figure, who stands
before a red brick wall, are excerpts from the official German announcement released June 11, 1942, the day the village was destroyed
and the majority of its inhabitants shot. Instead of representing the
event as a mass of dead villagers or a regiment of heartless Nazi soldiers, Shahn chose the solitary, anonymous victim, fists clenched de-

fiantly before the moment of execution. While forty thousand of these posters were ordered by a Czechoslovakian-American organization, the order was canceled by one of the "civilian morale 'experts'" because the poster's message was deemed too "violent."[9]

According to Brennan, the central figure in Shahn's other poster, *We French Workers Warn You . . . Defeat Means Slavery, Starvation, Death,* "simply wasn't an appealing-looking guy." And for Brennan, "appeal" was crucial if the poster was to be effective in conveying its message to the public at large.[10] He argued that so few of Shahn's posters were used because Shahn never reconciled the conflict between the poster as a work of art and a piece of propaganda. Shahn himself was aware of this problem, but viewed it in terms of recognizability, not appeal. For example, while he admired Picasso's *Guernica* (1937) as a painting, he felt it would be ineffective as an anti-war poster, not because it was "ugly," but because a "backlog of critical references" not available to the public was necessary in order to understand its meaning.[11]

Brennan rejected Shahn's welders poster because he thought that while it was a "wonderful picture," as a poster "it didn't mean anything and we couldn't use it."[12] The CIO-PAC could use it, however, and it became one of the best known, and most controversial, of Shahn's CIO posters.[13] For example, the editor of New York City's conservative newspaper *The Daily Mirror* described the poster as depicting "the face of President-Candidate Roosevelt wearing goggles and having a large helmet of some kind on his head. Alongside him is a Negro, also helmeted." The editor went on to state that Democratic claims of full employment after the war were misleading and that the poster was an appeal to racial prejudice. In addition, "the rise and absorption of the great Democratic Party into a mongrel and un-American organization like the Hillman-Browder party is the worst evidence of defeatism we have ever had in American history."[14]

The white welder in the poster does, in fact, resemble Roosevelt somewhat, and although it is not clear whether this was Shahn's intent,[15] the resemblance does make a visual connection between Roosevelt and the right to full employment after the war, which was a central issue for the Roosevelt administration as well as for the CIO. Full employment for all—black and white—after the war was also closely connected to postwar foreign policy. One of the primary objectives of the CIO in 1944, according to Philip Murray, was "to win the war, and then to cooperate generously with our Allies—Britain, Russia, and

China—in building a better world."[16] This better world meant full employment, at fair wages, not just nationally, but internationally. Yet the battle for full employment legislation begun by Roosevelt and Wallace was abandoned, ultimately, by Truman after 1945, just as the CIO's call for international cooperation with countries like Russia and China disappeared with the beginning of the Cold War.

Another of Shahn's 1944 CIO posters was *From Workers to Farmers . . . Thanks!* (Figure 4). As with *For Full Employment after the War,* the main concept for the poster—the wheat-filled hands—was produced while Shahn was in the employ of a government agency, this time the Office of Inter-American Affairs (OIAA).[17] And once again, while the OIAA did not make use of Shahn's image in its 1942 anti-fascist poster campaign, the CIO was more than willing to put it to use two years later to help rally the labor vote in the United States behind Roosevelt. Beneath the two large hands filled with grain in the center of the poster are the words: "From your hands has flowed abundant food to win the war. From ours, abundant tools. Together, we can produce a world of plenty for all." Twenty thousand copies of the poster were printed and distributed, appearing not only in Farmers' Union headquarters but also in CIO booths at county fairs. In 1944 ex-Governor Elmer A. Benson of Minnesota called it "one of the first, strongest, and most effective gestures in the direction of good will made by labor towards farmers."[18]

In addition to his work for the CIO-PAC, Shahn created at least one poster in 1944 for the National Citizens Political Action Committee (NCPAC), an organization of professional, civic, religious, and consumer groups who joined together in June 1944 to help elect a progressive president and Congress. The NCPAC was separate from, yet allied with, the CIO-PAC, with Hillman acting as chair of both organizations.[19] Shahn's poster appeared in at least three versions, one with the words "Our Friend" in the top left-hand section in English (Figure 5), one with a Polish translation underneath the English, and one with an Armenian translation. Approximately one thousand billboard versions of the poster were also printed.[20]

This poster/billboard includes the profile head of Roosevelt, which takes up the right third of the composition; a soldier carrying a child, for which Shahn's son Jonathan served as the model, on the left; and numerous raised hands across the foreground. One of these hands is black, the rest white. If they appear more naturalistic than other of Shahn's renditions of workers' hands, it is because the lithographer

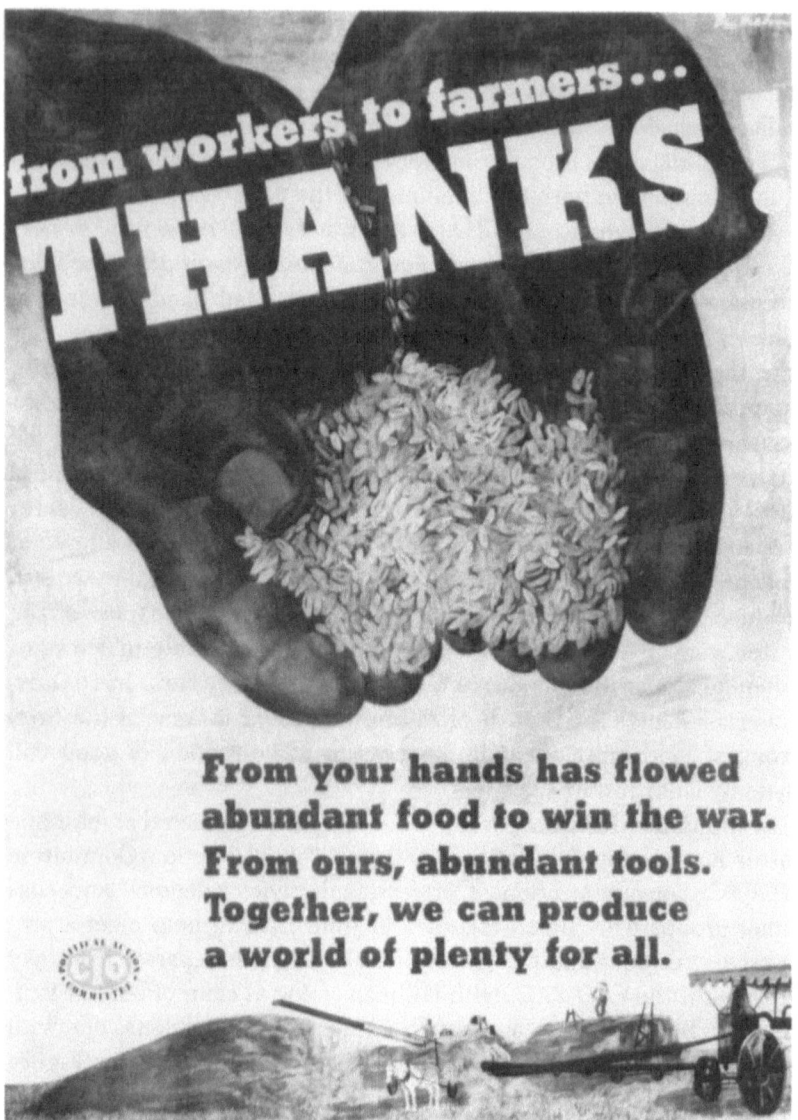

FIGURE 4

Ben Shahn, *From Workers to Farmers
. . . Thanks,* 1944
Photo-offset in colors
39½ × 29¾″
New Jersey State Museum Collection,
Trenton; Gift of Mr. and Mrs. Maurice
Rosenthal
Photographer: Dan Dragan

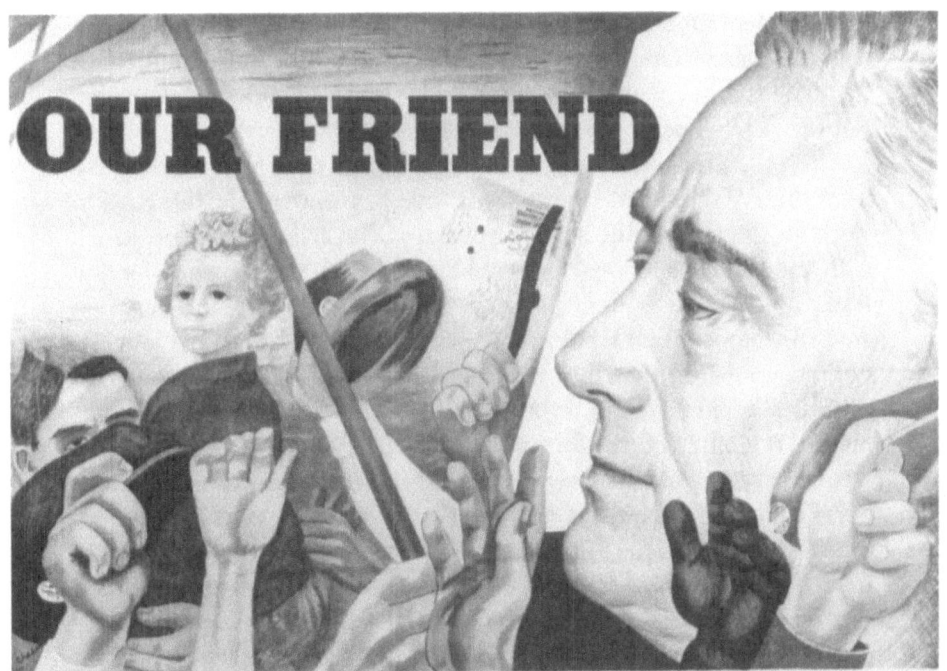

FIGURE 5
Ben Shahn, *Our Friend*, 1944
Lithograph in colors
30¹⁄₁₆ × 39⁷⁄₈"
New Jersey State Museum Collection,
Trenton; Gift of Mr. and Mrs.
R. George Kuser
Photographer: Geoffrey Clements

who printed the poster felt they should look more "life-like" and therefore altered them.[21] Some of the hands hold hats of different colors, shapes, and sizes. On the hats are buttons for the American Federation of Labor (AFL) and the CIO, and hat tickets for the Grand Lodge Ancient Order United Workmen of Washington, a fraternal benefit life insurance organization, and the National Farm Bureau. The red and white stripes of the American flag are visible in the top left corner. Roosevelt, a concerned look on his face, thus appears as the champion of the American working man (and, by implication, woman, though no women appear in the poster). The soldier attests to the president's role as commander-in-chief of a country at war and the child his concern for the nation's future. The poster thus summarizes the main themes of an election campaign that succeeded in returning Roosevelt to office in the fall.

After the successful 1944 campaign Shahn took a short reprieve from the PAC to devote more of his time to painting. He returned to work for the CIO in the summer of 1945. The arrangement he struck with them was as follows: he would work three days a week for the PAC, do his independent painting three days a week, and rest one day. In October 1946 Walter Abell, in an article entitled "Art and Labor," commented that this arrangement showed that work for organized labor had begun to "take its place, along with teaching and commercial art, among those forms of service to society through which the artist can secure an income, while at the same time devoting a portion of his time to independent creative effort."[22] Of course, Abell added, Shahn did not need to depend on labor or any other such sources for money. His independent painting was in great demand and provided him with an adequate income.[23] "But he values his participation in the labor field because he feels that such work enriches his life and broadens his creative horizons."[24]

Abell also pointed out that Shahn's welders poster was an example of how labor organizations were helping bring art to a broader audience, and how such art often functioned as an integral part of that audience's experience. "Shahn's *Welders* can speak to a factory worker much as a *Holy Family* spoke to a medieval monk," stated Abell. "It is of the tissue of his soul's experience; a symbol of his world and of his impulse toward a fuller life."[25] The purchase of the original painting for the poster by MOMA also proved, for Abell, that art produced for labor could be something more than propaganda of temporary significance. It could function, rather, as a permanent part of the nation's artistic heritage, preserved along with other great works of art in the country's major museums. Abell failed to mention, however, that the painting had been originally executed for the OWI.

We know today that Abell's assessment of the importance of organized labor as art patron and of Shahn's *Welders* as a working-class icon was unduly optimistic. Yet in October 1946 his words would not have seemed out of place. Not only had the PAC met with great success and visibility between 1944 and 1946, but the union rank and file had also flexed its muscle in a series of confrontations with management that made 1946 the greatest strike year in American history. A total of 110,000,000 working days were lost through strikes in 1946, whereas the pre-war high, reached in 1937, had been 28,424,000.[26]

The failure of the Truman administration to deal with these strikes became a major issue in the 1946 congressional campaign. The Republican Party argued that the "public's rights" had to be protected by legislation that would control strikes. The Democratic Party was split on the issue, with the conservative wing advocating harsher anti-strike laws and the more progressive wing trying to maintain the liberal-labor alliance established in the 1944 campaign. Truman himself vacillated between the two positions, on the one hand attempting to introduce legislation calling for the drafting of strikers into the army,[27] on the other vetoing the harshly anti-union Case bill.[28] Shahn sent a telegram to Alexander Smith, a member of the Senate Committee on Military Affairs, protesting such anti-labor legislation.[29]

These attacks on organized labor by both Republicans and Democrats decreased public support for the union movement and forced unions to step up their public relations efforts, which included, of course, the CIO's PAC, with Shahn in its employ. As in the 1944 campaign, the PAC argued that the public's rights would be protected by union strength, not by Republican legislation. But whereas its efforts had been closely aligned with the Democratic Party in 1944, in 1946 the PAC emphasized more general issues such as inflation and housing shortages and attempted to dissociate itself from Truman's administration.

These differences between the two campaigns can be seen in Shahn's PAC posters. In 1944 the portrait of "Our Friend" Roosevelt graced the walls of union headquarters and community billboards and the black and white welders working side by side for victory and full employment "epitomized the hopes of the liberal-labor alliance for a people's century after the war."[30] In 1946, with this alliance already weakening and with conservative gains on the increase, the images are more those of an organization and an ideal under attack. Instead of the open, wheat-filled hands of *From Workers to Farmers . . . Thanks!*, a large hand clenching the wrist of another, smaller hand, which in turn crushes a map of the United States, fills the center of *Break Reaction's Grip: Register/Vote* (Figure 6). The dark coat sleeve and white shirt cuff of the smaller arm indicate that this is the force of reaction (both Republican and Democrat) backed by big business. While it is shown

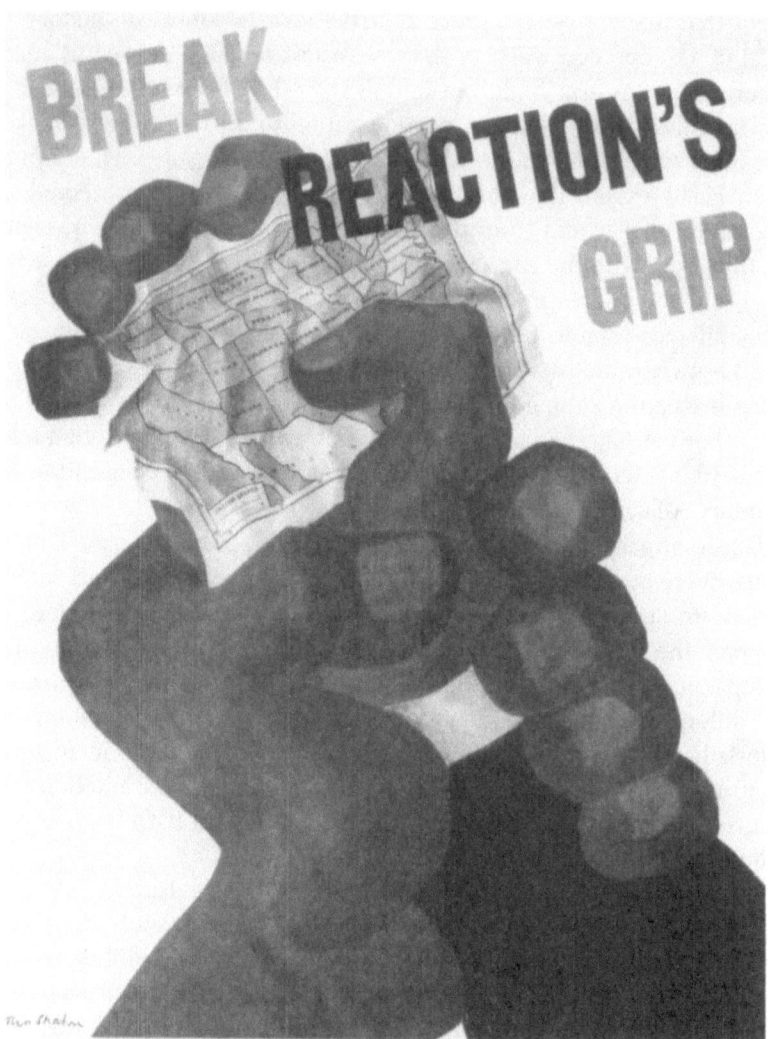

FIGURE 6

Ben Shahn, *Break Reaction's Grip: Register/Vote,* 1946
Photo-offset in colors
41¼ × 29"
New Jersey State Museum Collection,
Trenton; Purchase
Photographer: Dan Dragan

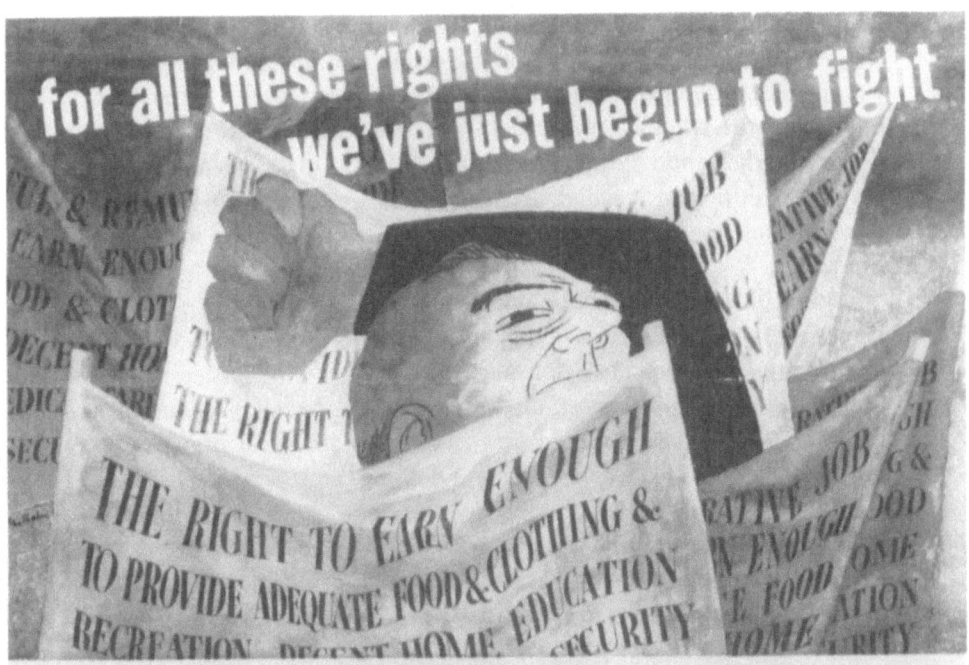

FIGURE 7
Ben Shahn, *For All These Rights We've
Just Begun to Fight: Register/Vote*, 1946
Lithograph in colors
28⅞ × 38¾"
New Jersey State Museum Collection,
Trenton; Gift of Mr. and Mrs. Michael
Lewis
Photographer: Dan Dragan

on the rise, it is also about to be pulled down by the superior strength
of the bare-armed progressive force of labor, though not before it has
put a considerable wrinkle in the national topography.

For All These Rights We've Just Begun to Fight: Register/Vote
(1946; Figure 7) depicts the militant struggle to protect the rights set
out by Roosevelt in his Economic Bill of Rights speech in January
1944: to earn enough to provide adequate food, clothing, recreation, a
decent home, education, and health care. The reception of this poster
within the CIO-PAC was not, however, totally positive, as evidenced

by the comments of Palmer Weber, head of the PAC's Research Division during the 1944 presidential campaign. Weber admired Shahn's commitment to images that the viewer would "recognize" rather than ones that were wholly "conceptual," yet he felt that in this poster "of a defiant worker amid sloganed pennons, [Shahn] drew a blank. It was his only failure and it failed because the image, though possibly related to the experience of Union Square, was meaningless to labor in the sticks."[31]

Weber did not elaborate on why the poster was meaningless to "labor in the sticks." Was it because such workers were unable to relate to militancy and defiance and slogans? The strike activities of 1946 tend to counter this suggestion. In addition Roosevelt, the author of Shahn's slogans, was still held in great esteem by most union members. A resistance to sloganeering and defiance was, however, present among at least a few union officials, who perceived an undesirable militancy in much of Shahn's work. One of Shahn's colleagues in the PAC felt this perception led to stacks of his posters being left unused in regional headquarters.[32] There may have been another reason, however, for this particular poster's lack of success with certain individuals—the ambiguous way in which Shahn chose to depict the scene.

Preliminary studies for the poster indicate that Shahn tried out at least two different designs.[33] In one, the left half of the poster is filled with the head of a male figure, either looking forward or down, with the text above and to the right. In the second set of studies, the head and shoulders of the figure are centered in the composition, and the right hand is raised in a fist level with the figure's head. In one of the second group of drawings, small rectangular forms suggesting placards are visible behind and to the right of the figure.

The final poster is strikingly different from these early studies. The vague outlines of placards have been transformed into a series of large banners. The text—"for all these rights we've just begun to fight"— floats above the figure's head, suggesting the chant of a crowd. The number of banners also suggests the presence of a multitude of individuals, although there is, in fact, only a single figure visible. His left fist is extended above and behind his head in a revolutionary gesture, creating a greater sense of momentum than in the earlier studies. Yet, at the same time, he appears overwhelmed by the banners surrounding him, which both obscure the lower half of his face and appear to hamper his very movements. Words box the figure in, giving voice to his concerns while, in the case of the banners, physically silencing him. It is this combination of empowerment and immobilization that may have contributed to the poster's mixed reception.

Shahn also produced less "militant" posters for the 1946 campaign. In one such poster, *Warning! Inflation Means Depression: Register/ Vote* (Figure 8), a worried figure holds his hand, no longer clenched defiantly, over his mouth. The same figure had appeared in an earlier painting, *1943 A.D.* (1943), with barbed wire in front of him and an additional piece of barbed wire around his forehead, an obvious reference to Christ's crown of thorns. This figure had also appeared in a war poster designed by Shahn that same year, the barbed wire around the forehead now replaced by a strand of wire extending across the whole of the image. In the 1946 CIO poster, Shahn has removed all references to war—the barbed wire and the men pushing wheelbarrows that appear in the background of both earlier works. Yet he has not replaced these referents with concrete signs of current union struggles. Even the worried gaze, once associated with a visible condition of imprisonment, is now directed at a less tangible inflation and depression. While action and urgency are suggested in the caption and in the exclamation point of "Warning!," the figure himself appears fixed to the spot, unable to engage even in the action of speech.

The fact that Shahn considered an image created during wartime suitable for a peacetime political campaign suggests the tenuous nature of this peace in 1946. The battles between unions and management during this year often took on, in fact, a warlike aspect, with unions fighting to defend the gains won in the thirties against the onslaughts of conservative representatives of both parties. Battles on the broader political front were also taking place. During the first nine months of the year there was still hope that the postwar era would be a "century of the common man." Henry Wallace had coined this phrase in a speech delivered in May 1942, when he was Roosevelt's vice-president. The phrase was an indirect reference to an article published the previous year by Henry Luce in which Luce outlined his vision of a postwar "American century." Whereas Wallace advocated extending the New Deal to world proportions, Luce supported a form of benevolent imperialism, one that would oppose social revolutions. In addition, while Wallace's emphasis was on the stimulation of trade relations with other nations, Luce considered the opening up of the world for American business ventures of equal, if not greater, importance. Trade relations were possible with socialist and communist countries; unrestricted capitalist investment was not.[34] Eric Sevareid

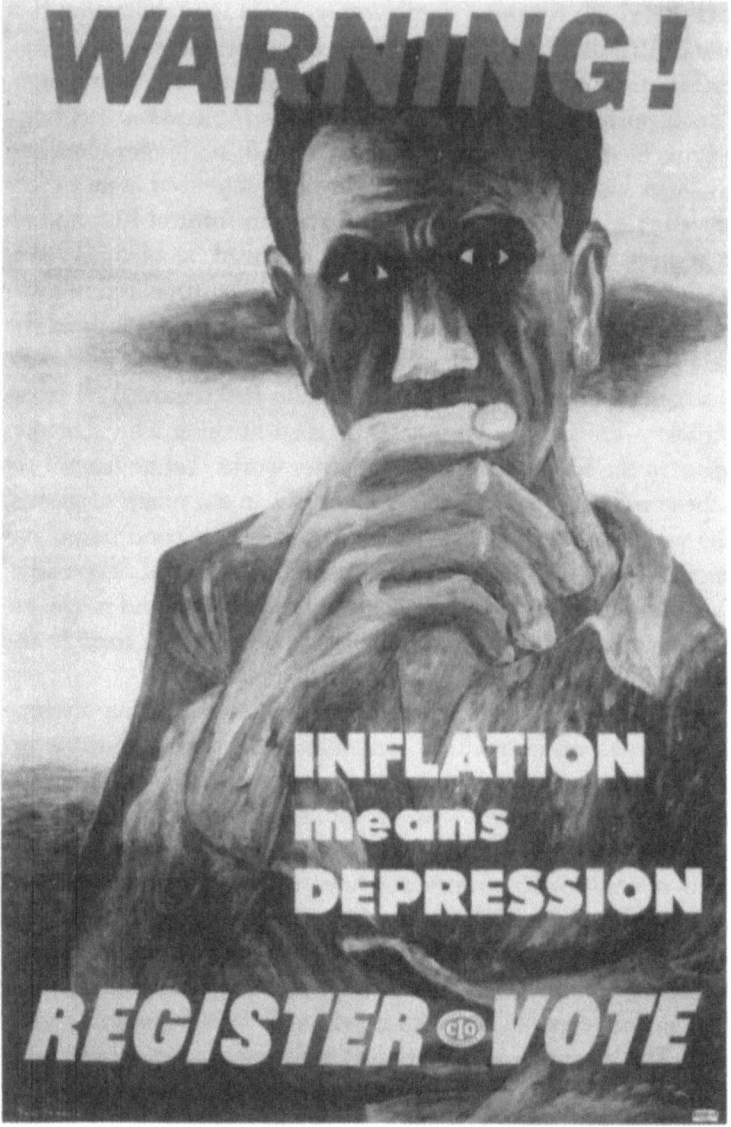

FIGURE 8

Ben Shahn, *Warning! Inflation Means
Depression: Register/Vote*, 1946
Photo-offset in colors
41⅛ × 27¾"
New Jersey State Museum Collection,
Trenton; Museum Purchase
Photographer: Geoffrey Clements

wrote Edward R. Murrow from London in the summer of 1942 that the fate of Europe and the world in general after the war depended on whether the ideas of Henry Wallace or Henry Luce dominated U.S. domestic and foreign policy.[35]

The ideas of Henry Luce were, in fact, winning out by 1946, and the hope for a "century of the common man" grew increasingly dim as the year progressed, particularly after Wallace was forced to resign as Secretary of Commerce on September 20 because of his opposition to Truman's foreign policy. It grew even dimmer after the Republicans won control of Congress in November. At the same time, rifts that had begun to appear earlier in the year within the CIO were widening under pressure from the right. Workers were increasingly being forced to either abandon (or deny) their associations with the left, particularly the CPUSA, or leave their unions. Wallace, once the hero of the CIO and its choice for vice-president in 1944 over Truman, fell into disfavor. Many of those who left the employ of the CIO, Shahn among them, maintained their allegiance to Wallace and formed the core of the Progressive Party effort of 1948. But in November 1946, prospects for a progressive political movement of any sort, and particularly one based within the union movement, did not look good. Had Abell written his article on art and labor for the December rather than the October issue of *Magazine of Art*, it might not have been so optimistic.

Trouble in the Labor Movement

Shahn began the year 1947 working on an exhibit for the United Auto Workers (UAW-CIO) to be held in New York City in January. He was in charge of designing the texts that were to accompany eight large panels and determining the general layout. The purpose of the exhibit, like many of Shahn's earlier projects for the CIO-PAC, was to point out the control and abuse of Congress by big business and to encourage industrial, agricultural, and service workers to vote for prolabor candidates.[36] This was to be among the last of ..ahn's efforts for the CIO. While he subsequently withdrew from active involvement in PAC projects, he did not, however, abandon his attempts to express the concerns and struggles of workers in the United States. In fact, he devoted a considerable amount of time in 1947 to exploring various ways in which to visually articulate the struggle between labor and big business.

One set of images in particular addressed this struggle. In a watercolor sketch[37] Shahn depicts two men locked in physical combat. The

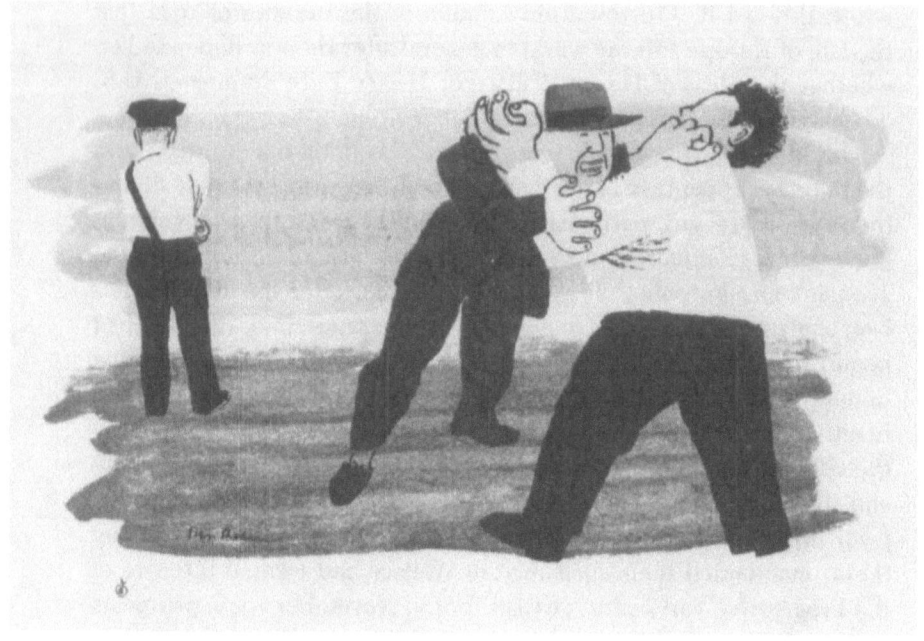

FIGURE 9

Ben Shahn, *Laissez-Faire*, 1947
Serigraph in colors
14 × 21″
New Jersey State Museum Collection,
Trenton; Gift of Mr. and Mrs. Michael
Lewis
Photographer: Joe Crilley

man on the left wears a suit, hat, and tie, signifying his identity as a member of the conservative establishment—either a businessman or a politician, probably the former. The man on the right wears a white shirt or pullover and his head is bare, attributes usually given by Shahn to workers. The faces of both men are clearly visible, the former in full face, the latter in profile. While the businessman is on higher ground than the worker, the worker appears to be holding his own in the struggle in which they are engaged.

This sketch appears to have been a preliminary study for the serigraph *Laissez-Faire* (Figure 9), which includes the same two fighting men, similarly attired. The title of the serigraph reinforces the suggestion that the figure in the suit is a businessman.[38] In this version, however, the businessman's left hand, not visible in the watercolor, is grasping the collar of the worker's shirt, obscuring his face in the process and giving the businessman an obvious advantage. Also present in this version and not in the watercolor is a third figure to the far left—a policeman with his back to the other two men.

In the painting *Trouble* (Figure 10), the two fighting men are located in the center foreground. But now not only is the businessman grasping the chin of the worker, but the worker's right hand, not shown in the other two images, is thrown across his eyes, signifying both distress and defeat. The policeman is also absent, and while the watercolor and serigraph contain only general areas of wash to indicate foreground and background, the background in the tempera painting

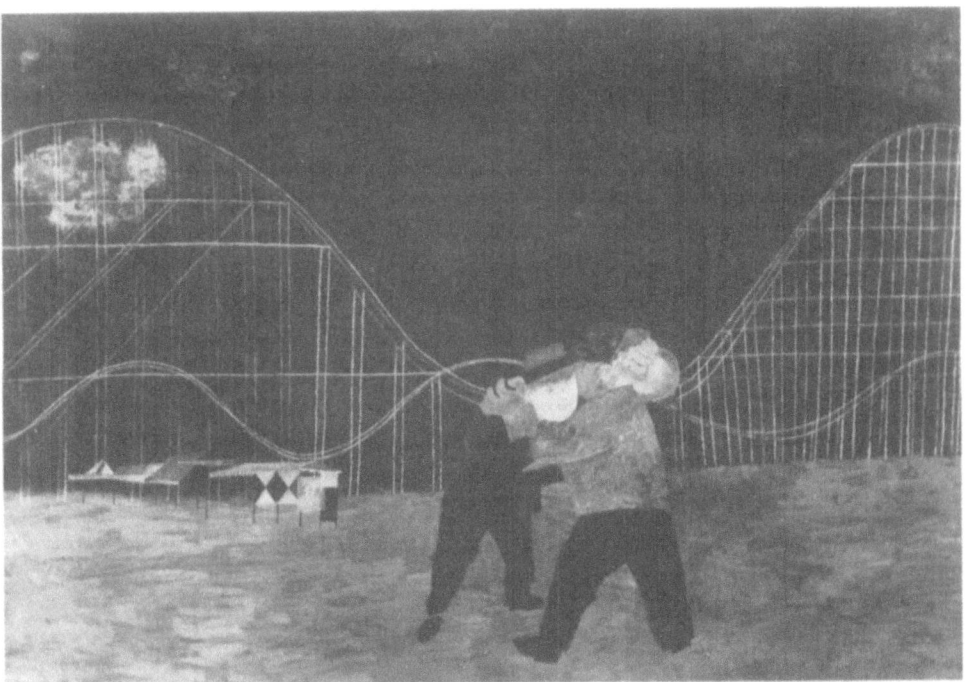

FIGURE 10
Ben Shahn, *Trouble*, 1947
Tempera on plywood
24 × 36″
Collection: Sheldon Memorial Art Gallery, University of Nebraska–Lincoln;
F. M. Hall Collection

is occupied by an elaborate rollercoaster structure and a row of empty canopied stalls.

Shahn's work for the CIO-PAC during the 1946 campaign, in particular his anti-business poster *Break Reaction's Grip* (Figure 6), and the events of 1946–1947 affecting the situation of organized labor in the United States provide insights into the meanings of these three images. The display of panels Shahn worked on for the UAW at the beginning of 1947 depicting the evils of big business and its Republican supporters was part of a massive campaign organized by the labor movement to protest the proposed Taft-Hartley legislation. In addition to a stipulation requiring officers of unions to file affidavits with the Department of Labor declaring they were not members of the Communist Party or any organization supporting it, the act established a sixty-day cooling-off period after the end of a contract during which strikes were prohibited. It also outlawed the use of mass picketing to stop company-hired scabs from entering a factory, and secondary boycotts, an important tactic in pressuring employers to settle a strike.[39]

While the AFL and CIO leadership denounced the act, they ultimately complied with the requirement that all officers sign the non-communist affidavits. In the UAW, all CPUSA members were removed from the executive and those in the rank and file found it increasingly difficult to voice their political opinions. Shahn was among many who chose, at this time, to shift their allegiances and services from the CIO to Wallace and the Progressive Party.

One final clue to the meaning of Shahn's three images can be found in a series of illustrations he executed for an article on labor organizing for the November 1946 issue of *Fortune* magazine. *Fortune* had begun publication in 1930 under the direction of Henry Luce. Luce conceived of it as a magazine concerned with examining the "ethics of business," one that would attempt to draw the line "between the gentleman and the money-grubber, between the responsible and the irresponsible citizen."[40] To this end Luce hired Archibald MacLeish, Dwight Macdonald, Margaret Bourke-White, and others to investigate various aspects of business. These writers and photographers often produced critical exposés that created a certain amount of animosity toward the magazine in the business world. But while Luce allowed his writers a large amount of critical freedom, he made it clear that such freedom was to have a reformist, rather than revolutionary, bent. Private enterprise was to be improved, not destroyed.[41] Predictably, by the late forties Luce had tightened the reins on his writers, insisting that the magazine exhibit a more supportive attitude toward private enterprise and that it "assist in the successful development of American Business Enterprise at home and abroad."[42]

Two of *Fortune's* art editors in 1946, Leo Lionni and Deborah Calkins, were friends of Shahn who admired his work and shared many of his political sympathies.[43] As an artist actively involved in labor campaigns, his suitability for the *Fortune* article was obvious. He was, in fact, working for the CIO when *Fortune* contacted him, and later recalled that Philip Murray saw no harm or conflict of interest in his accepting the commission, despite the anti-big-business nature of the PAC's 1946 campaign.[44] Perhaps both Murray and Shahn felt that the greater the coverage of the federation's drive, the better. Shahn had few qualms about working for a corporation like Time, Inc., as long as he was allowed to carry out the commission on his own terms and as long as the job offered a formal, personal, or moral challenge.[45] In order to gather ideas, Shahn went south for a month, interviewing a variety of people—the owners of "hate sheets," the managers of factories, workers—and executing numerous sketches,[46] although, in the end, he also drew heavily on photographs he had taken in the mid-1930s for the Resettlement Administration/Farm Security Administration (RA/FSA).

The article, entitled "Labor Drives South," discussed the attempts of both the AFL and the CIO to organize non-union industries in the South, particularly the textile industry.[47] This southern drive was not a united effort, however, for the rivalry that had begun with the CIO's split from the AFL in 1937 continued into the forties. This rivalry is alluded to in one of Shahn's illustrations, a rural landscape in which a "Vote CIO" poster on the side of a barn is balanced by an AFL flyer attached to a telephone pole that proclaims "Be American! Join the American Federation of Labor." The AFL charged on a number of occasions that the CIO was influenced by the CPUSA and thus was un-American. The caption for the illustration and the billboard with the large eye and the even larger word "Secrets!" that is located between the CIO poster and the AFL flyer refer to the Oak Ridge atom workers, who voted CIO despite AFL Red-baiting.

For the most part, however, the line drawings and full-color illustrations by Shahn that accompanied the article depicted quiet or congenial moments in the lives of southern workers—a man playing a guitar or sitting in a rocking chair holding a child or entering a church—

rather than AFL-CIO rivalry or picket lines or clashes between workers and police. This was, in fact, in keeping with the article's presentation of the southern drive as predominantly conflict-free. In comparing it to the organizing drives of 1934 and 1937, the author commented that "there are no road barricades to halt the union flying squads, no machine guns peeping over the roofs of defiant mills, no sheriffs deputizing the members of citizens' committees, no herding of strikers into state stockade camps."[48]

That Shahn might have disagreed with this interpretation of the 1946 drive is suggested by his submission of a drawing of a policeman with his back to the viewer—the same policeman that appears in *Laissez-Faire*—facing two men seated across the street on the curb. The drawing was rejected because it contained a mood of tension and impending violence which, according to the editor of the magazine, did not exist in the southern drive.[49] The drawing of the policeman appeared a few months later, however, in the January 13, 1947, issue of *New Republic*, then edited by Henry Wallace. The policeman now gazes across an empty street at a CIO organizing headquarters, with his right hand resting on his holstered gun (Figure 11). This was the only illustration in an article that presented a less conciliatory picture of relations between unions and factory owners during the southern drive.[50] According to the author of the article, Ralph G. Martin, the 1946 drive, while not as violent as those of the 1930s, was not totally free of conflict. Union organizers were subjected to continual verbal and physical harassment, and considerable pressure was brought to bear on workers who showed support for unionization. The source of Shahn's policeman was, in fact, a photograph of a sheriff during a 1935 strike in Morgantown, West Virginia, which Shahn had taken on his first photographic trip for the RA/FSA (Figure 12).

While the article Shahn illustrated for *Fortune* did not come out strongly against union organizing, the editorial in the same issue of the magazine clearly outlined *Fortune's* policy with regard to unions. Just as American businesses needed to be prevented by legislation from creating cartels and monopolies, so too did unions need to be regulated to prevent them from forming industry-wide bargaining units that would interfere in the establishment of "competitive prices."[51] Union demands for high wages were blamed for rising prices, despite the fact, omitted from the *Fortune* editorial, that companies such as U.S. Steel had recently used wage increases won by unions to raise prices up to twice as much as necessary to cover the cost of the wage

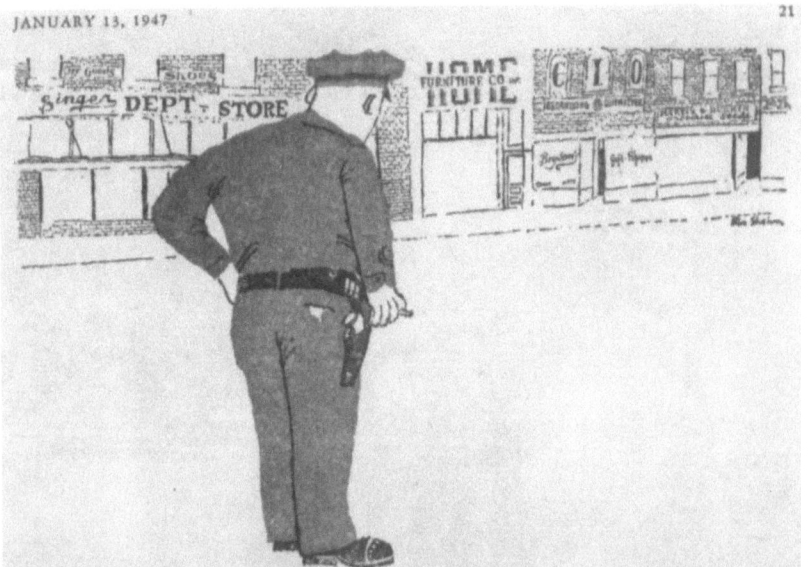

first families, she has entrée every-where and her influence is tremendous. Almost everybody who is anybody down South is either her cousin or friend, and hardly anyone ever says no to Lucy Mason.

She has a special way of dealing with sheriffs. When one sheriff waved a pistol at a Negro picket line and threatened to bury them all in the local graveyard, Lucy went into action. She used words like "federal prosecution" "civil rights" and "FBI" until she had the sheriff scared silly. It was all a mistake, he said, and it would never happen again. It hasn't.

The threat of an FBI investigation is a strong one. Occasionally when the incident is serious enough and Lucy files a formal complaint, an FBI man will come down to look around. Usually, all he has to do is to get the sheriff or somebody aside and say, "Lock, brother, if you don't watch out you'll be getting yourself in trouble. You can't do this. . . ."

As for the organizers themselves, they know exactly what they can and can't do. Each of them has a clearly

written, comprehensive booklet called "Your Civil Rights."

The CIO's Strategy

IF THERE is an over-all strategy to the CIO drive, it's to unionize the big, tough companies first. Once they're in, it will be easier to get the smaller ones. But if they first unionized all the smaller manufacturers, many of them would have to go out of business because they wouldn't be able to pay higher wages and still compete with the bigger companies. In getting the big boys, the CIO must organize all their factories at the same time. Otherwise, the corporations can play checkers with their plants and workers, closing up one plant and shifting the non-union workers elsewhere.

Textiles are putting up the toughest fight, with Bibbs and Cannon in the lead.

But the worst working conditions are not in textiles: they're in wood-working and tobacco. So far the CIO hasn't lost a single election among tobacco workers.

Nobody knows the CIO membership potential in the South. The ones who hate the CIO call their drive "the second invasion of the carpetbaggers." The others look at the 15.5-cent-an-hour wage increase at the Lafayette Cotton Mills in Georgia and at the company in Danville, Virginia, which agreed to pay for life and hospitalization insurance for employees and their immediate families. They look at Gadsden, Alabama, where one out of every five persons is a CIO member and the town has had its face lifted with a dozen civic improvements.

These are the Southerners who know that their South of 26 million people has the most inadequate facilities for education, housing and health of any section of the country. For Southern progressives, the CIO is a hope. More money for workers means better working conditions, decent homes, better communities, more education, improved medical care. And more educated workers means more politically conscious ones, means *finis* to the Bilbos and the Rankins. It means a new South.

FIGURE 11
Ben Shahn, Drawing of a policeman, in
January 13, 1947, issue of *New Republic*, p. 21
Photographer: Stephen Cahill

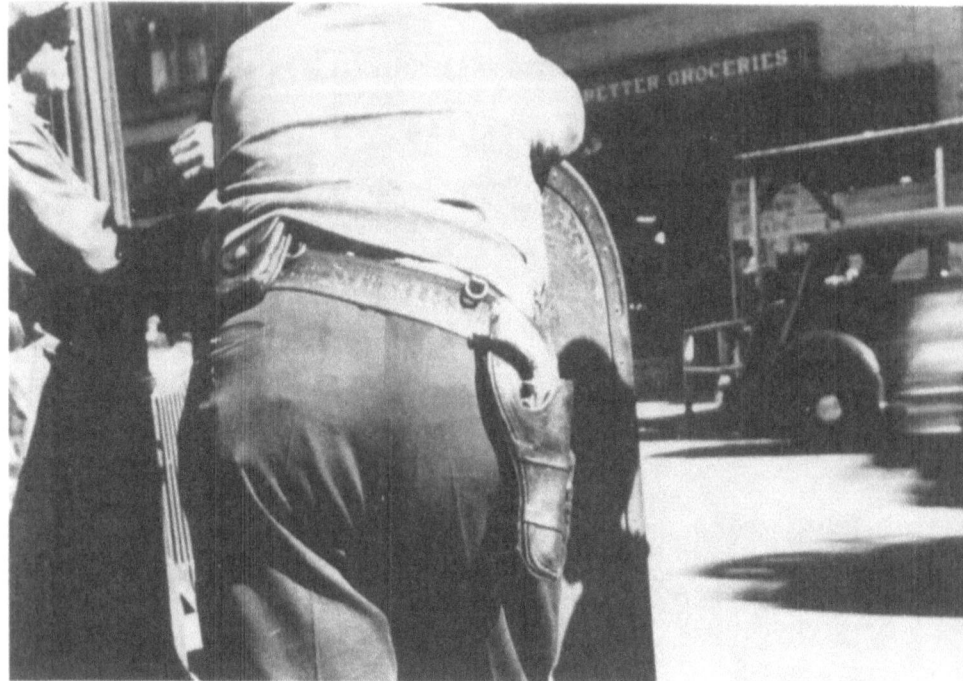

FIGURE 12
Ben Shahn, *Sheriff during Strike, Mor-*
gantown, West Virginia, 1935
Black and white photograph
Courtesy of The Harvard University
Art Museums (Fogg Art Museum); Gift
of Mrs. Bernarda Shahn

hikes.[52] *Fortune's* call for legislation regulating unions rather than
"a hysterical prohibition of strikes or a campaign of union busting"[53]
was answered the following summer with the passage of the Taft-
Hartley Act.

In returning to the three images discussed at the beginning of this
section, therefore, it is clear that Shahn's initial conceptualization of
the image of *Trouble* was of a relatively balanced fight, or at least of a
fight in which labor met the onslaughts of big business with grim de-
termination. In the serigraph, labor is losing ground, while the policeman, representative of law and the state, refuses to become involved.
What appears to be the ultimate defeat of the worker in the painting is
represented as the defeat of the individual, alone in a setting one usually associates with gaiety, crowds, and relaxation. Shahn has omitted

from his three versions of *Trouble* the signs or captions that often allow us to identify the activities in his paintings and posters. But there are enough iconographic clues within the three works themselves to allow us to view them as a gloss on contemporary events.

Censorship in the Art World

Events outside the field of organized labor were also drawing Shahn's attention in 1947. A new organization, Artists Equity Association (AEA), was formed that year, with Shahn as one of its founding members. Unlike the American Artists' Congress, an organization in which Shahn had also been involved and which was founded in 1935 as part of the Popular Front campaign against fascism, the AEA's primary focus was the economic security of artists.[54] It dealt with such issues as jury and rental fees, copyright, dealer relationships, industry-artist relationships, teaching positions, and publishing.[55] It was open to all artists whose work had been accepted in a major exhibition, who had a recognized dealer in the fine arts field, or who had other qualifications that established their status as professional artists.

But the AEA soon became embroiled in political issues as well. The editor of *Art News*, Alfred M. Frankfurter, described Artists Equity as "the desperately needed organization of artists cutting across divisions of Left and Right, of progressives and academicians—something, as it should be, between a labor union, a trade association, and a guild."[56] This desperate need was, in part, the result of a growth in the purchase, display, and reproduction of the work of living American artists over the previous decade.[57] But it was also the result of an art world that had become increasingly divided, on both political and aesthetic grounds. In writing his editorial, Frankfurter had one particularly divisive incident in mind. AEA's most important immediate task, he stated, was "to see the State Department case resolved with dignity to artists and art instead of with the disgrace which now surrounds them, both in the eyes of their gleeful detractors and of the public."[58] What was this event that caused Frankfurter so much concern and that, indeed, galvanized much of the art world?

At the end of April, Secretary of State George C. Marshall had announced the cancellation of "Advancing American Art," an exhibition of contemporary American art put together the previous year by J. Leroy Davidson, a member of the State Department, in response to the requests of a number of foreign countries for such an exhibition.[59] The exhibition was to present a positive image of the state of American painting to an international art world that tended to view the United States as a materialistic and technological, rather than artistic, nation. It was also to present "a conceptual image of the United States as a nation of humanistic, unprejudiced, and strongly individual people."[60] Seventy-nine oil paintings were purchased by the State Department for approximately $50,000. They, along with thirty-five watercolors, were then divided into two sections, one of which was sent to Europe and the other to Latin America.[61] At the time of the cancellation, the two wings of the show were in Haiti and Czechoslovakia. Shahn's paintings *Hunger* (1942–1943), *The Clinic* (1944–1945), and *Renascence* (1946) were among the works recalled.

The response of the art world to the cancellation of the show was swift. On May 5 over six hundred artists and friends met at the Capitol Hotel in New York to protest Marshall's action. The meeting was called by the Art Division of the Progressive Citizens of America (PCA), an organization founded in December 1946 out of the union of the Independent Citizens' Committee of the Arts, Sciences and Professions (ICCASP) and the National Citizens Political Action Committee (NCPAC). Both the ICCASP and the NCPAC had been created in 1944 (the former as the Independent Voters Committee of Arts and Sciences, the latter under the sponsorship of the CIO) in order to support and raise funds for the reelection of President Roosevelt.[62]

In the Program for Political Action adopted by the PCA, the organization claimed that the government had "fallen to men of shocking bigotry and ignorance, men dominated by the same stupid arrogance that brought the nation to its knees fifteen years ago." Because of this state of affairs a new national organization was needed to "seek unity among progressives . . . combat political apathy, which is reaction's weapon . . . [and] enlist millions of people in year-round action on national, state and local issues."[63] It was to be "independent of all political parties," and while it supported the policies of Henry Wallace, Wallace himself was not a member, feeling that his new position as editor of the *New Republic* prevented his formal affiliation with the group.

The founders of the PCA were not the only progressives to voice their concerns about the current political climate. In January 1947 Americans for Democratic Action (ADA) was founded in an attempt to prevent the PCA from becoming the rallying point for postwar liberals. Unlike the PCA, the ADA was stridently anti-communist in its membership regulations and attracted such notable Cold War liberals as Stewart Alsop, Sidney Hook, the Reverend Reinhold Niebuhr, and Arthur M. Schlesinger, Jr. Philip Murray, head of the CIO, had originally endorsed the PCA, but other CIO leaders, including Walter Reuther of the UAW, had committed themselves to the ADA. This prompted Murray to withdraw his endorsement of the PCA in mid-February and to ban any CIO affiliation with either organization in order to avoid a split in the federation.[64]

The first meeting of the executive committee of the Art Division of the PCA was held in New York on January 22, 1947. Among the original aims of the group was the establishment of regular membership meetings "at which one political speaker and one craft speaker would present [the] latest developments in the political scene affecting the artist-as-citizen."[65] It was fitting, therefore, that one of the Art Division's first actions was to organize a meeting to protest the State Department's cancellation of its art exhibition. What emerged from this meeting was a petition containing 1,500 names directed toward President Truman and Secretary Marshall, urging the continuation of the exhibition, and a resolution authorizing a delegation of artists to travel to Washington to register an official protest.[66]

Another goal of the Art Division of the PCA was the production of monographs on key issues, such as discrimination in the art world. The division published, therefore, the findings of the Washington delegation in a pamphlet entitled *The State Department and Art*. The delegation had discovered that the cancellation of the State Department exhibition was part of a larger attack on the whole Cultural and Information Division of the State Department by right-wing Congressmen such as Republican Representative Fred Buseby of Illinois. Buseby claimed that "more than 20 of the 45 artists were definitely New Deal in various shades of communism," and cited, among others, Milton Avery, Stuart Davis, Philip Evergood, and Ben Shahn.[67] The fact that Shahn's painting *Hunger* had been reproduced as a poster (Figure 13) for the CIO's anti-Republican congressional campaign of 1946 after it had been purchased by Davidson for the State Department further angered Republican congressional representatives.[68] What they seem to have forgotten, or been unaware of, was that the image had originally been conceived by Shahn for a government agency, the OWI, as an anti-war poster. According to the PCA pamphlet, Republican Congressman John Taber of New York used his position as Chairman of the House Committee on Appropriations to destroy most of the State Department's cultural program by cutting the Information

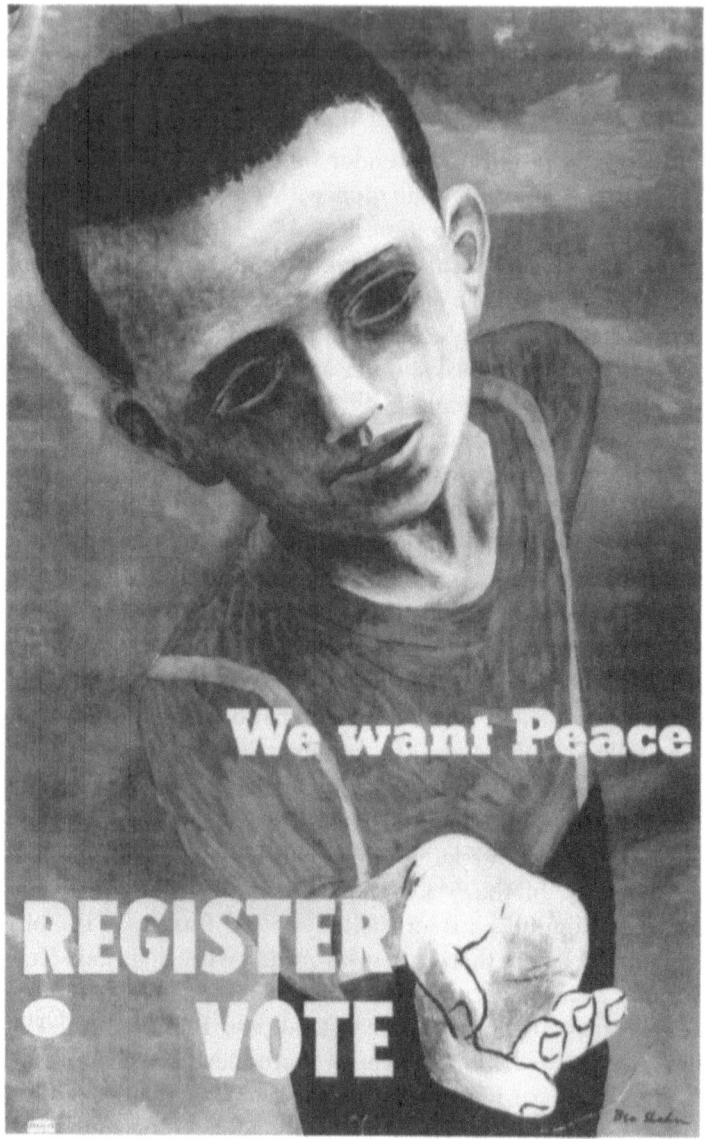

FIGURE 13

Ben Shahn, *We Want Peace: Register/
Vote,* 1946
Lithograph in colors
41⅜ × 26⅞"
New Jersey State Museum Collection,
Trenton; Purchase
Photographer: Dan Dragan

and Cultural Division's budget 48 percent and scuttling the entire art project.[69]

While the political affiliations of the artists were the focus of congressional attacks on the exhibition, criticisms were also raised regarding the style and content of the paintings. Many were described as "incomprehensible, ugly, and absurd" and Yasuo Kuniyoshi's *Circus Rider* elicited the much-publicized response from President Truman: "If that's art, I'm a Hottentot."[70] Hearst newspapers, including the *Baltimore American* and the *New York Journal American,* reproduced a number of works from the show, particularly those by Stuart Davis, John Marin, and Shahn, often inserting derogatory captions as comments on their questionable content and value.[71]

Among the artist organizations that objected to the State Department's exhibition were the American Artists Professional League, the National Academy of Design, the Salmagundi Club, and the Society of Illustrators. Their members, primarily concerned with reproducing surface appearances in their work, objected to modern art on both moral and aesthetic grounds. The concepts of order, conformity, clarity, and control were of the utmost importance to these artists. By supporting modern art, the government was symbolically legitimizing the values associated with that art—freedom, change, lack of control, ambiguity, and risk.[72] The works in the exhibition contained few traditional American scenes or landscapes, confronted the emotional traumas and moral contradictions of war, and spoke in an "international," or some claimed "foreign," art language of abstraction and expressionism. This was not the ideal of America or American art that conservative forces wanted projected abroad. The fact that the government was providing financial support to modern artists at a time when the art market was growing increasingly competitive undoubtedly contributed to the intensity of the attacks on the State Department show.

The most effective means of discouraging this support in 1947 was to label modern art communistic. The Truman administration, extremely sensitive to accusations of communist infiltration within its ranks, was quick to publicly dissociate itself from anything even remotely connected with the "Red Menace." Following his cancellation of the State Department show at the end of April, Secretary of State Marshall announced on May 6 that there would be "no more taxpayers' money for modern art."[73] The paintings from the show were subsequently sold as "surplus" by the War Assets Administration the following June, after having been on exhibit at the Whitney Museum for one month.[74]

The policies and activities of the New Deal era also became increasingly associated, in the minds of many, with communist subversion. Art produced under government sponsorship during the thirties and early forties was subjected to close scrutiny, and within a few months of the State Department fiasco Shahn was once again the focus of the criticisms of conservative politicians. The subject this time was a pair of murals for the Social Security Building in Washington, D.C. (Figures 14 and 15).

Shahn had been awarded the $19,980 commission by the Treasury Department in November 1940 as part of a program established in 1934 to decorate federal buildings, particularly post offices, with murals. Three hundred and seventy-five designs had been submitted and the four-artist jury—Edward Biberman, Kindred McLeary, Franklin Watkins, and Marguerite Zorach—had arrived at a unanimous decision, praising Shahn's designs for their "variety in tempo and texture" and "sombre, but good color."[75] Two other artists, Seymour Fogel and Philip Guston, also received mural commissions. Fogel's two panels, *The Wealth of the Nation* and *The Security of the People*, were painted in the building's lobby, while Guston's three-panel *Reconstruction and the Well-Being of the Family* was located in the auditorium. Shahn's two murals, approximately nine feet high and sixty feet long, were situated on opposing walls of the entrance of the north-south corridors and illustrated the theme *The Meaning of Social Security*. They were based, in particular, on a passage from an address Roosevelt had made to Congress:

> Among our objectives, I place the security of the men, women and children of the Nation first. This security for the individual and for the family concerns itself primarily with three factors. People want decent homes to live in; they want to work; and they want some safeguard against misfortunes which cannot be wholly eliminated from this man-made world of ours.[76]

Each mural was organized into three sections: unemployment, child labor, and old age on the east wall; work, the family, and social security on the west. Shahn conveyed his enthusiasm for the mural commission to Edward Bruce, who, along with Edward Rowan, administered the Treasury Department's mural program, in the following words: "To me, it is the most important job that I could want. The building itself is a symbol of perhaps the most advanced piece of legislation enacted by the New Deal, and I am proud to be given the job of interpreting it, or putting a face on it."[77] He later added that "it seems to me that in all my work for the past ten years, I have been probing into the material which is the background and substance of Social Security . . . all of it having to do with the problem of human insecurity."[78]

Shahn did not begin work on the murals until December 1941, a delay caused, in part, by his decision to change from "fresco buono" to tempera. This required replastering the walls and waiting several months for them to dry. He made the change because he felt the murals' proximity to the viewer (they come almost to the floor of the hallway) required more subtle effects.[79] In the meantime, of course, the United States had entered World War II, and during the seven months Shahn took to finish his murals, the halls of the Social Security Building were traversed by military as well as civilian personnel, with many comments directed Shahn's way. A rigger who worked on the construction of the building approved of the panel on steel construction, while a war contractor of handball courts criticized the court in Shahn's mural as faultily proportioned. One of the guards was reminded of his home state of Washington by the wheat farmer, while a man from Iowa felt that one of the men in overalls was the "spit'n'image" of his friend Ed Talbot. And an Army colonel, who approached Shahn while he was eating in the cafeteria, told him that "what you're painting up there on the wall is important to keep in front of all of us while we're fighting this war."[80] Shahn summarized his response to all of these comments a few years later:

> I'm not sure what I think about Tolstoi's definition of great art as the kind that pleases the most people. I suspect it's one of those half truths. I don't know. But I do know I get a kick out of being able to paint in the same picture "the spit'n'image of Ed Talbot" and the war aims of an Army colonel, while all the time other pictures of mine are hanging in the Museum of Modern Art.[81]

Five years after their completion, the murals once again drew the attention of Washington officials. On June 27, 1947, an article appeared on the front page of the Washington *Evening Star* commenting on a letter from the Federal Security Administration (FSA) to the Public Buildings Administration (PBA) requesting that Shahn's murals be removed or destroyed because of adverse criticism (the FSA had moved into the Social Security Building). Mrs. Ruth Thorne, assistant to the Director of Information of the FSA, was quoted as saying that

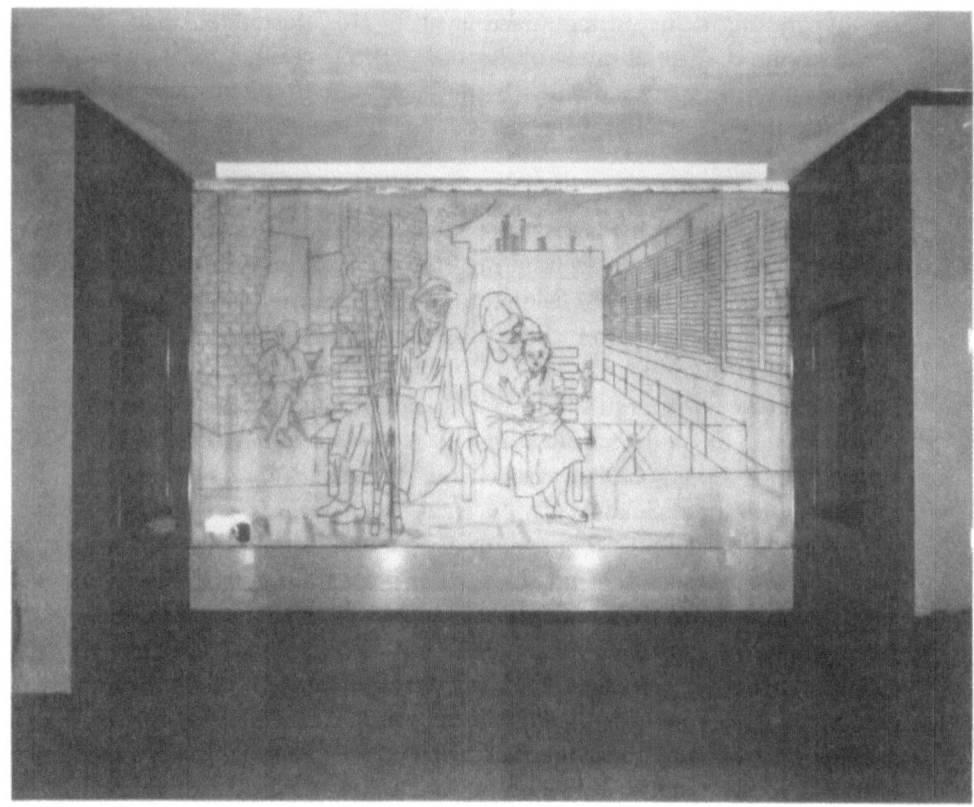

FIGURE 14

Ben Shahn, Mural, Social Security
Building (now Wilbur J. Cohen Federal
Building), 1940–1942
Cartoon, east wall, detail
Commissioned by the Section of Fine
Arts, Public Buildings Administration,
United States Treasury
Photograph courtesy of National Ar-
chives, 121-PS-8250

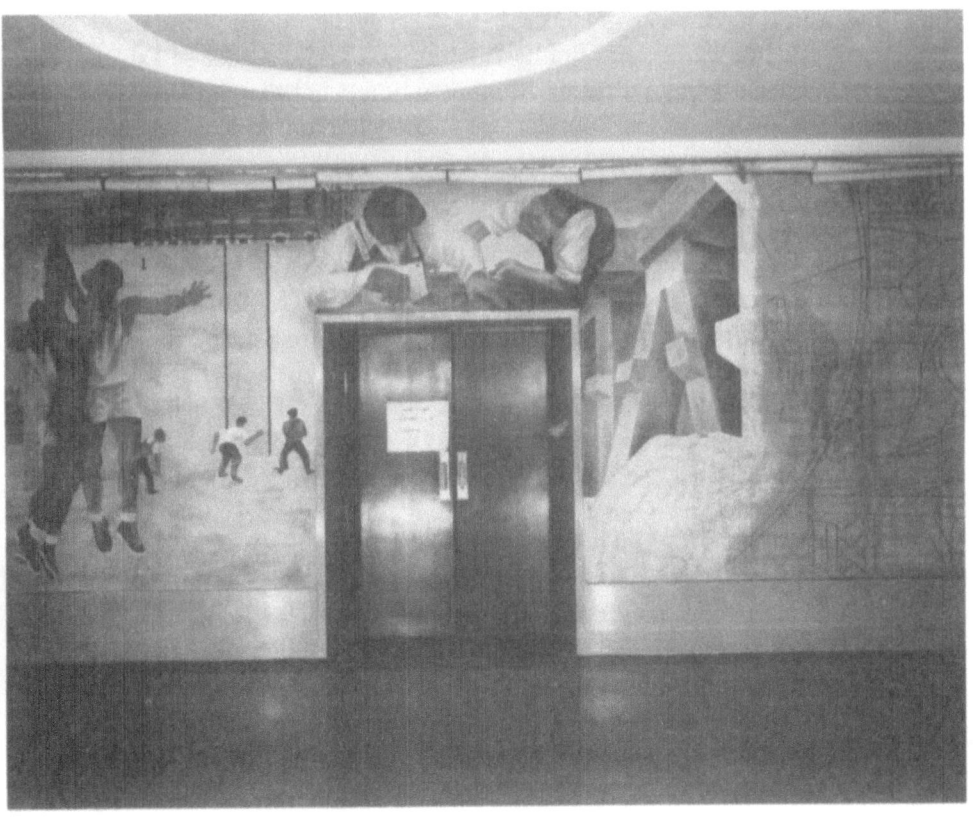

FIGURE 15
Ben Shahn, Mural, Social Security
Building (now Wilbur J. Cohen Federal
Building), 1940–1942
West wall, in progress
Tempera
Commissioned by the Section of Fine
Arts, Public Buildings Administration,
United States Treasury
Photograph courtesy of National Ar-
chives, 121-PS-8251

the murals were no longer suitable for the new occupants of the building—which included the Public Health Service, the Office of Education, and the Food and Drug Administration—and that, in her opinion, the people in the murals "are in poor circumstances and look quite pathetic."[82]

Even before the *Evening Star* article appeared, phone calls had been made and letters exchanged within the art world trying to head off the destruction of the murals. On June 26 George G. Thorp, assistant director of the American Federation of Arts (AFA) wrote to the Executive Director of the AFA, Hudson Walker, reassuring him that information was being gathered on the FSA request and that Juliana Force, first vice-president of the AFA, and James Thrall Soby were being kept apprised of the situation.[83] Of obvious concern to all was the possibility that the murals would be removed quickly and quietly before anyone knew what was happening. Having worked on Diego Rivera's ill-fated Rockefeller Center mural, Shahn was especially aware of the speed with which such destruction could be carried out.

Soon after the *Evening Star* article came out, Alfred H. Barr, Jr., of MOMA wrote to Francis P. Douglas at the *Evening Star's* city desk commending him for giving publicity to this attempt to destroy the murals. Shahn "had to deal with tragic human subject matter," stated Barr, and naturally could not treat it "in the spirit of Pollyanna." The most famous mural in the world, Michelangelo's *Last Judgment*, was "not very gay either." Shahn was generally recognized as one of the leading American artists of his generation both at home and abroad, noted Barr, and the destruction of his murals would be an act of "major vandalism." He added that "the ignorance and reactionary prejudices concerning modern American painting recently displayed in several high quarters in Washington is humiliating to every American interested in his country's reputation as a center of culture."[84]

The same day that the *Evening Star* article appeared, Shahn received a letter from Alan Reitman, Director of Public Relations for the CIO-PAC, assuring him that the murals would not be taken down and that he and others had "managed to block the thing in one of the Congressional subcommittees."[85] Shahn also received further assurances from James Thrall Soby in a letter of July 2:

> The Washington murals are in no apparent danger. This from Admiral
> Peebles, who is in charge of Washington buildings and now begs every-

body not to raise a fuss for fear the Hearst papers will pick it up and get at Congress. The fact is, however, that they were in very real danger.[86]

While Hudson Walker wrote to Shahn as late as July 24 expressing his concern over the unfavorable comments being voiced in Washington about his Social Security Building murals,[87] the combined protests of Soby, Reitman, Barr, and others managed to prevent them from being removed.[88]

Government antagonism toward modern art and the resulting threats and acts of censorship were thus of central concern to artists in 1947. In its pamphlet on the Washington delegation's findings, the Art Division of the PCA announced that on October 25–26 the National Arts, Sciences and Professions Council of PCA would hold a national conference in New York to discuss the question of cultural freedom and civil rights. A similar meeting on the West Coast had already been held on July 10 in Beverly Hills. The theme of the meeting had been "Thought Control in the United States," and among the talks presented was "The Attack on the American Artist" by Edward Biberman. Biberman criticized the cancellation of the State Department show and compared the recent assaults on modern artists to those of Hitler.[89]

While Shahn was not one of the original members of the PCA's Art Division,[90] he became increasingly involved in the division's activities as the year progressed, joining in campaigns to protest the censorship of Anton Refregier's murals in the Rincon Annex of the San Francisco Post Office[91] and the firing of ten writers and directors in Hollywood who had been cited by the House Committee on Un-American Activities (HUAC).[92] He would become even more involved the following year, when the PCA formally endorsed Wallace's candidacy at its second annual convention in mid-January and became officially affiliated with the new Progressive Party. In the early months of the PCA Art Division's existence, however, Shahn was busy with another project that attempted to fuse art and politics.

Bernarda Bryson Shahn recalls a March 1947 luncheon meeting at the Algonquin Hotel in New York with Shahn, Bob Osborne, Leo Lionni, David Stone Martin, and William D. Pawley, who at that time was the U.S. ambassador to Brazil. Pawley had invited them there to tell them of a Latin American magazine called *Topaz*, modeled on the political magazines of early-nineteenth-century France, which contained a number of political cartoons. Pawley was interested in providing the financial backing for a similar magazine in the United States and wanted to know if they, in turn, would be interested in organizing it.[93] Despite Pawley's conservative politics, the group decided to take him up on his offer.

On April 9 Shahn, Bryson Shahn, Betty Chamberlain, Adolf Dehn, William Gropper, John Groth, Bob Osborne, and Mitchell Siporin met to discuss the general form the magazine was to take. They decided it would be primarily an artist's magazine, with writers producing captions or text for the illustrations, reversing the usual process of having the artist illustrate the writer or editor's ideas. It would also be humorous and satirical. Among the subjects proposed at that time were France, Clare Booth Luce, and Thomas Dewey; suggested writers were Earl Wilson, James Agee, Kenneth Fearing, and e. e. cummings. The magazine was to have a fully cooperative form of organization, with a rotating editorial board of three artists and with all general matters coming before the full membership of the group.[94]

By November 17 they had produced a more finished proposal. The name of the magazine was to be *Mugwumps*, a term referring to individuals who bolt from their party's policies, though not necessarily from the party itself, to support alternative positions.[95] The choice of this particular name suggests the group's dissatisfaction with the current leaders and policies of the Republican and Democratic parties and perhaps a willingness to support the growing third-party movement in the United States. The magazine would be composed of 75 percent drawings and cartoons and 25 percent text and would sell for ten cents at newsstands, once a month to begin with, fortnightly if it was successful. The list of topics now included housing, the atom bomb, anti-labor bills, Russia, the United Nations, and more.[96] Unfortunately, *Mugwumps* never got past the dummy stage, but much of the energy and many of the ideas explored by the group were undoubtedly put to use in the upcoming Progressive Party campaign.[97]

A Tribute to Shahn

The decision to have a major retrospective exhibition of Shahn's work in the fall of 1947 was made by MOMA's Exhibition Committee the previous April. James Thrall Soby was appointed director of the show. According to his assistant Dorothy Miller, Soby's enthusiasm for Shahn's work was a major factor in the museum's decision.[98] But Shahn was not a stranger to the Museum of Modern Art. In 1930 his work had been included in the exhibition "46 Painters and Sculptors under 35 Years of Age."[99] Two years later MOMA's Lincoln Kirstein had invited him to participate in a mural show. Shahn submitted two paintings, a montage of three pictures from his 1931–1932 series on the trial of Nicola Sacco and Bartolomeo Vanzetti, found guilty of murder in 1921 and executed in 1927, and an enlargement of one section of the mural. The latter depicted the Lowell Committee, headed by Harvard University's president A. Lawrence Lowell and charged with reviewing the court's findings after protests of racial and political bias on the part of the presiding judge; Judge Webster Thayer; and the coffins of Sacco and Vanzetti (Figure 16). The inclusion of unflattering likenesses of four public figures, however, produced objections from some of the museum trustees. Shahn subsequently received an offer of $2,000 for the second painting, which would have prevented it from being hung in the show.[100]

Shahn refused this offer, and when Kirstein informed him that this work would not be exhibited, a group of Shahn's supporters suggested organizing a "Hang Shahn Committee." In the end, both of Shahn's paintings were included in the show, and he received a telegram from Diego Rivera congratulating him on his success. In recalling this incident Shahn commented: "I was in my glory. The big money had wheeled out its heavy artillery and then wheeled it back without firing a shot. I had won my first battle."[101]

Shahn's subsequent encounters with the museum were much less combative. Over the next decade and a half individual works of his appeared in exhibitions held both in the United States and abroad,[102] and in 1943 eleven of his canvases were included in the show "American Realists and Magic Realists," organized by Dorothy Miller. The criteria for inclusion in the show were stylistic. Paintings had to display a "'sharp focus and precise representation,' whether the subject has been observed in the outer world—'realism,' or contrived by the imagination—'magic realism.'"[103] This particular mode of representation had fallen out of favor with the art world in the early twentieth century, noted Miller, but had recently "enjoyed a revival of interest on the part of a number of artists." She added that the public, of course, had never lost interest in this type of painting, for

no other style of painting appeals so naturally to the great majority of people, and in this sense it is a truly democratic style, offering no barrier

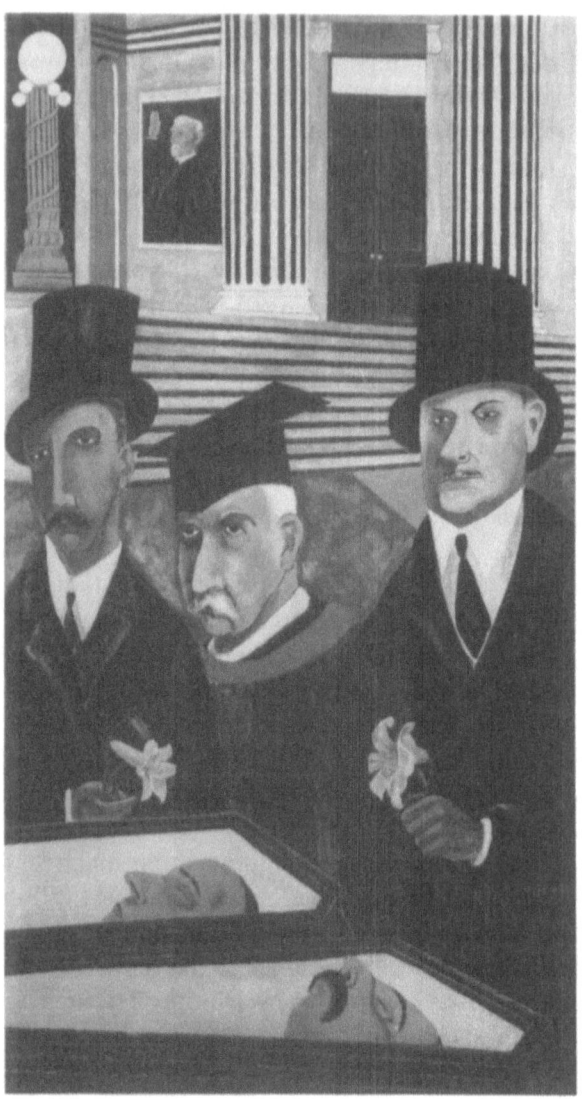

FIGURE 16

Ben Shahn, *The Passion of Sacco and Vanzetti*, from the Sacco and Vanzetti series of 23 paintings, 1931–1932
Tempera on canvas
84½ × 48″
Collection of Whitney Museum of American Art, New York, Gift of Edith and Milton Lowenthal in memory of Juliana Force 49.22

of technique between the artist and the untrained eye. Now, after periods of impressionist, abstract and expressionist art, it is once again of interest to the cultivated taste, as it has always been to the general public.[104]

In 1943 Miller had reason to believe that such democratic art forms might be in the ascendancy, just as many believed that a people's democracy led by Roosevelt and Wallace was an inevitability after the war. The events of postwar America, however, would, in both cases, prove otherwise.

Shahn's works were purchased, as well as exhibited, by MOMA. By 1943 *Handball* (1939) and *Bartolomeo Vanzetti and Nicola Sacco* (1931–1932) were already included in the museum's permanent collection. The latter had been donated by Abigail Rockefeller, who had bought the painting in 1932, the year in which the entire Sacco and Vanzetti series had been exhibited at the Downtown Gallery. According to Philip Wittenberg, she had wanted to purchase the complete series because "come the Revolution, I can fill the windows with these, and the House of Rockefeller may survive."[105] Unfortunately, Wittenberg had already purchased one of the paintings.[106]

Shahn also came into brief contact with another member of the Rockefeller family as an assistant to Diego Rivera on his *Man at the Crossroads* mural for Rockefeller Center. The inclusion of the head of Lenin in the mural had prompted Nelson Rockefeller to request its removal in a letter dated May 4, 1933. The destruction of the mural was due, at least in part, to Rivera's refusal to grant this request. Shahn organized a parade to protest the proposed destruction and helped Rivera draft a response to Rockefeller's letter.[107]

Shahn's MOMA retrospective in the fall of 1947, therefore, was the culmination of a seventeen-year relationship with the museum, a relationship that had not always been conflict-free. In fact, while Soby was hanging the retrospective, he was informed that one of the MOMA trustees disapproved of the inclusion of Shahn's CIO posters. Soby refused to remove the posters and, with the backing of the museum's director, René d'Harnoncourt, they remained in place.[108] Shahn's retrospective was also the culmination of a seventeen-year struggle to express, in visual form, the stories that were, for him, more important than formal experimentation for its own sake.

What was the response to Shahn's exhibition? How did critics position him within the highly volatile art world of 1947? Many of the reviews reflected the themes presented in the essay by Soby discussed earlier: Shahn as the opposite of the "pure" painter; Shahn as a financially successful and distinctively American artist who engaged in political as well as artistic activities. The evaluation of these characteristics varied, however, as did the interpretation of the meaning of Shahn's images and his artistic talents.

One of the more favorable reviews of Shahn's show was a short article by Betty Chamberlain in the October issue of *Art News*. Like Soby, Chamberlain described Shahn's reputation in concrete terms: "Shahn has achieved extraordinary popularity in a very short time. His four one man shows since 1930 have all sold rapidly, and so far there seems to be a purchaser almost as soon as each picture is finished."[109] Shahn's method of working was of particular interest to Chamberlain:

> For years Shahn has alternated between periods of solitary work in his shop at home and periods of work in the midst of social activity. In his own shop he stores up material and ideas and puts them down in easel paintings . . . When a mural commission or a job to make government or union posters has come along, he can call upon the stored-up ideas. "It is like breathing," he says, "the work in my shop is the intake while the work on the jobs is the outgo."[110]

According to Shahn, this combination of activities had worked out well so far and he hoped that it would continue to do so in the future, for though he was at present in a period of shop work, he knew that the upcoming year was election year and that "some work is going to have to be done about it."[111]

Chamberlain also pointed out an interesting development in Shahn's use of architecture and architectural ornamentation in his painting. In his early Sacco-Vanzetti series it filled the background and functioned "as abstract designs in addition to being expressive symbols of the character in the drama." In *Walker Greets the Mother of Mooney* (1932–1933) "the house itself is eloquent about Mooney's background and his mother's reactions." With the war period, things changed. The architectural details became more baroque and were no longer "the full stop to the picture; they stepped to one side and left room for greater depths and richer colors."[112] While the horizon was abruptly cut off by the red brick wall in both *Vacant Lot* (1939) and *Nazi Brutality* (Figure 2) it reached to what Chamberlain called "a surrealist infinity" in works such as *East 12th Street* (1947). In this painting two walls are placed at diagonals in the left and right sections of the painting, leaving the center empty except for three roller-skating figures, who follow the line of the left-hand building into the distance.

Shahn's obsession with detailed depictions of architecture and his considerable talent in this respect can undoubtedly be traced to his apprenticeship as a young man in Hessenberg's lithography shop, where he was required to engrave on stone exact perspectives of brick plants or chain factories or textile mills for letterheads and labels.[113] While Chamberlain points to the change in the nature of the architectural elements and details in Shahn's paintings and their role as primary background elements, she does not venture to comment on the significance of this change. With the horizon abruptly cut off, one is forced to confront the images in the foreground—the rubble and the claustrophobic existence of urban life for the boy in *Vacant Lot;* the horror of the execution of the men of Lidice, Czechoslovakia, by the Nazis in the OWI poster *Nazi Brutality.* One is also often able to locate the foreground events by reading the architectural details ("the house itself is eloquent about Mooney's background"). Opening up the background to a "surrealist infinity," on the other hand, causes the images in the foreground to lose some of their primacy, the eye being drawn away from them by the well-marked diagonals of the walls or roadways. The standardization of architectural elements (baroque, classical) also makes it more difficult to establish a specific time and place.

In a work not discussed by Chamberlain but included in the exhibition, Shahn creates a space somewhere between the abrupt truncation of *Nazi Brutality* and the "surrealist infinity" of *East 12th Street.* At first glance, *Spring* (Figure 17), painted in 1947, appears suffused with a sense of calm and well-being. The couple is enjoying the freshness of spring on a lush green lawn. Two children skip by in the distance. The painting would be described the following year as "a twentieth century American *fête champetre*—the public city park in place of the aristocratic groves of Watteau and the riverside picnics of Courbet and Seurat."[114] Yet the plant in the woman's hand is a thistle, both beautiful and threatening, and she holds its sharp thorns uncomfortably close to her companion's face. Indeed, the lower half of the young man's face is a dark red, and his hand is raised in a protective gesture, as if to ward off the advances of the young woman. The sharply receding fences that meet at the horizon to the right of center pull us away from the figures. Yet the woman's bright red dress keeps drawing us

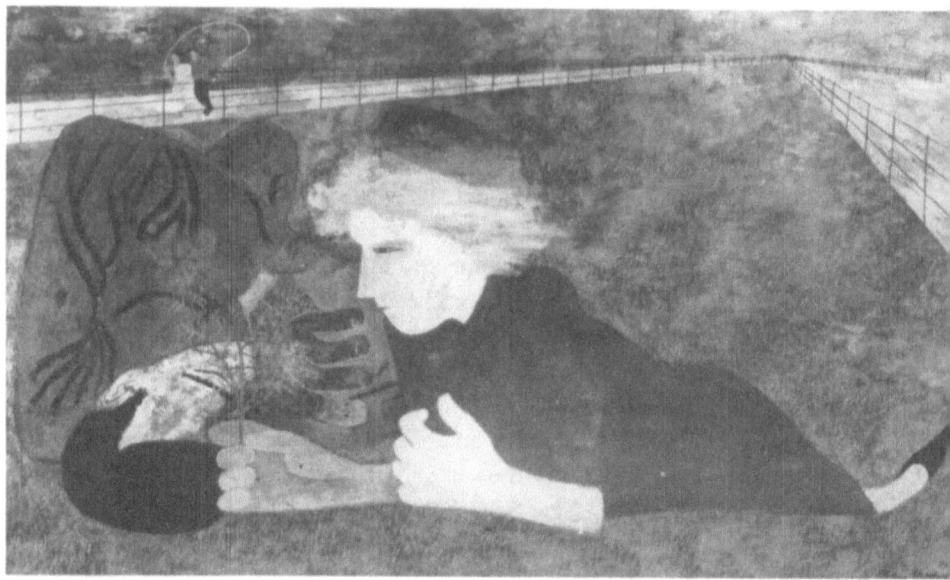

FIGURE 17
Ben Shahn, *Spring,* 1947
Tempera on masonite
17 × 30″
Collection: Albright-Knox Art Gallery,
Buffalo, New York; Room of Contempo-
rary Art Fund, 1948

back, creating a sharp, staccato rhythm, which is broken somewhat by
the red and yellow tops of the skipping children.

Ultimately, the image is unsettling. It appears to offer the viewer a
choice—escape into the empty and unknown distant landscape or remain in the foreground and confront the troubling relationship between the two figures, with its potential mistrust and deception (the
carefree days of childhood cannot be recaptured). Yet it denies that
choice by not allowing us to rest at either point on the picture plane.
The painting was certainly a fitting metaphor for the spring of 1947,
when talk of another world war clouded the future and the search for
communists sowed suspicion and mistrust among the survivors of a
more optimistic New Deal era.

Spring was also an indication of Shahn's move away from docu-
mentations of specific historical events, with their recognizable architectural forms, toward the development of a symbolic language that
could, in his mind, better represent the changed nature of postwar

social relationships. In the mid-1950s Shahn commented retrospectively on this change in his work. After his photographic journeys of the late thirties he believed that "the incidental, the individual, and the topical were enough; that in such instances of life all of life could be implied." But after the war, he came to feel that this was not enough. He began to question, along with many artists, the value of portraying only the visible appearance of historical events. "I wanted to reach farther, to tap some sort of universal experience," he stated, "to create symbols that would have some such universal quality." At the same time, he did not want to return to the impersonal generalities and statistics he had rejected in the late thirties. For Shahn, the universal experience was "that private experience which illuminates the private and personal world in which each of us lives the major part of his life."[115]

Robert M. Coates, in a review for the *New Yorker,* commented on this combination of the particular and the universal in Shahn's work. According to Coates, Shahn possessed the ability "to combine an appearance of matter-of-factness and realism with an enormous atmospheric suggestion, an ability to make concrete images flow effortlessly into the symbolic." As an accomplished draftsman, Shahn evinced "a rigid respect for the limitations of the picture plane that [made] many of his designs seem almost abstract."[116] Shahn was thus both a realist and a symbolist, adept at both draftsmanship and abstraction.

Coates perceived this flow from the concrete to the symbolic in the content, as well as the form, of Shahn's painting. His work "was already proving itself ill-adapted to the blunt purposes of direct propaganda," causing him to turn, therefore, to personal commentary. "He is less passionate than he is compassionate," states Coates; "he satirizes instead of denouncing." Recently Shahn had moved away from a "wry commentary on life around the corner" to "a slightly freer use of fantasy." These developments in Shahn's work—from direct propaganda to wry commentary to use of fantasy—were positive moves in Coates' mind, extending the implications of his work. *The Red Stairway* (1944; Figure 38) represented not only a crippled man climbing a staircase but also the "endless frustrations of mankind."[117]

Yet there were many critics who resisted speaking about Shahn's work in terms of fantasy or explorations of the limitations of the picture plane (two characteristics often referred to in descriptions of the work of the abstract expressionists) and who insisted, instead, that the narrative, political element in Shahn's work was still primary. In a review for *Art Digest,* Ralph Pearson claimed that Shahn's goal was to produce an art of storytelling and social commentary, a goal he attained "with distinction." According to Pearson, Shahn's success in this respect was of particular importance because of the growing number of people who were of the opinion that "the exact opposite of this course"—i.e., the creation of an art based on aesthetic sensation alone, was of greater relevance for contemporary artists.[118] An artist and teacher as well as a critic, Pearson believed that the fundamental tenet of modern art was "designed creation." An artist was not to copy reality but to transform it into a more meaningful imagery through a recognizable order and design. This belief was accompanied by a faith in the power of the artist, as an artist, to change society, to have an effect on the outside world. For Pearson, great art required a combination of both aesthetic value and social commentary, a combination that he felt was present in Shahn's work.[119]

Another critic approved of Shahn's social commentary, although not without certain reservations. In her review for the Communist Party paper *People's World,* Ann Leonard found the exhibition "remarkable" and the artist someone who "has assimilated a rich variety of experiences, yet who continues to respond with an honest sensitivity attuned to the working people from whom he comes." Yet the worker's family, as portrayed in Shahn's work, at times

> becomes an object of dismay, almost to the point of revulsion. . . . It is often in his treatment of faces that the artist betrays either a confusion or a somewhat unhealthy adjustment to his subjects. Perhaps it stems from a little too much pity, a little too much concern over what he may feel to be weak and helpless elements in society.[120]

For the CPUSA in the late 1940s, art was above all a political weapon and as such had to be a source of strength and inspiration rather than of pity, confusion, or resignation. Art could not be divorced from the politics of the artist or the changing dictates of the party. When, early in 1946, Albert Maltz, a party member, tried to argue that a work of art must be viewed "as to its real quality—its deep evaluation of life, character and social scene" rather than "as to whether or not it was the proper 'leaflet' for the moment," he was soundly chastised by party officials and forced to recant.[121] Gone were the days of Popular Front alliances and "communism as twentieth-century Americanism," a slogan formulated by Earl Browder during his tenure as CPUSA leader from 1935 to 1945. Browder had even dissolved the CPUSA in

1944 and created, in its stead, the Communist Political Association (CPA). The CPA had then put its organizational support behind Roosevelt and had worked, primarily through the CIO-PAC, to help ensure his reelection.

Browder's reformism was brought to an end, however, in the summer of 1945, when he was ousted from the leadership of the CPA by his opponent William Z. Foster, who immediately reconstituted the CPUSA. In addition, the snowballing of anti-communist sentiment and legislation in the late forties and early fifties resulted in the CPUSA closing ranks and conducting its own purges of those unwilling to follow the policies of the CPUSA leaders, which were now more closely aligned with those of Stalin and the Russian Communist Party than they had been during Browder's leadership. In the area of culture, this meant the implementation of the policies of Andrei Zhdanov, which, in the Soviet Union, had led to the crackdown on dissident writers and the subordination of art to politics. In the spirit of "Zhdanovshchina," therefore, Eugene Dennis, general secretary of the CPUSA, condemned the Maltz article in a mid-February 1946 meeting of the National Committee as "bourgeois-intellectual and semi-Trotskyist."[122]

The harshest review of Shahn's show was written by someone Eugene Dennis might well have dismissed in similar terms—Clement Greenberg.[123] Greenberg found the artist's technical skills wanting—his color was tawdry and artificial and his drawing banal. Greenberg did not stop there, however:

> Ben Shahn's gift, though indisputable, is rarely effective beyond a surface felicity. What his retrospective show at the Museum of Modern Art (through January 4) makes all too clear is how lacking his art is in density and resonance. These pictures are mere stitchings on the border of the cloth of the painting, little flashes of talent that have to be shaded from the glare of high tradition lest they disappear from sight.[124]

On the positive side, Greenberg allowed that Shahn had been at least momentarily successful in his use of a "quasi-expressionist, half-impressionist" style, derived from pre-cubist artists such as Cézanne and Vlaminck. And unlike Coates, who saw Shahn's interest in photography as having been responsible for an unfortunate hint of the mechanical in his work,[125] Greenberg saw it as having had a positive influence. Out of this interest Shahn had developed "the formula which remains responsible for most of the successful pictures he has painted since then: the flat, dark, exact silhouette placed upstage against a re-

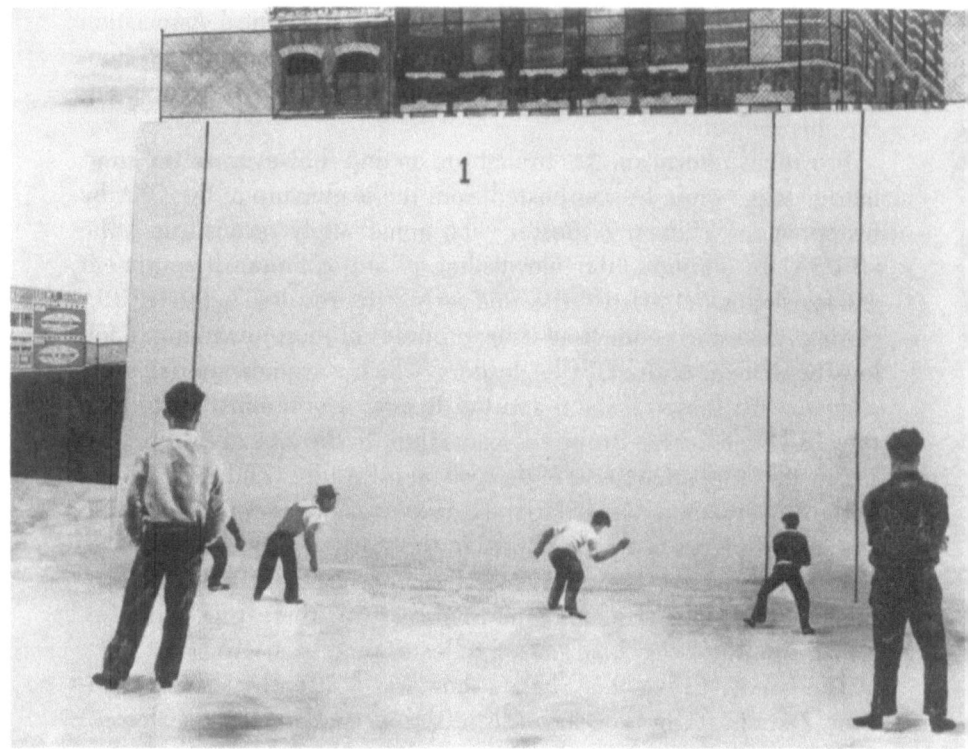

FIGURE 18

Ben Shahn, *Handball*, 1939
Tempera on paper over composition
board
22¾ × 31¼″
Collection, The Museum of Modern
Art, New York; Abby Aldrich Rockefeller Fund

ceding empty, flat plane that is uptilted sharply to close the back of the
picture and contradict the indication of deep space." *Handball* (1939;
Figure 18) and *East 12th Street* (1947) were two pictures that issued
from this formula. Indeed, Greenberg commented further that Shahn
was "more naturally a photographer than painter . . . surest of himself
when he orients his picture in terms of dark and light." [126]

Shahn's experiences as a photographer had, in fact, had an influence
on the development of his painting, although this influence was not
limited solely to the area of formal concerns. During the course of his
employment as a photographer for the RA/FSA from 1935 to 1938

Shahn took approximately six thousand photographs.[127] He conceived of them both as "sketches" for future paintings and as documentation, a record of a certain moment in history. In 1944 he commented that, as a group, he and the other photographers

> had only one purpose—a moral one I suppose. So we decided: no angle shots, no filters, no mats, nothing glossy but paper . . . We tried to present the ordinary in an extraordinary manner. But that's a paradox because the only thing extraordinary about it was that it was so ordinary. Nobody had ever done it before, deliberately. Now it's called documentary. . . . We just took pictures that cried out to be taken.[128]

The facts presented in RA/FSA photographs, however, were not left totally to the discretion of the photographers. They were provided with "shooting scripts" listing the types of things Roy Stryker, the head of the photographic section (officially called the Historical Unit) of the RA/FSA, would prefer to have photographed, such as families listening to the radio and gatherings on street corners.[129] The end result was a group of photographs marked by a sense of "compassion rather than collective struggle."[130] There were few photographs of striking workers or lynchings or clashes between the unemployed and the police (or, at least, few that were printed and distributed); instead, one finds run-down farm houses and small-town gas stations or tenant farmers who confront the photographer with blank or worried stares.

Shahn's choice of compassion rather than collective struggle as the overriding theme for his photographs was part of a more comprehensive re-evaluation of the subject matter of his work. Having left the urban environment of New York City, with its strikes and organized political agitation, he had, in his own words,

> crossed and recrossed many sections of the country, and had come to know well so many people of all kinds of belief and temperament, which they maintained with a transcendent indifference to their lot in life. Theories had melted before such experience. My own painting then had turned from what is called "social realism" into a sort of personal realism. I found the qualities of people a constant pleasure . . .[131]

What Shahn found lacking in the theories about art and politics debated in the meetings of the Artists' Union and John Reed Clubs was a consideration of the "qualities of people," the beliefs and temperaments of particular individuals that allowed them to survive economic crises. He began to place greater emphasis in his paintings, therefore, on the private moments of individuals rather than their public struggles, believing that an understanding of such private moments would help make more effective the public struggles to extend the rights and improve the lives of American workers, particularly through the labor movement and the New Deal policies of the Roosevelt administration. By the mid-thirties Shahn was also becoming increasingly impatient with the factionalism within the organized left, especially between supporters of Stalin and Trotsky. It was this infighting, and in particular attacks on Trotsky supporter Diego Rivera, that, according to Shahn, led him to sever his ties with *Art Front* late in 1935.[132]

While Shahn drew extensively on his store of photographs for ideas for his paintings throughout the forties, by the end of the decade the relationship between the two had become a point of contention for the artist. For example, the influence of his photography on his paintings had been the focus of an article in the May 1946 issue of *U.S. Camera*, and Shahn had not been particularly pleased with the way the paintings and photographs had been mechanically juxtaposed.[133] In a letter sent just before the opening of his MOMA show, Soby informed Shahn that he had vetoed a request from the *New York Times* for some of his photographs for an article on Shahn as a painter and a photographer because he thought it would "turn into another U.S. Camera article, which you hadn't liked—nor I."[134] In an earlier letter thanking Shahn for his comments on the text for the 1947 Penguin book, Soby had added that he worried considerably about the tendency to connect Shahn's painting and photography too closely. He had tried, therefore, "to qualify whatever I said about your photography by pointing out how different the paintings are in final conception and spirit."[135]

In keeping with his intentions as outlined in this letter, Soby noted in the Penguin text that Shahn's "approach to photography was almost certainly dictated by his vision as a painter," and that "while Shahn's painting often records a photographically arrested reality, its impact is quickened by the most exacting and imaginative painterly means." Paintings such as *Handball* and *The Welders*, while derived from photographs, stood on their own as completely separate images. "In brief," stated Soby, "Shahn uses photography as other artists use preliminary sketches, and from its notations proceeds under the compulsion of a painter's inner vision."[136]

Shahn admitted in the *U.S. Camera* article that he used photography "to make notes for future paintings." But he also pointed out that he was interested in the medium as a means of documentation and not in trying to make an "art" out of photography in the sense of attempting to create painterly or "otherworldly" effects.[137] Both Shahn and Soby tried, therefore, to distance Shahn's paintings from his photographs, giving primacy to the former. Greenberg's praise of Shahn as a photographer was thus a double-edged compliment.

In summing up his review, Greenberg struck the same dismissive note with which he had begun it, describing Shahn's work as "derivative" and as "essentially beside the point as far as ambitious present-day painting is concerned." Greenberg did not blame Shahn alone, however, for the failings of his art. "Shahn has a genuine gift," stated Greenberg, "and that he has not done more with it is perhaps the fault of the milieu in which he has worked, even more than his own."[138] The nature of this milieu was quite evident in 1947, as it is now in retrospect. It was composed of the union hall, the campaign headquarters, and the semi-rural garment-worker community, as well as the studio. It was filled with people engaged in political as well as artistic discussions and actions. It was the lifeblood of Shahn's politics and aesthetics. If such a milieu was detrimental to the development of significant art, what was to take its place? And exactly what type of art would emerge from this new milieu to assume the role of "ambitious present-day painting"?

Greenberg provided his answers to these questions in various articles over the next few years. One such article, "The Present Prospects of American Painting and Sculpture," had already appeared in the October 1947 issue of the British journal *Horizon,* a month before his review of Shahn's exhibition. In this essay Greenberg lamented the sorry state of contemporary American art and placed the blame for this situation on the poverty of middle-class cultural taste. The use of art as part of a campaign to educate the middle and lower classes in order to provide buyers for the products of a burgeoning cultural market had succeeded in both "raising the lowest standards of consumption" and bringing "the highest down to meet them." Greenberg saw this improvement of middle-class taste and its attendant mass cultural market as dangerous, because it "seduc[ed] writers and artists into rationalizing and packaging for mass distribution even the most pretentious products."[139]

This was not the first time Greenberg had attacked the philistinism of the middle class or bourgeoisie. In his 1939 article "Avant-Garde and Kitsch," he had advocated the creation of an elite cadre of artists whose duty it would be to preserve the best of bourgeois culture from the confusion and violence of the times.[140] Without such an avant-garde, the arts would fall prey to kitsch, an imitative art which developed in industrialized capitalist and totalitarian societies to amuse a mass proletariat who could not appreciate true culture. Hitler, Stalin, and Mussolini used kitsch as their official culture to ingratiate themselves with the masses, who preferred kitsch because it was easily recognizable and required little effort to enjoy. To provide the masses with true art would require providing them with the leisure time necessary to appreciate this art, which would mean a restructuring of the means and relations of production that would result in socialism. This was obviously not what fascist governments wanted, nor was it what the liberal, reform government of the United States wanted, no matter how much social-welfare legislation it might enact. The avant-garde, therefore, faced with the hostility of the masses and the shrinking support of the ruling classes, who were becoming too materialistic to support true art, could merely act as the preservers of whatever living culture was left until the inevitable appearance of socialism.

Greenberg's attack on middle-class taste in 1947, however, was not phrased as part of a larger socialist program. Rejecting the CPUSA policy of art as a political weapon on the one hand and the humanist ideals of social liberals (whom he labeled "Whitmanesque blowhards" in his *Horizon* article) on the other, Greenberg and a number of abstract artists, including Barnett Newman and Robert Motherwell, came to believe that artists were unable to comment directly upon social conditions in their work.[141] As early as 1944 Robert Motherwell had remarked that

> the materialism of the middle class and the inertness of the working class leave the modern artist without any vital connection to society, save that of opposition; . . . modern artists have had, from the broadest point, to replace other social values with the strictly aesthetic. . . . so long as modern society is dominated by the love of property . . . the artist has no alternative to formalism.[142]

Such sentiments led, ultimately, to the statement issued by Motherwell and Harold Rosenberg in 1947: "Political commitment in our times means logically no art, no literature. A great many people, however, find it possible to hang around in the space between art and political action."[143]

For Greenberg, the preservation of a vital culture in the United States depended upon the existence of a milieu that would foster a rational, disengaged art, an art that exhibited a "contempt for nature in all its particularity"[144] and that rejected the mistaken notion that, in the face of current events, painting had to be "epic poetry," "theatre," "an atomic bomb," or "the rights of Man."[145] The major New York art dealers of 57th Street and MOMA could not be relied upon to create such a milieu or encourage such an art. They were, according to Greenberg, major exponents of middle-class, bourgeois taste. The fate of avant-garde art would depend, therefore, in true avant-garde fashion, on the young ("few of them over forty") and struggling artists below 34th Street who were living in cold-water flats, painting in the abstract vein, and having little, if any, reputation beyond their immediate circle of friends.

While Greenberg did not name Shahn in his *Horizon* article, it is clear that, for Greenberg, Shahn was everything an important and ambitious artist should not be. His work was purchased by industrial corporations, labor unions, government bureaus, and art collectors of varying political persuasions. He was a popular, not alienated and unappreciated, artist and had 57th Street approval. He was over forty years of age and lived in a small town. He had respect, rather than contempt, for "nature in all its particularity."

Greenberg's opinions, while influential, were by no means the final word on any particular artist in 1947. His evaluation of the contemporary American art scene was countered, in fact, in the same issue of *Horizon* by Soby in an essay on Shahn and Morris Graves. As in his Penguin essay, Soby described Shahn's Russian background, his hatred of injustice, his anti-mysticism, and "his reverence for reality as opposed to myth, his belief in and conscience toward present circumstance."[146]

According to Soby, Shahn had benefited stylistically from "cubism and its later, abstract ramifications," as well as from French symbolism and German expressionism. In terms of content, his most recent work had become less satirical and more elegiac. He had moved from stressing "the effect on the individual of organized and oppressive social forces" to portraying "the individual in terms of private emotional experience." Yet, for Soby, no matter how gracious or spiritual he had become, Shahn was still concerned with the public benefit to be gained from his art and had successfully fused propaganda with aesthetics in his many posters. He had also remained decidedly American, in both his subject matter and "the pulse and nerves of his paintings." He had managed to combine the American realist tradition of

John Singleton Copley, Thomas Eakins, and Winslow Homer with the romantic tradition of Washington Allston, the Hudson River School, and Albert Pinkham Ryder.

Soby's final paragraph contained an explicit reference to the opinions of critics like Greenberg. The work of Shahn and Graves demonstrated convincingly that "neither of our two great pictorial traditions [realism and romanticism] is anywhere near spent, though the self-conscious modernists, who hold that all art begins with Cézanne and Picasso, would have us think otherwise."[147] The careers of Shahn and Graves also proved, in Soby's mind, that American painters could look wherever they liked for inspiration without losing their "indigenous sense of direction." Thus, for Soby, contemporary American artists could draw inspiration from current international artistic developments, while, at the same time, remaining part of a distinctly American artistic tradition. To aspire to "epic poetry" or to comment on "the rights of Man" were among the strengths, rather than the failings, of such an art.

In the end, Soby was also more flexible than Greenberg, willing to acknowledge the importance of abstract or nonobjective art. It was, in fact, the inflexibility of Greenberg's position that caused much of the criticism directed at him in the coming years. Shahn would join in this criticism, questioning whether formal experimentation alone was sufficient reason for the creation of art. From 1948 onward he would increasingly take to the podium to express his opinions and to defend the integrity of what he termed humanistic content and socially relevant art.

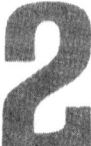

WALLACE, DONDERO, AND ROOSEVELT, N.J.

Because the artist is sensitive, he is more sharply
aware of a cold breeze blowing from somewhere. He
doesn't quite recognize what it represents, but he's
conscious of its presence. Perhaps it's another
depression, another war. But the reality is that artists
are sensing something in the wind, and the need exists
for them to come together again in search of a little
warmth to take off the chill of isolation.

—MITCHELL SIPORIN
Woodstock Art Conference, 1947

The Progressive Party Campaign

In August 1947 the Woodstock Art Association and Artists Equity
sponsored the First Annual Woodstock Art Conference. In the midst
of the State Department controversy and the growing censorship of
both art and artists, the conference was a rallying point for individuals
within the art world who were concerned about the protection of the
rights of artists and the reputation of modern art.[1]

Yasuo Kuniyoshi, in a talk entitled "What about the Artist?," called
upon artists to engage in a concerted effort to make known their place
in society. "I should like to see the artist write about himself, and
others, lecture on art . . . promote an open encounter that permits
discussion and critical evaluation," stated Kuniyoshi. Another of the
speakers, theatrical producer, director, and critic Harold Clurman,
also encouraged artists, critics, and lecturers "to find ways of communicating to the public the nature and meaning of art." The artist
Mitchell Siporin found the conference "a sign of the beginning of the
end of a kind of misanthropic miasma that enveloped the artist during
the war period," an attempt "to break through the isolation that enclosed him."[2]

Not all artists and critics, however, wanted to break through the isolation that enclosed them. In January 1948 Greenberg wrote that

Isolation is, so to speak, the natural condition of high art in America. . . .
Isolation, or rather the alienation that is its cause, is the truth—isolation,
alienation, naked and revealed unto itself, is the condition under which
the true reality of our age is experienced. And the experience of this true
reality is indispensable to any ambitious art.[3]

Not surprisingly, Shahn opposed Greenberg's position on isolation and shared with Kuniyoshi, Clurman, and Siporin the belief that modern artists had an active role to play in society, and that part of this role was to make modern art understandable to the general public. To this end Shahn undertook numerous speaking engagements at universities and museums and appeared on radio and television throughout the late forties and early fifties. Often included in these talks were commentaries on contemporary political, as well as artistic, developments.

While Shahn had been invited to participate in conferences or give lectures before 1948,[4] such invitations increased in number from this year onward. In addition, his willingness to accept these invitations grew after the events of 1947–1948, which provided him with two of the most important issues he felt needed to be discussed—the rise of abstract or nonobjective art and of a reactionary and repressive political climate.

In order to better understand Shahn's public statements regarding art and politics in 1948, it will help to examine first one of the major political and artistic activities in which he was involved that year—the presidential campaign of Henry Wallace. As in the CIO-PAC days, Shahn created posters and leaflets and, in general, helped supervise the publicity aspects of the campaign, an important job considering the hostile attitude of the press toward the new party.[5] The Progressive Party headquarters was located on Park Avenue in Manhattan, and Shahn came in from Roosevelt, New Jersey, two or three times a week. As with the CIO-PAC campaigns, he was concerned not only with providing images and designs for pamphlets or posters, but also with making sure the party's limited resources were well spent. For example, in addition to working as a volunteer, he also undertook the time-consuming production of his own color separations for his posters rather than having them done at the printers.[6]

Undoubtedly the best-known of the various images Shahn created during these months was the large painting of Truman and Dewey—*A Good Man Is Hard to Find* (1948; Figure 19)—that appeared behind Wallace at the Progressive Party convention in July 1948. Poster and postcard versions of the painting were also produced and distributed nationally. In this image Truman, in shirt-sleeves and suspenders, sits at an old-fashioned piano while Dewey, in a formal suit, sprawls across its top. The sheet music in front of Truman includes "There Goes That Song Again," "A Good Man Is Hard to Find," "Blest Be the Tie That

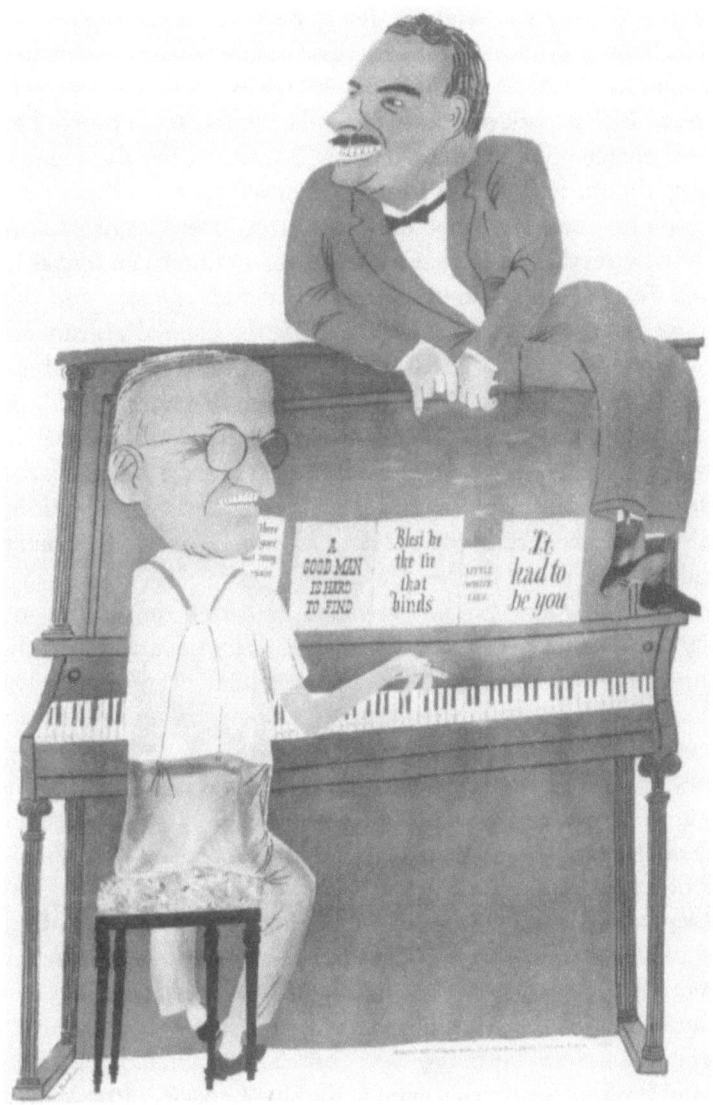

FIGURE 19

Ben Shahn, *A Good Man Is Hard to
Find*, 1948
Lithograph in colors
43⅝ × 29¾"
New Jersey State Museum Collection,
Trenton; Gift of New Jersey Junior and
Community College Association
Photographer: Dan Dragan

Binds," "Little White Lies," and "It Had to Be You." While the home-spun, old-fashioned Truman is presented as a somewhat more likable character than the beady-eyed city slicker Dewey, the painting's primary message is that both politicians are playing the same tune, that the only real choice open to voters dissatisfied with either the Democratic or Republican Party is the Progressive Party.

Shahn had often engaged in political caricature. Dewey's profile, in fact, was lifted directly from an earlier serigraph entitled *Vandenberg, Dewey, and Taft* (1941). In another painting of 1948, *Dewey and the Ventriloquist,* the politician is shown seated on the knee of a business-man who "operates" him. A third portrait of Dewey, this time full-face, appeared in the July 5, 1948, issue of *New Republic.*[7] In all of these images, the insincerity and untrustworthiness of the politicians is indicated by their toothy, frozen smiles, while their physical weak-ness is alluded to by their undersized arms, hands, and feet. This is in stark contrast to the serious expressions and/or large hands Shahn gave to the politicians and workers he admired.

In the case of Truman, Shahn conveyed an added sense of vacu-ousness by omitting the eyes behind Truman's spectacles. A slightly more sympathetic version of Truman appeared in an early watercolor study, where the absence of the furrowed brow and an upward tilt to the right eyebrow give the president a less sinister look.[8] The setting and figural arrangement of the painting can also be traced to a press photograph of actress Lauren Bacall's visit to the White House in 1948. The photograph shows Bacall perched atop a piano with Truman at the keyboard.[9]

Photographs of Shahn at work on the Truman and Dewey painting and of the painting itself behind Wallace at the convention appeared in newspapers across the country.[10] A slightly different version of the im-age also appeared on the front page of the September 1948 issue of *Uncensored,* the newsletter of the New York State Council of the Arts, Sciences and Professions. In this version the sheet music "Little White Lies" is replaced by "Dear Old Gang of Mine." The illustration accom-panied an article by Wallace in which he optimistically (and errone-ously) predicted that "The Progressive Party Is Here to Stay." In keeping with Shahn's image, Wallace claimed that the Democratic and Republican parties were basically the same, and condemned their warmongering, pro-business, and anti-labor attitudes. To add to the sarcastic visual commentary on the physical and moral weaknesses of Truman and Dewey, a quote from Shakespeare was inserted beneath

Shahn's illustration: "What a piece of work is man! How noble is reason, how infinite in faculty, in form and moving how express and admirable! In action how like an angel! In expression how like a god!"[11]

By September 1948, however, few believed that the Progressive Party was a viable political force. Eight months of concerted attack from without, coupled with dissension and defections from within, had drastically weakened the party.[12] Shahn himself objected to the degree to which the CPUSA was attempting to influence the running of the campaign,[13] though he, like Wallace, was more concerned with the detrimental effect of Red-baiting on the party's reputation and on American liberalism in general, than with the actions of American Communists themselves.[14] As late as October 20 Shahn still felt strongly enough about Wallace's candidacy to sign a "We Are for Wallace" statement that was published in the *New York Times*. Sponsored by the National Council of the Arts, Sciences and Professions, the statement included a quote by Wallace in which he claimed that

> there is no misunderstanding or difficulty between the U.S.A. and the U.S.S.R. which can be settled by force or fear and there is no difference which cannot be settled by peaceful, hopeful negotiations. There is no American principle or public interest, and there is no Russian principle or public interest which would have to be sacrificed to end the cold war and open up the Century of Peace which the Century of the Common Man demands.[15]

Shahn had also made public his evaluations of United States foreign policy earlier in the year. The occasion was a conference on art education held at MOMA:

> We witness the depressing spectacle of our own country faring forth on her maiden voyage into world politics without anything in the way of philosophical belief or moral principle. In dealing with world affairs we have not asked ourselves merely what is right. We know better than what is right, we know what is expedient. That our expediency has so often proved *inexpedient* (as well as wrong and unjust) ought to attest to the powerful logic of our maintaining human values—even in diplomatic affairs.[16]

Wallace did not have the broad base of support from both organized labor and the business sector of America that he needed to achieve his century of peace and of the common man. The CIO-PAC had joined with the ADA in carrying out the bulk of the campaign against the Progressive Party in 1948, using tactics that were simple and devastating.

They portrayed Wallace as peculiar and pathetic, presented his party as a front for communism, and accused him of intentionally splitting the liberal vote, thus ensuring the election of a reactionary President and Congress and the destruction of the New Deal.[17] In the meantime, Truman campaigned as a populist, promising to end the nation's fears of another depression by safeguarding and extending the social gains of the New Deal. The success of these tactics was borne out by Truman's victory and the Progressive Party's meager showing at the polls.

The defeat of Wallace marked the end of a political era for Shahn, as it did for social liberals in general. Those committed to this liberal tradition would now have to attempt to maintain it within a series of smaller organizations, such as the Emergency Civil Liberties Committee (ECLC), rather than within a national political party or labor organization. On both an individual and an organizational level, they would also have to come to terms with the new Cold War liberalism of the ADA. Shahn faced another question as well. Since the 1930s he had been continuously involved in the creation of public art—posters, murals, photographs—first for the RA/FSA, then the OWI and CIO-PAC, and finally for Wallace. Where would he now turn for access to this mass audience? One answer to this question surfaced in the form of commercial assignments for various broad-based publications.

From the Topical to the Universal:
The Hickman Story

In 1949, Bernarda Bryson [Shahn] observed that Shahn was interested in documenting, in graphic form, "aspects of important sociological questions which are increasingly pricking at the conscience of thoughtful Americans."[18] Over the next decade and a half Shahn would focus a considerable amount of his artistic attention on such themes—racial prejudice, slum housing, safety standards in mining, education, computer technology, nuclear testing—in the context of commercial assignments.[19] And out of such assignments would develop many of his major paintings. Commercial work would thus provide him not only with his larger audience, but also with many of the basic ideas for his fine art work, ideas once derived from his photographic trips and OWI and CIO-PAC activities. One example of this combination of fine and commercial art can be found in a commission Shahn accepted for the illustration of an article in a 1948 issue of *Harper's Magazine*.

Russell Lynes, art director for *Harper's*, asked Shahn early in 1948 to make the drawings for an article by John Bartlow Martin on a tragedy that had occurred the previous year in Chicago.[20] A black man named James Hickman, after having lost four of his children in a tenement fire, shot the landlord he believed was responsible for setting the fire. Bartlow described in detail the background and character of Hickman—an honest, hardworking, religious man—and the deplorable housing shortage and racial discrimination that had forced him to accept a barely habitable apartment for himself, his wife, and his seven children. Hickman was arrested and indicted for first degree murder. His defense committee, set up by Mike Bartell of the Socialist Workers Party and two union men, Willoughby Abner and Charles Chiakulas, pleaded him innocent due to temporary insanity. Hickman was found guilty of the lesser charge of manslaughter and placed on probation for two years.

After examining the factual and visual material surrounding the story, Shahn decided that the universal implications present in this event—the human dread of fire, the pity evoked by such a disaster, the racial injustice and relentless poverty that had pursued Hickman throughout his life—required a symbolic rather than factual depiction. After working out a series of such symbols, however, he rejected this approach, for "in the abstracting of an idea one may lose the very intimate humanity of it, and this deep and common tragedy was above all things human." Shahn returned, therefore, to the familiar aspects of family life—the Hickmans' clothes and furniture—and on that level made his "bid for universality and for the compassion that [he] hoped and believed the narrative would arouse."[21]

The drawings that appeared in the *Harper's* article presented aspects of the intimate, everyday reality of the Hickmans' lives—their small wooden shack in Mississippi, the tenement house in Chicago, the ornately carved chest of drawers, with a family picture on one side and a picture of Christ with a child on the other. Yet there were elements within these illustrations that were drawn from sources outside of the Hickman story. Two of the tenement buildings closely resemble the house in New York from which Shahn and his brothers and sister, more fortunate than the Hickman children, escaped a fiery death (Figure 20). And a drawing of Hickman, arm thrown across his face at the news of his children's deaths, is taken directly from a 1946 painting, *Sing Sorrow.* By recycling such images—the flame-topped tenement, the gesture of sorrow—Shahn hoped to convey a sense of compassion

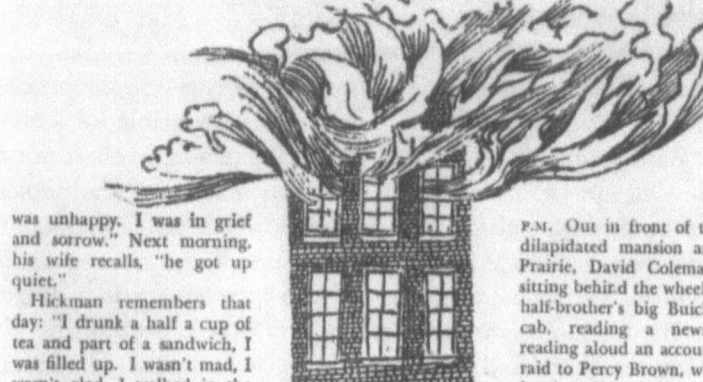

was unhappy. I was in grief and sorrow." Next morning, his wife recalls, "he got up quiet."

Hickman remembers that day: "I drunk a half a cup of tea and part of a sandwich, I was filled up. I wasn't mad, I wasn't glad, I walked in the . . . living room, I reached under the bed in the cash box, I took the key off my side and unlocked it, reached in for this automatic, picked it up and laid it down. You just got to go through with it. I laid it down again. I walked back and sat down beside my wife, I ain't spoke nothing to her. I walked back to the cash box, I picked up this gun, I knocked the safety off of it and wanted to see if it would hang. I put it back down, I can't go through with this. The voice kept speaking, you know your promise." This "promise" was the vow he had made to God to protect his children. "The third time I picked up this gun, I put eight in the magazine, knocked the safety off and threw one in the barrel." Still he paced the house and yard in torment; once he got a block away. But he came back: "The word was so sharp it was cutting like a two edge sword. . . . The third time I didn't return no more."

He caught a bus, transferred to a streetcar, and got off at 26th and Indiana. Coleman lived a few blocks away. "I stood there on the street. I didn't want to go through with what it was telling me. . . . [But] this was a vow that I made to this family in 1923 . . . and the answer is I wouldn't back up. So I walked on down to Prairie." It was a little before 1:00

"I cannot understand how she escaped. . . . It was a miracle. The Lord was with her."

P.M. Out in front of the big dilapidated mansion at 2720 Prairie, David Coleman was sitting behind the wheel of his half-brother's big Buick taxi-cab, reading a newspaper, reading aloud an account of a raid to Percy Brown, who was leaning through the window.

Hickman came up the sidewalk. "He had some rent tickets in his lap. . . . I walked up to him and spoke to him and friendly talked. I wanted peace with all mankind. 'How do you do, how are you feeling this morning, Coleman?' 'What do you want with me?' 'I come to ask you something about this arrest warrant, of the $100 and causing this disturbance,'" that is, the fire. Coleman replied "Yes, but I ain't going to pay you." Hickman recalls, "My mind got scattered. I took out my automatic and blazed him twice. He said: 'I'll pay you.' I said: 'It's too late now. God is my secret judge.' I said: 'You started that fire.' He said: 'Yes, I did.' I shot him twice more. . . . I thought he was dead." He wasn't but he died three days later.

Hickman walked down the street and away, the automatic still in his hand. He missed a streetcar, walked on, farther than he needed. "I had put a heavy load down and a big weight fell off of me and I felt light." He took a streetcar home and asked his son Charles, "Where is your mother? He said, down to Arlene's. I said, 'Tell her to come here, I got something to tell her,' so she came. . . . She said . . . 'They will find you.' 'I know.'" He waited till 4:15 P.M. before the

FIGURE 20

Ben Shahn, Drawing of burning building, in August 1948 issue of *Harper's Magazine*, p. 51
Photographer: Stephen Cahill

aroused by the recognition of the typical in the specific, a compassion he felt historical documentation alone could not convey.[22]

Not convinced that he had fully expressed his sense of the enormity of the Hickman fire, or that small drawings could convey this enormity, Shahn further explored the Hickman images in his painting. He had retained one image from his second, symbolic, stage of drawings in the published illustrations—a highly formalized wreath of flames that appeared atop the burning tenement building. It was this image that formed the basis for his painting *Allegory* (Figure 21). The lion-

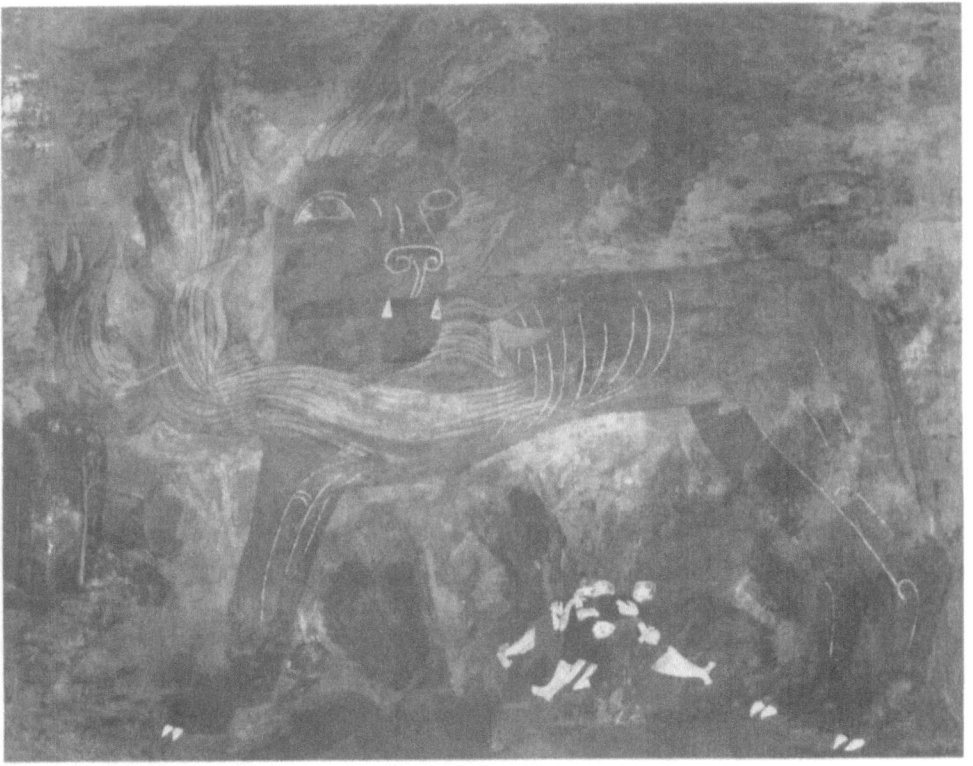

FIGURE 21
Ben Shahn, *Allegory*, 1948
Tempera on panel
36 × 48"
Collection: Modern Art Museum of Fort Worth
Gift of W. P. Bomar, Jr.
Photographer: Bob Wharton

like beast with the flaming mane and the four children lying in a heap beneath it represented, for Shahn, all that he had ever felt about fire and the helpless and innocent that it destroys, as well as the fear of wolves that had been with him from his early years in Russia. He sought to create an image of "the emotional tone that surrounds disaster" rather than of the disaster itself,[23] though without abandoning recognizable imagery.

Shahn had completed another series of drawings for *Harper's* earlier in 1948, again for an article by John Bartlow Martin.[24] In the tradition of the muckraking journalists of the first decades of the century, Martin exposed the gross negligence and bureaucratic red tape that had led to the deaths of 111 men in an explosion at the coal mine in Centralia, Illinois.[25] Two of the paintings that emerged from these drawings—*Miners' Wives* (1948) and *Death of a Miner* (1949; Figure 22)—maintain recognizable settings and details, yet suggest, through faces left blank or an absence of references to a specific event in the title or painting itself, a more general portrayal of the anguish felt in the face of death or disaster. The latter painting included a schematized fire-beast above the running miner, a symbol of fire/death/destruction that would appear time and again in Shahn's work.

In recognition of the significance of his work, Shahn was cited twice in the early months of 1948 as among the most important contemporary American artists. The first mention came in an article by Alfred M. Frankfurter for the January issue of *Art News*. Titled "The Year's Best: 1947," the article summarized the results of voting by the editorial staff of *Art News* in categories ranging from "the most important old master acquired by an American public collection" to the most significant modern exhibition and the ten best one-person shows.[26] While the winner of the most significant modern exhibition was the abstract-expressionist annual at the Chicago Art Institute, no abstract expressionists were among the ten best one-person shows, which included exhibitions of the work of John Marin, Pablo Picasso, Joan Miró, Arthur Osver, Maurice Sterne, Shahn, Max Beckmann, Karl Knaths, Roberto Matta, and Walter Stuempfig. Frankfurter felt obliged to note, however, that there had been an unusual paucity of nominations that year in the category of best one-person shows—fewer than fifteen—and that, in fact, the categories of the acquisition of the most important modern American painting and the most important modern sculpture had to be omitted due to the unwillingness of the editorial staff to so much as nominate a work or works for consideration.

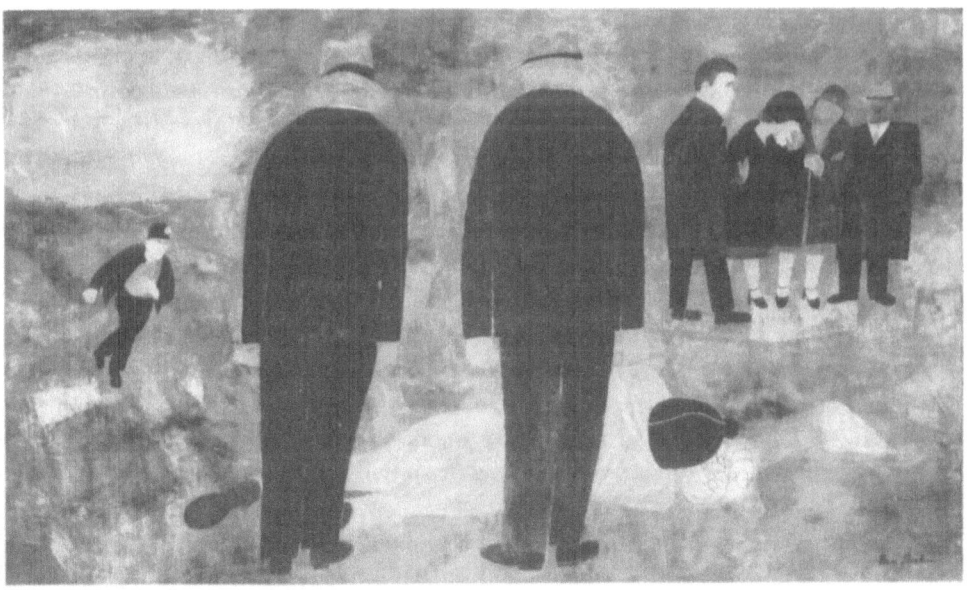

FIGURE 22
Ben Shahn, *Death of a Miner*, 1949
Tempera on muslin, treated with gesso,
on panel
27 × 48″
Collection: The Metropolitan Museum
of Art, Arthur H. Hearn Fund, 1950
(50.77)

This reticence on the part of the *Art News* editorial staff may have been due to their low evaluation of the modern art being produced by contemporary Americans. But it may also have been an indication of the changes rapidly taking place in American art at this time. While Greenberg was proclaiming the superiority of the more abstract versions of modern art, which were being taken up by an increasing number of young artists, many important critics and museum directors still preferred and defended the work of individuals such as those on *Art News'* list. The views of the two sides were aired publicly on a number of occasions throughout 1948, with heated debates not only over the relative merit of individual styles, but also over the degree to which modern art should be intelligible to the layperson.[27]

A month after Frankfurter's article appeared, another list was pub-

lished, this time by *Look* magazine.[28] Rather than rely on the nominations and votes of its editorial staff, *Look* contacted sixty-eight leading
museum directors, curators of painting, and art critics across the country and asked them to name the ten best American painters (thirty-
nine replied). The winners, in the order of number of votes received,
were John Marin, Max Weber, Yasuo Kuniyoshi, Stuart Davis, Shahn,
Edward Hopper, Charles Burchfield, George Grosz, Franklin Watkins, Lyonel Feininger, and Jack Levine (the last two artists tied for
tenth place). *Look* also asked the winning artists to list their choices
for the ten best American painters. Three-quarters of the artists they
named were the same as those chosen by the directors and critics.

For the author of the *Look* article, the winning list registered "more
advanced opinion than might have been expected," though "the sur-
realists and very abstract work" were almost totally rejected, as was
the "old-fashioned, ultra-realistic painting still favored by large sections of the public." To sum up, the *Look* poll produced "a high
quality, middle-of-the-road selection that will be questioned both by
arch conservatives and by the most advanced abstractionists."[29] Museum directors, curators, and critics were not alone in their prefer-
ence for the middle of the road. In April Arthur M. Schlesinger, Jr.,
voiced the opinion that the "hope of the future lies in the widening
and deepening of the democratic middle ground."[30] But before this
ground could be widened, it would narrow considerably as the Cold
War heightened and what remained of the left and its liberal sympathizers was either silenced or forced underground or transformed
into a liberalism far removed from its thirties counterpart.

Dondero, Communism, and Modern Art

In a review of the Whitney Museum's Annual Exhibition of Contemporary American Painting, which opened November 13, 1948, Henry
McBride, art critic for the *New York Sun*, singled out Shahn's painting
Allegory and subjected it to "a curiously McCarthian analysis."[31] While
indicating that he admired Shahn's skill as a painter, McBride added
that he preferred to ignore "the politics or the morals" of his artists,
which, in Shahn's case, was a particularly difficult thing to do. He
claimed to discern in the bright red coloring of the beast a "subtle trib-
ute to our quondam friend but present enemy, the Soviet Republic,"
and went on to comment that he had always thought the political implications in Shahn's work to be "of the shadiest. The shade often is
red, and it is this time." McBride hoped that the attention of the pub-

lic would be focused upon "the art rather than the insinuation," as he would "certainly hate to see Ben Shahn boxed up with the Dean of Canterbury and sent away to wherever it is they send disturbers of the peace."[32]

While Shahn was no stranger to such hostility, he was particularly disconcerted by this attack, coming as it had from someone he had looked upon as a friend. Such attacks were not unusual, however, after 1947, particularly with the defeat of Wallace in November 1948, which all but silenced the primary public voice of protest against the Cold War rhetoric and policies of both Democrats and Republicans. A month later, Alger Hiss, a prominent figure in the Roosevelt administration and, at the time, president of the Carnegie Endowment for International Peace, was indicted on two charges of perjury. The indictment marked the end of a six-month-long espionage investigation by the House Committee on Un-American Activities (HUAC). With its sensationalizing and use of former members of the CPUSA who had turned informers, it set the pattern for the committee's future investigations and harassment of New Dealers and CPUSA members alike.[33]

The identification of "traitors" and individuals deemed "un-American" because of past affiliations or present unpopular opinions became a common pastime for both politicians and private citizens. On four separate occasions in 1949—March 11, March 25, May 17, and August 16—Republican Representative George Dondero of Michigan presented statements in Congress attacking modern art as communistic and singling out particular artists, galleries, and art organizations. While only the latest in a string of invectives directed at modern art since the Armory show of 1913, Dondero's attacks bore the marks of an increasingly irrational Cold War rhetoric.

The focus of Dondero's March 11 attack was an art exhibit organized by Carroll Aument of MOMA for the naval hospital at St. Albans, New York. The exhibit was held in the ship's library for two weeks starting January 17. In order to accommodate the bedridden patients, paintings were brought around to the various wards by different participating artists, who explained "the difference between the aims of the painters following the classical and modern trends of thought."[34] The representative from Michigan found three aspects of this exhibition objectionable: a number of the artists had communist affiliations; the patients were thus a captive audience for communist propaganda; and the taxpayers' money was being spent to support communist art. To

support his claims, Dondero cited seventeen artists and their communist affiliations, which ranged from a favorable review in the *New
Masses* to support of Henry Wallace. The list of "communist affiliations" after Shahn's name was one of the longer ones: John Reed Club;
American Artists' Congress; Artists' Union; State Department show;
ACA (American Contemporary Art Gallery); *New Masses* art auction,
March 24, 1942; National Council of the Arts, Sciences and Professions; support of Wallace; assistant to Diego Rivera on the Radio City
mural.[35]

Dondero devoted the major part of his speeches in Congress on
March 25 and May 17 to exposing the "communist affiliations" of two
artists' organizations—Artists Equity Association (AEA) and the American Contemporary Art Gallery (ACA).[36] In referring favorably to a
number of artists' groups in his May 17 speech, Dondero also revealed
the sources of his "art expertise" (he was a lawyer by profession). In
his concluding remarks, he called upon "the loyal, patriotic, clean-
minded, right-thinking artists of this country [to] band together and
purge their establishment of this social disease [of communist modern
art]." Just as labor organizations were throwing out communists and
communist sympathizers, so too must "such powerful and healthy organizations as the National Academy of Design, the American Artists
Professional League, the Allied Artists of America, the Illustrators Society, and the American Watercolor Society . . . gird themselves for
battle in a common cause, and throw the Marxists out." And just as
the right and center were joining forces in their battle against communism in the political arena, so too, in the art world, must "the reluctant warriors of the right and center take up their swords" against the
lists and juries that were loaded against them, and "smite for the right
and purge them, as it is their duty to do."[37]

Finally, on August 16, in a presentation titled "Modern Art Shackled
to Communism," Dondero defined, in specific terms, exactly what it
was about modern art that was so threatening to the moral fiber of the
United States.[38] He began by rejecting the claim that modern art
could not be communist because art in Russia was realistic. Communist art in the United States (i.e., modern art) was different from communist art in Soviet Russia (i.e., socialist realism) because each served
a different purpose. While socialist realism was "the medium of con-
trolled propaganda," meant to delude Russian workers, modern art
was "the weapon of destruction . . . Communist art outside Russia is
to destroy the enemy, and we are the enemy of communism." This

destruction would be achieved through the erosion of "the high standards and priceless traditions of academic art."[39]

Without claiming that his list was all-inclusive, Dondero identified six of the infamous "isms" of modern art and the manner in which they operated as instruments of destruction:

> Cubism aims to destroy by designed disorder.
> Futurism aims to destroy by the machine myth. . . .
> Dadaism aims to destroy by ridicule.
> Expressionism aims to destroy by aping the primitive and insane. . . .
> Abstractionism aims to destroy by the creation of brainstorms.
> Surrealism aims to destroy by the denial of reason.[40]

Many of the artists attacked by Dondero would not have disagreed with his claim that the "isms" of modern art acted as destructive forces. What they would have disagreed with, however, was Dondero's evaluation of what was being destroyed. For the Dadaists, World War I was proof that the traditions and values of the ruling elites of Europe, of which academic art was a part, were no longer viable and needed to be destroyed or ridiculed. World War II reinforced this sentiment among modern artists and served to enlarge the list of traditions marked for destruction.

Instead of attacking the American Contemporary Art Gallery (ACA), as he had in his May 17 address to Congress, Dondero focused on a much more powerful institution on August 16—the Museum of Modern Art in New York. Among the various "crimes" committed by MOMA that revealed its communist sympathies was the financing of a trip to New York by the British art critic Herbert Read in 1948. Read, a supporter of surrealism, was brought to New York to take part in the same Conference of the Committee on Art Education at which Shahn spoke. Read was thus provided, according to Dondero, with an audience of "1,000 American art educators and teachers, offering their bared breasts for free injections of the evil virus of the 'isms,' anti-Christian, antisanity, antimorality, and anti-American."[41]

Another of MOMA's "anti-American" activities was the publication and distribution "of a booklet on Ben Shahn, that proponent of social protest in art . . . [who] would seem to be one of the pets of the Museum of Modern Art." Not only was Shahn a "Communist-fronter and member of the John Reed Club," but he also hung out in the thirties with such "disreputable" characters as Diego Rivera, José Clemente Orozco, and David A. Siqueiros. Shahn and MOMA were thus doubly condemned in 1947–1948—by Greenberg for their aesthetic conservativeness and by Dondero for their political radicalism.

While Greenberg agreed with Dondero that overt politics had no place in art, he did not advocate, as did Dondero, the policing of the art world by right-wing congressmen. According to Dondero, "when art becomes art with a social or political protest . . . it ceases to be free, and having entered the ideological and political field, it is properly subject to the restrictions we have always placed upon politics and political writers."[42] In addition, while Greenberg claimed that abstract art was "uninflated by illegitimate content," either religious or political, and displayed a "radical inadaptability to the uses of any interest, ideological or institutional,"[43] Dondero found Jackson Pollock, Robert Motherwell, and William Baziotes practitioners of an "abstractivism or nonobjectivity . . . spawned as a simon pure, Russian Communist product."[44] By insisting on the foreign nature of this and all other modern art, Dondero contributed to the controversy raging over what type of art was truly "American" and forced the supporters of both Shahn and the abstract expressionists to define in more precise and convincing terms the nationality and nationalism of their respective artists.

Responses to Dondero's congressional speeches were not long in coming. On June 16 Representative Charles A. Plumley introduced into Congress a letter from Hudson D. Walker, executive director of Artists Equity, clarifying the aims of the association. Contrary to the charges leveled by Dondero, Artists Equity, according to Walker, had no interest in or influence on the political thinking of its members. It was concerned primarily with the economic welfare of artists.[45] A few weeks later *Saturday Review* carried an article by James Thrall Soby in which he compared Dondero's recent attacks on modern art to those of Hitler and Stalin. Soby condemned, in particular, Dondero's call for some form of "proper supervision" of art critics who were too enthusiastic in their support of modern art.[46] Alfred Frankfurter echoed Soby's protests in an editorial in *Art News* that same month.[47] "Indeed," commented Soby, "almost the only encouraging factor in the current witch hunt is that it has united American art circles in protest as I have never seen them united before."[48]

A final set of invectives was issued by Dondero to Congress on October 13 in response to an article by Emily Genauer in the September issue of *Harper's*. Genauer had been one of the critics named by Dondero in his May 17 speech as having been "very kindly" toward "left-wing, so-called artists." Genauer's article, "Still Life with Red Herring,"[49] covered much of the same material as the earlier criticisms of Dondero. She countered his claim that the St. Albans Hospital exhibition was a communist plot, as well as his attack on the National Institute of Arts and Letters. Part of her article, however, was based on an interview she conducted with Dondero in June, and she quoted him as follows:

> Modern art is communistic because it is distorted and ugly, because it does not glorify our beautiful country, our cheerful and smiling people, and our great material progress. Art which does not portray our beautiful country in plain, simple terms that everyone can understand breeds dissatisfaction. It is therefore opposed to our government, and those who create it and promote it are our enemies.[50]

Genauer followed Dondero's quote with two similar passages condemning modern art drawn from the statements of Lenin and Stalin in order to prove how similar Dondero's tactics and sentiments were to those of the leaders of Soviet Russia. "It is a paradox, and a frightening one," she stated, "to behold an elected representative of the people naïvely and inadvertently following the Moscow line about art, and demanding that the communist techniques of constraint be applied to American artists and critics."[51]

Dondero responded to Genauer's article by denying having made the statements attributed to him, though the sentiments were correct, and by questioning the accuracy of both her quotes and her interpretation of the material at hand. Genauer's twisting and distorting of the facts was no surprise, claimed Dondero, as "distortion, ridicule, and the warping of values is typical of the art, the so-called modern and contemporary art, which Miss Genauer has so persistently championed and promoted in her literary work." As for her comparison of his statements with those of Stalin and Hitler, Dondero found no fault with the similarity, and instead commended these two leaders for recognizing, as he did, the "incontrovertible fact" that the art of the "isms" was repulsive and destructive.[52]

But it wasn't simply the similar sentiments regarding modern art that worried Genauer. More importantly, she objected to Dondero's call for a curtailment of the freedom of expression of artists and critics. Dondero did not directly address this concern, but instead repeated his accusations and his "facts," a tactic that would soon be used to great effect by another member of Congress, Senator Joseph McCarthy.

A Call for Peace

One aspect of Genauer's article to which Dondero took particular exception was her presentation of the St. Albans Hospital art exhibition as a humanitarian venture aimed at giving the physically disabled patients a new interest in life. He was convinced that the show was a communist plot, not only because fifteen of the artists had "Red affiliations," but also because the publicity surrounding the show was "perfectly timed to harmonize with the Communist peace offensive, which reached its highest point at the so-called peace conference at the Waldorf Astoria Hotel from March 25 to March 27."[53] Was it a coincidence, he asked, that *Look* carried an article on the show in its April 12, 1949, issue, which was sold at the newsstands on March 29, a day after the peace conference had closed? And was it even a further coincidence that one of the illustrations in the article was "a propaganda picture in every sense of the word"? The photograph in question contained, in Dondero's words,

> a convalescent sailor studying a modernistic painting, but centered, featured, and magnified in this picture is the gruesome steel apparatus [artificial legs] that this unfortunate man must wear for the rest of his life. This picture is harrowing, disturbing to the emotions, and is a powerful plea for "peace at any price." The caption with the picture says, in part, "These paraplegics want to remind the world of the terrible toll of war."[54]

Dondero hastened to add that he, like every other American, wanted a permanent peace, "but this is a period in our history when we are preparing for defense against a Communist power which, determined to dominate the world, hides behind a false front of world peace, designed to undermine the moral stamina of our people."[55] Anyone who argued for peace in 1949, therefore, or produced a painting or photograph condemning the evils of war, was a communist or communist sympathizer.

This was not the first time Soviet Russia had been accused of engaging in a "peace offensive." Such was the phrase used to describe its decision to sign the Nazi-Soviet Non-Aggression Pact in August 1939 and its subsequent effort to discourage American entry into the war. Of course, many in the United States were also against becoming involved in this military conflict, at least until Japan bombed Pearl Harbor in December 1941. By that time the Soviet Union had also dropped its "peace offensive," having been invaded by Germany in June of that year.[56]

Shahn had marked these events of 1939–1941 with a painting entitled *Spring (Democracies Fear Peace Offensive)* (1940). Two men sit on either side of a third chair, on which rests a newspaper. The headline is clearly visible: "Democracies Fear New Peace Offensive." The figure on the right partially covers the headlines of a second copy of the same paper with his right leg and stares off to the right, suggesting a lack of concern about the events described in the paper. The other figure, however, gazes downward deep in thought, possibly pondering the consequences for the United States, France, and Britain (the democracies referred to in the headlines) of a continued accord between Hitler and Stalin.[57]

At the end of the forties the word "peace" was again fraught with references to Soviet-American relations. It had come to signify, for Dondero and many other Americans, "not merely the absence of war, but also a particular conception of world order, the 'Weltanschauung' of the Soviet Union, the Pax Sovietica. In the same way, the word 'freedom' symbolized the opposing, rival world order, the Pax Americana."[58] Thus there began a concerted effort on the part of government agencies, particularly the Justice Department, to destroy the organized peace movement in the United States. Visas were denied to those foreigners wishing to come to the United States to lecture on peace. The Peace Information Center (PIC), the American Peace Mobilization, and the American Peace Crusade were all ordered to register as agents of a foreign power and were listed by the Attorney General as subversive organizations.[59] The failure of the officers of the PIC, headed by W. E. B. Du Bois, to register resulted in their indictment by a federal grand jury in February 1951.[60]

The Soviet Union had, indeed, initiated a "peace offensive" at the end of the forties, partly in response to the Cold War pronouncements of the American government, which presented Soviet Russia as an immediate military threat to Europe and, ultimately, to the rest of the world. The first Soviet peace congress was held at Wroclaw, Poland, in August 1948 and was attended by a delegation from the United States that included representatives from the arts.[61] Early in 1949, the Soviets withdrew all of their demands on Germany, particularly with regard to the issue of German rearmament. In April they also began lifting the Berlin blockade, begun in June 1948.[62]

Whether, in fact, a Soviet military threat did exist at this time is unclear. The Soviet Union had borne the brunt of the resistance against Hitler's armies and was certainly in no shape economically to launch another major military offensive.[63] More than 20,000,000 Soviet citizens had been killed as opposed to 300,000 American soldiers. In addition, over 70,000 towns and villages had been destroyed and 25,000,000 people left homeless. But the Soviet Union did pose a real threat to American interests in Europe in another way. Its primary role in the defeat of Hitler had won it many friends in Europe. In addition, the heroic actions of the communists in the Resistance movements in occupied Italy and France increased the prestige of the Communist Party in these countries. Indeed, when the war ended it seemed that both countries would elect communist governments, though American intervention helped prevent this from happening.[64] Because so much of the rationale behind American foreign policy at this time was based on the existence of an oppressive, militaristic, tyrannical image of the Soviet Union as opposed to a just, democratic image of America, the maintenance of both images became of utmost importance. Exactly how the American government attempted to do this, and the role of art in its efforts, will be examined in more detail in Chapter 4.

Despite the government's actions in 1949, the peace movement in the United States was not suppressed, and many American citizens continued to participate openly in various national and international peace conferences. One such gathering was the Cultural and Scientific Conference for World Peace held in New York City under the sponsorship of the National Council of the Arts, Sciences and Professions in March 1949.[65] Another conference was the American Continental Congress for World Peace, held in Mexico City from September 5 to September 10. Shahn was one of the members of the United States group of the Continental Committee, along with W. E. B. Du Bois, Linus Pauling, and Paul Robeson.[66]

While Shahn did not attend the conference in Mexico, he was present at another gathering in New York City in October of that same year, a Bill of Rights conference organized by the Civil Rights Congress. As one of its sponsors, he was invited to give a brief presentation on the invasion of the rights of individuals in the creative arts. Paul J. Kern, a lawyer and sponsor of the conference, wrote to Shahn regarding its urgency: "The fact that we are spending over 40 million dollars a year for secret police is alarming enough! Add to it the indiscriminate methods of those police . . . and no individual is now safe against the smears, telephone tapping, 'mail covering' and unsubstantiated gossip."[67] Bernard De Voto was more graphic in his response to the actions of the FBI at this time: "We are shocked. We are scared. Sometimes we are sickened. We know that the thing stinks to heaven, that it is an avalanching danger to our society."[68]

The text of Shahn's presentation is unavailable, but we can assume with some certainty that he was critical of the activities of the FBI and of congressmen like Dondero, and that he objected strongly to the transgressions of justice and basic human values that were being carried out by American government officials both at home and abroad. "One of the great and tragic characteristics of the atomic age," he had noted to an audience at Smith College earlier that year, "is that human values—morality, if you will, have not kept pace with scientific achievements. Thus we have the horrible spectacle of Hiroshima, accented by that of a ranking general who had his birthday cake baked in the shape of the bomb explosion."[69]

Shahn felt artists could help revive these human values by creating work that "broadened and enriched the human spirit" and by remaining politically engaged. In clarifying his position on the artist's involvement in politics he cited a Greek distinction: "To the Greeks the word 'idiot' was opposite in its connotation to the word 'politic.' The idiot was one without understanding of or participation in political matters." To be politically engaged implied "the obligation and need of the individual (working in cooperation with others) to do something about the evils of his time."[70]

Shahn spoke at yet another gathering in 1949, the Seventh Annual Conference on Art Education held at MOMA from March 18 to March 20, in which he reiterated his appeal to all artists to work together in order to bring new dimensions to the spirit and imagination of men and women. Shahn's co-panelists were Balcomb Greene and Robert Motherwell, whom he described, respectively, as "an abstractionist and a non-objectivist." Shahn hoped that such stylistic differences would not interfere with artists' willingness to cooperate with each other in the creation of new spiritual dimensions, though he noted that the nonobjectivist would probably have the least to contribute. For while a knowledge of the arrangement of shapes and colors and lines was an essential part of any artist's aesthetic equipment, such qualities were "not the stuff of man's ultimate values. To make them the object of painting seems to me to question the worth of art activity itself."[71]

Balcomb Greene also wanted artists to provide inspiration for the community, but he was less optimistic about their ability to do so. To inspire, artists had to communicate, and in 1949 such communication was hindered by a political-economic system that attempted to sell art as it sold other perishable products, that mediated between the artist and the public in such a way that the message of the artist was often obliterated. Greene was also less optimistic than Shahn about the possibility of cooperative action, whether in art or politics:

> We know we are inadequate in collective action and as people. Our political-economic system is cooperative and ingenious in its organization but not cooperative in distribution. We have observed that our nation can cooperate magnificently for war but cannot as yet do this for peace.[72]

In commenting thus, Greene gave voice to the feelings of many Americans who were concerned about the warlike atmosphere that filled the halls of Congress and the pages of major newspapers and journals. The success of Mao Tse-tung's communist forces in the summer of 1949 and the explosion of an atomic bomb by the Soviet Union on September 22 of that same year increased the Cold War hysteria and further diminished hopes for peace.

In the Key of Roosevelt, N.J.

While Shahn spoke about the creation of new spiritual dimensions, of revealing the deeper realities of human relationships, political decency, and social injustice through art, what type of art was he producing and for whom? An article in the May 1949 issue of *Art News* helps provide an answer to this question. Under the title "Ben Shahn Paints a Picture," Thomas B. Hess traces the painting *Nocturne* (1949; see frontispiece) "from the first glimmer of idea to the final touch of the brush."[73]

Nocturne was executed in January and February 1949 and was inspired, according to Hess, by Shahn's own community environment. Indeed, Hess felt the work could be subtitled "in the key of Roosevelt, N.J." A brief look at the origins of the town and Shahn's relationship to it, therefore, is in order. Roosevelt, originally named Jersey Homesteads, was one of the first of the planned communities undertaken by the RA/FSA in the mid-1930s. It was built as a new home for a group of Jewish garment workers from New York City, most of whom had emigrated from Eastern Europe and most of whom were members of the International Ladies Garment Workers Union (ILGWU). In addition to individual homes and a community center, the RA/FSA constructed a garment factory, to be run cooperatively by the town's residents, and provided land for cooperative farming.[74]

As a member of the Special Skills Division of the RA/FSA at the time, Shahn was involved in the day-to-day decisions regarding the inclusion of works of art in the planned communities. Special Skills had committed itself to "a program of placing some permanent piece of art work of quality—whether murals, easel paintings, sculpture or other decorative ornaments—in every Resettlement community." The works would "be placed in community centers or elsewhere on community property where everyone alike may share their enjoyment."[75] This art program was part of a larger cultural and educational program that emphasized the importance of art works and cultural activities—classes in fine and applied arts, singing groups, and orchestras—in helping "to bind the homesteaders into harmonious social units, to maintain and build up morale through the experimental and construction period, and to relieve the strain of insecurity until economic stabilization had been accomplished."[76]

When the idea arose for a mural in the Jersey Homesteads community center, the director of Special Skills, Adrian J. Dornbush, turned to Shahn, who began working on the designs in the spring of 1936.[77] Shahn envisioned the mural (Figures 23–26) as a history of the town's residents, documenting their arrival in the United States, their employment in the crowded and oppressive sweatshops, and the improved working and living conditions obtained through union organizing and the programs of the Roosevelt administration. What finally materialized, however, was not a literal history, but a series of scenes drawn from memories of Shahn's own past, fragments of his earlier paintings and photographs (the coffins of Sacco and Vanzetti appear in the upper lefthand corner), recorded historical events, and conversations with members of the community. Almost everyone in Jersey Homesteads went at one time or another to watch Shahn paint, speaking with him in Yiddish and arguing with him about customs and scripture.[78] He often sketched his visitors, including at least one of them, Irving Plungen, in the crowd below the labor leader in the center of the mural.[79]

It was at this time that Shahn met Albert Einstein, who lived in the nearby community of Princeton. This meeting with Einstein, plus the fact that the scientist had been a friend of the garment workers' cooperative since its inception,[80] may well have been the impetus be-

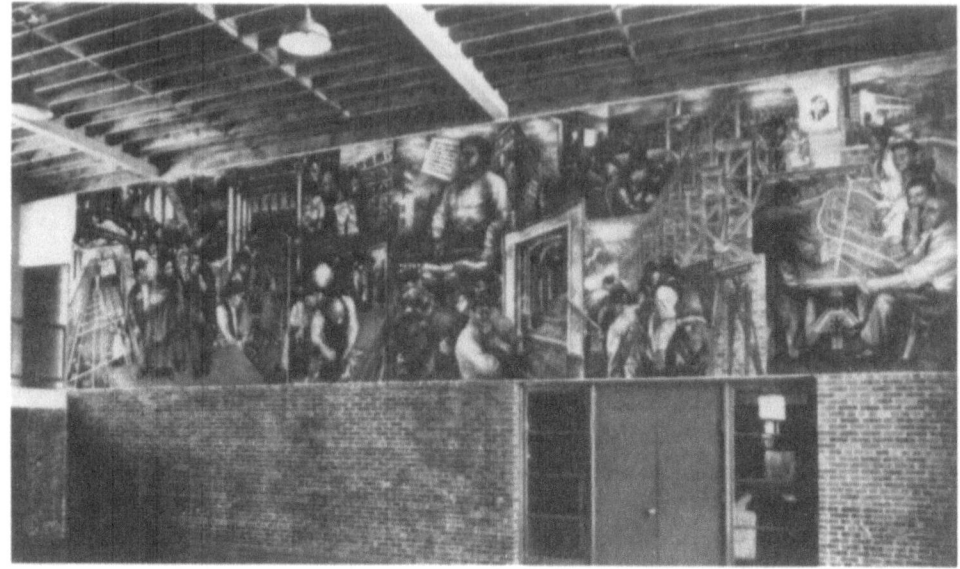

FIGURE 23

Ben Shahn, Mural, Jersey Homesteads
(now Roosevelt, N.J.), 1937–1938
Fresco
12 × 45'
Commissioned by the Farm Security
Administration (FSA)

FIGURE 24

Ben Shahn, Mural, Jersey Homesteads
(now Roosevelt, N.J.), 1937–1938
Detail, left section
Photograph courtesy of Stephen L.
Taller

FIGURE 25

Ben Shahn, Mural, Jersey Homesteads
(now Roosevelt, N.J.), 1937–1938
Detail, center section
Photograph courtesy of Stephen L.
Taller

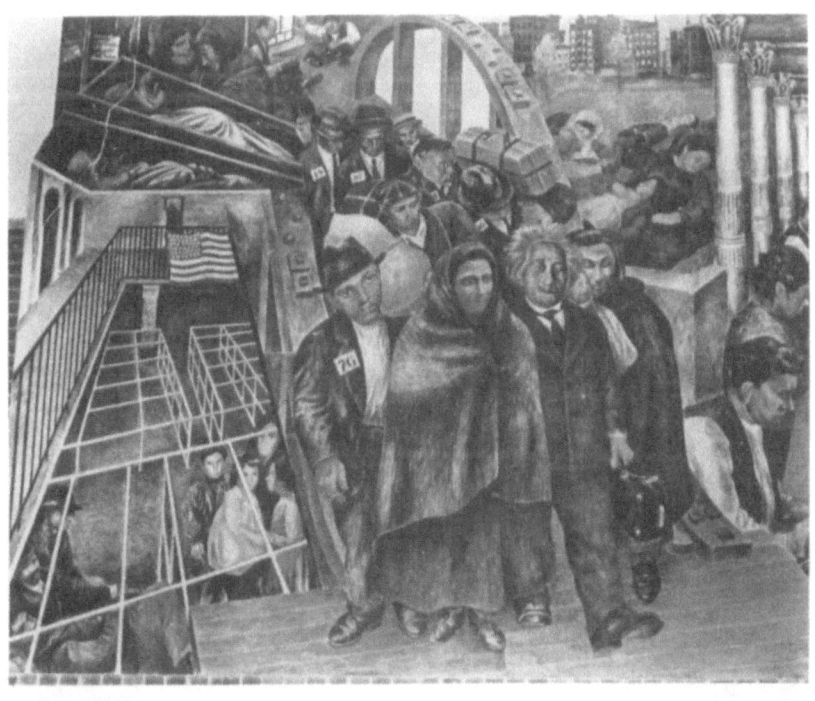

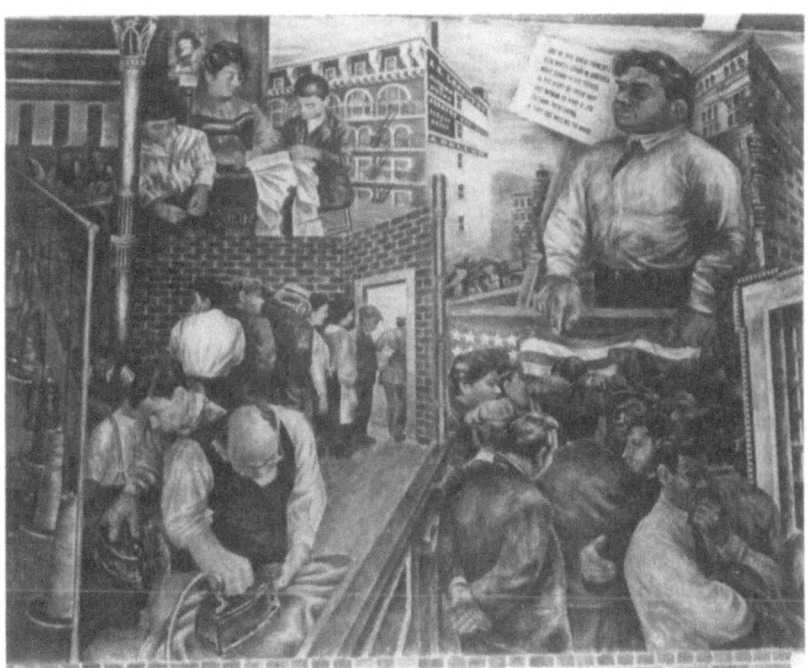

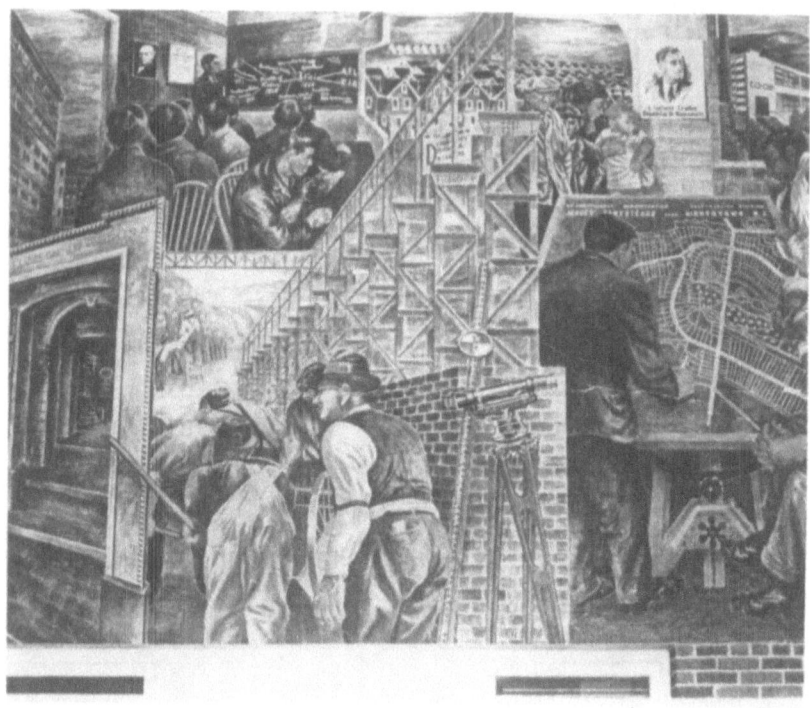

FIGURE 26
Ben Shahn, Mural, Jersey Homesteads
(now Roosevelt, N.J.), 1937–1938
Detail, right section
Photograph courtesy of Stephen L.
Taller

hind Shahn's inclusion of him in the mural leading the group of immigrants down the gangplank.[81] Einstein had also renounced his German
citizenship and left Germany after Hitler came to power in 1933. His
presence in the mural, along with the Nazi soldier in the top left corner holding a sign in German reading "Germans, beware: don't buy
from Jews," added to the mural's anti-fascist sentiment.

The highlighting of Einstein and the Nazi soldier, however, was
somewhat misleading, for most of the town's inhabitants had, like
Shahn, come from Eastern Europe, not Germany, and had arrived between 1880 and 1920, not in the 1930s. After 1920 a series of laws were
passed which sharply curtailed the immigration of all nationalities to
the United States. Shahn's emphasis on Germany can be attributed, in

part, to his active involvement in the Popular Front campaign of the late thirties against fascism. Again, however, the suggestion in the mural that the United States was welcoming Jewish refugees from Nazi Germany with open arms was not reflected in actual government policy at this time, which imposed tight restrictions on such refugees.

The mural was ultimately a celebration of the accomplishments of the ILGWU and the Roosevelt administration, despite the fact that the cooperative factory and farmlands that were to provide Jersey Homesteads' economic base were already failing by the time Shahn's mural was completed. The community survived, however, though somewhat disillusioned, and Shahn was drawn back to it with his family, settling there in 1939 and remaining until his death in 1969. The town had much to offer Shahn: a cohesive Jewish culture; a sense of both newness and tradition; proximity to the art world of New York City and the intellectual environment of Princeton; and residents who believed strongly in the value of social reform. In 1944 Shahn viewed his New Jersey mural as his most successful. "People really look at it," he commented. "They know it by heart. To them it's like the building, a part of the community."[82]

By the late 1940s, Jersey Homesteads had undergone a number of changes, not the least of which was the assumption of a new name, Roosevelt, in 1945 in honor of the president whose death that year had so saddened the nation. While many of the original Jewish garment-worker settlers were still there, new people, some of them non-Jewish, had moved in after the war. Many were artists or writers or musicians, drawn in part by Shahn's presence in the community. Another factor contributing to their arrival was the government's decision in 1947 to end its subsidy of the town's expenses and to sell the houses to its inhabitants or to other interested buyers at an average price of $4,200 each. Add to this the beginning of the inexorable migration from the city to suburban areas, and Roosevelt was destined to alter in both its ethnic and its economic composition.[83]

In his 1949 article, Hess presents the town as the epitome of the unified, idyllic community. "A few hundred yards from Shahn's house are friends with whom he can discuss ethics, aesthetics, politics and food; the same distance in another direction one can hunt deer." Roosevelt had also become a sort of mecca for folk singers, and Shahn spent many evenings in local bars listening to both visitors and residents sing and play their guitars. There were also innumerable community concerts, where everything from "The Streets of Laredo" to Hebrew chants was heard. Thus, according to Hess, "the subject of *Nocturne*—two men singing at each other with that peculiar intensity that differentiates good folk singing from crooning—has often been seen in Roosevelt."[84]

Hess fails to note, however, that the arrival of folk singers and artists and New York businessmen, coupled with what many viewed as the abandonment of the community by the government, created a sense of protectiveness among the original settlers and a suspicion of newcomers. This suspicion was exacerbated by the national mood of distrust and anxiety fueled by the Cold War pronouncements of government officials and private citizens alike. And even though the war was over and unemployment figures were still low, concern about future employment prospects was aroused by the Truman administration's claims that there would be another depression if Europe were not rebuilt in order to provide a market for American products. Technological developments had also created further confusion among Roosevelt's residents:

> What was this thing the papers called automation? . . . What was a computer? Could it really think like a man? Was it maybe going to replace the garment workers at their sewing machines? And, if an atom bomb were to hit New York, was the fallout going to reach Roosevelt?[85]

In fact, in the same issue of *Fortune* that contained "Labor Drives South," two physicists had written about the future revolution in cybernetics. "Nowhere is modern man more obsolete than on the factory floor," claimed E. W. Leaver and J. J. Brown. "Modern machines are more accurate and untiring than men."[86]

The town of Roosevelt was also particularly vulnerable to attacks of treason and "un-Americanness," having been associated, from its very inception, with the forces of communism. The headlines of a Philadelphia newspaper in 1936 proclaimed "New Deal Raises a Little Soviet," the subhead adding "Soviet-Inspired Project near Hightstown to Have 'Co-operative' Needlework Factory; Director-in-Chief Is Russian-Born." The author of the article went on to point out that "200 carefully selected families, headed by a Russian-born little Stalin, will be running their 'co-operative' full blast not 50 miles from the birthplace of American Democracy."[87] Jersey Homesteads was six miles from Hightstown, a stronghold of the Ku Klux Klan. And Freehold, the county seat, even into the fifties and sixties, "had kept its two fire companies kosher, so to speak; one was pure WASP, white American Protestant, the other pure WAC, white American Catholic."[88]

The relationship between the town of Roosevelt/Jersey Homesteads and the Communist Party was complex. While the janitor of the community center had known Lenin in Zurich and the gas station attendant had been a crew member on the *Potemkin* at the time of the abortive Russian Revolution of 1905,[89] the opinions of the ILGWU leaders and the history of the union itself undoubtedly carried great weight in determining the town's overall attitude toward the Communist Party. During its early years (1900–1909) the ILGWU was a conservative union suffering from a series of disastrous strikes, internal problems, and raids from the more radical Industrial Workers of the World (IWW). Its fortunes changed with the successful settlement of a shirtwaist makers' strike and a cloak makers' strike in 1910, and the Triangle Shirtwaist Company disaster in 1911. A fire had broken out on one of the top floors of the building, and because the fire exits had been locked to keep the employees in and the union organizers out, the workers, primarily young Italian and Jewish women, were unable to escape. One hundred and forty-six died in the eighteen minutes it took to bring the fire under control. This tragic fire and loss of lives further strengthened the resolve of the ILGWU to improve the working conditions of garment workers. Shahn included a reference to this fire in the central section of his mural, where an oversized male figure addresses a crowd of workers in front of the Triangle Shirtwaist Company building.

The presence of a new generation of union leaders, Jewish socialists or Bundists who had fled Russia after the failed revolution of 1905, was also an important factor in the expansion of the union. Sidney Hillman and David Dubinsky were among these Bundists. They brought with them a commitment to the principles of European social democratic unions, with their concern for a wide range of social issues—social insurance plans, cooperative housing, educational and cultural programs—as well as for wages and working conditions.

After the successful Russian Revolution of 1917, however, and the establishment of the CPUSA, a serious struggle developed between Communist Party members and Jewish socialists over control of the garment unions (in 1914 the Amalgamated Clothing Workers of America was formed with Sidney Hillman as president to represent the men's clothing industry). The struggle dragged on throughout the

1920s, involving physical as well as verbal confrontations. The socialists managed to maintain their control, but the often brutal and demoralizing battles left a rigid anti-communism within the union leadership and rank and file and a greater willingness to unite with reformist rather than revolutionary groups.[90]

The Depression made serious inroads into union control within the garment industry. Sweatshops multiplied and strikes failed. But with the election of Roosevelt as president of the nation and Dubinsky as president of the ILGWU in 1932, the fortunes of the union changed. A combination of reform and pro-union legislation and Dubinsky's personal energy resulted in an expansion of membership, successful strikes, and the establishment of the thirty-five-hour work week for over 90 percent of the dress workers. When a split occurred in the Jewish Socialist Party over whether or not to support Roosevelt, Dubinsky sided with those who favored participation in the New Deal coalition. According to Irving Howe, President Roosevelt subsequently "became an adored figure in the Jewish unions, with the social reforms of his administration signifying the kind of concrete goals that, for most Jewish workers, would gradually replace the ideal of socialism."[91]

Shahn's Roosevelt/Jersey Homesteads mural was in keeping with the general sentiment of Dubinsky and many of the union members who lived in the town. While communist sympathizers had encouraged Shahn to include Earl Browder, the leader of the CPUSA, in the group of men around the planning table in the right section of the mural, he did not follow their suggestion. Instead, he included Senator Robert F. Wagner, a key force in the establishment of the National Labor Relations Board; John Brophy, director of the CIO; Sidney Hillman, president of the Amalgamated Clothing Workers of America; Dubinsky; and Heywood Broun, president of the American Newspaper Guild. On the wall behind the group is a poster of President Roosevelt.

The classroom scene to the left of this group of men, with its portrait of Samuel Gompers on the wall, treats the history of the American Federation of Labor (AFL) and the CIO, not the CPUSA. It was undoubtedly inspired by the elaborate education program the ILGWU had instituted as part of its efforts to improve the lives of its members. But it is also likely that the circumstances of Shahn's meeting with Einstein were at least in part responsible for the particular subject matter that is being discussed in the classroom scene. In the summer of 1937

Benjamin Brown, whose dreams of a cooperative community and lobbying efforts in Washington were key factors in the government's decision to found Jersey Homesteads, decided to build a labor college on his farm two miles from the town.[92] He had already collected a large library of books dealing with the history of labor, and called together a group of individuals to help construct a college around this library. Among the group were Einstein, the architect Kurt Holtzman, and Shahn. Holtzman was asked to develop a physical design for the college and Shahn to conceive a visual arts training center. Both did their homework, Shahn producing "a plan for apprenticeship training in presswork and graphics of all sorts from posters to college publications, from books to labels."[93]

The name of the institution was to be Veblen College, after Thorstein Veblen, the American writer and social critic. Its main educational purpose was "to develop in its students a strong social motivation, a humanistic social intelligence, and the social techniques for the new technological age."[94] The choice of Veblen as the college's namesake was also motivated by a wariness of possible communist intrusions into the community at the level of symbols. It was argued that "left-wing as well as liberal parties will respect the college for its name, while at the same time the name will prevent such party labels as communist being easily attached to the college, thus aiding to maintain its non-sectarian character."[95] Unfortunately, at the second gathering of the college's supporters in September 1937, quarrels broke out among the professors who were to staff the college. Because no consensus could be reached, the plan for the college was ultimately abandoned.[96]

No matter how hard members of the community tried, however, the association between Roosevelt/Jersey Homesteads and the Communist Party stuck. In 1948 the town was one of the few localities where Wallace's Progressive Party carried the election. With such a voting record, it was no surprise that residents who told people where they lived were often asked, "Isn't that the town full of communists?" One such resident, Stanley Reiss, grew tired of having to defend his patriotism and joined with approximately sixty other Roosevelt residents to form the Civic League. According to one of the town's residents, Edwin Rosskam, the Civic League's intent was to rid the town of Reds, although Reiss himself believed that the purpose of the organization was to help Roosevelt take its place in Monmouth County as a borough instead of being given a special title. Unless it was a good one, like you say New Hope is noted for its lovely art—right?—or the Bronx Zoo for its fourteen striped zebra. That would be OK, but when you get around to Roosevelt, the best we could hope for was that it was a town loaded with communists, or worse yet, Jew-communists.[97]

The league published a monthly paper, the *Civic League Reporter*, in order to help expose those it deemed unpatriotic. In recalling his involvement in the league's activities, Si Pinkster admitted that "it was a pretty lousy situation. . . . it was the McCarthy type of thing and we were sucked into it. We went out of our way to hurt people." Shahn became the focus of much of the league's vitriol. In response he attended league meetings and sat there without saying a word; no one had the courage to tell him to leave. "The man had enough guts to come in and tackle us all in his own quiet, pleasant little manner," stated Pinkster. "He beat us. By just being there he beat us."[98]

While Shahn served as a member of the town council from 1945 to 1948, he subsequently withdrew from public office for a number of years, though he did not withdraw from political activity. The Wallace campaign had dampened his enthusiasm for the Progressive Party, yet he still produced art work and gave speeches on its behalf in the first part of 1949 and supported James Imbrie, the retired businessman who ran as the Progressive Party's gubernatorial candidate for New Jersey in 1949.[99] He also continued in his efforts to improve the living and working conditions of the local migrant black workers through state legislation and through publicizing examples of maltreatment. When some chicken coops housing a number of migrant workers burnt down, Shahn was among a group that determined the landlord had delayed in calling the fire department in order to collect the insurance money. Shahn subsequently took photographs for the press to help raise money for the workers' resettlement.[100]

Thus, while Shahn was still able to enjoy a sense of belonging to a coherent community in 1949, it was a community divided along much the same lines as the rest of the country. The deer were not the only ones being hunted a few hundred yards from Shahn's house. Young FBI men knocked on Shahn's door and the doors of other Roosevelt residents or rifled through their mail, and neighbors were pitted against neighbors in attempts to prove their patriotism. This, then, was the Roosevelt in which Shahn painted *Nocturne*, a town that partly welcomed the presence of new residents and talent and ideas and partly closed in on itself in fear of a return of the persecutions so many of its inhabitants had come to the United States to escape. In the process, they participated in a new, distinctly American form of persecution.

In presenting his analysis of *Nocturne,* Hess did not trace similar motifs or changes in the style of Shahn's painting in general over an extended period of time. He chose to focus, instead, on the immediacy of the painting's creation, its locus in Shahn's Roosevelt environment. To support this analysis, a number of photographs were interspersed throughout the article—Shahn working in his studio and walking among the trees that surrounded it, a man playing a guitar in Roosevelt, Shahn's son silhouetted against a lemon plant, the work bench and paints in the studio. We must, indeed, look to Roosevelt for an understanding of *Nocturne,* but not just the Roosevelt described by Hess. Is there evidence in the painting of that other aspect of the town's 1949 reality omitted from Hess' description—the anger, suspicion, anxiety, and fear produced by national and international events?

When Henry McBride commented that the shade of Shahn's work was often red, he was referring not only to Shahn's palette, but also to the political implications of Shahn's work. Shahn did, in fact, use the color red more often in his paintings of the late forties and early fifties than at any other point in his career. Whereas bright red is often used in earlier works to highlight certain elements, primarily architectural (e.g., the rafters in *Willis Avenue Bridge* [1940], the stairway in *The Red Stairway* [1944], and the bridge in *Cherubs and Children* [1944]), in paintings such as *Allegory* (1948), *Nocturne* (1949), and *City of the Dreadful Night* (1951), red dominates. Why did Shahn choose to use this color so extensively during this particular period? Were his reasons political or aesthetic or both?

Shahn was obviously aware of the association between the color red and communism. After McBride's review, and possibly earlier, he was also aware that his use of the color was being viewed by some as a political statement. As a color, red is effective in conveying the sense of intense emotion, particularly anger. Its association with fire and blood also makes it suitable for the depiction of crises or disasters. In the case of *Nocturne,* the sense of intensity on the part of the guitar player is conveyed not only by the red coloring of his face, but also by his expression, which Hess interprets as the angry look that often appears on the faces of folk singers. He also attributes the "violent red-lead hue" of the bench ironwork to a color it actually acquires for a few days each spring.

But the fact that folk singers sometimes screw up their faces in anger while singing or that the ironwork on benches sometimes turns bright red for a few days in the spring is not enough to explain why Shahn chose this particular expression or color for this particular painting. He had painted musicians and singers before—*Jesus Exalted in Song* (1939), *Pretty Girl Milking the Cow* (1940), *Four Piece Orchestra* (1944)—but in none of these paintings does he endow the participants with the intensity of those in *Nocturne*. In *The Blind Accordion Player* (1945) and *The Violin Player* (1947) the musicians do convey a sense of distress, caused in the first instance by the death of President Roosevelt, but in both cases it is a distress directed inward. The brows are furrowed but the lips are pressed tightly shut and the eyes, if not closed, stare blankly ahead. *Nocturne* is one of the few paintings by Shahn in which a sense of action, in this case verbal, is depicted; *Trouble* of two years earlier is another.

Nocturne is also one of the few paintings by Shahn in which the figures look directly at each other. The overriding sense gained by an overview of Shahn's work of the 1940s is one of either isolation or immobilization. Having abandoned "social realism" for "personal realism," Shahn first produced images of individuals absorbed in a game or a small task or a reflective moment, usually alone—*Sunday Painting* (1938), *Seurat's Lunch* (1939), *Vacant Lot* (1939). When there are two or more figures, they almost invariably look in different directions, have their backs turned toward each other, or are absorbed in different activities—*Willis Avenue Bridge* (1940), *Girl Jumping Rope* (1943), *World's Greatest Comics* (1946). His paintings of the struggles of unions or the aftermath of war often exhibit this same individual reflection or suffering.

In *Nocturne* not only are the two figures engaged in the same activity, but their eye contact indicates that they are cognizant of this fact. They are unified by both their singing and their anger. The figure on the left wears the clothes Shahn consistently uses to identify manual workers—the white shirt with no tie, the simple brown or black jacket and pants. The flowered shirt of the guitar-player, however, sets him slightly apart. He could be a manual worker as well, but he is more than likely a professional folk singer, inspiring his audience through song. This interpretation would be in keeping with Shahn's often-expressed belief in the power of art to reaffirm human values, to create a sense of community. This power was particularly important in 1949, when communities like Roosevelt were being torn apart and when the ability of individuals to express their anger or objections was limited by a fear of being labeled a traitor.

One such professional folk singer who may have served as inspiration for Shahn's painting was Pete Seeger. After having performed for the armed forces in the Pacific during the war, he returned to the United States and entered progressive politics, recording for Folkways Records and gaining a reputation as "the bard of the Wallace movement." He and Shahn would undoubtedly have run into each other in 1948 at the PCA headquarters in New York City, where Seeger often went to participate in the party's program of folk songs for political action.[101]

In 1949 Seeger formed the Weavers, a group that met with great success. But this success was soon undone by the blacklisting of the early fifties. Many in the United States had recognized, indeed, the power of popular music and moved to defuse it, through both blacklisting and, at times, acts of violence. On August 27, 1949, a concert in Peekskill, New York, was organized by Paul Robeson to raise money for the Harlem Chapter of the Civil Rights Congress. It was halted by a group of Legionnaires, who barricaded the roads to the concert area, stoned the concertgoers, and burned chairs, platforms, and songbooks. The concert was rescheduled for the following week. While the protection of 3,000 security guards (longshoremen, fur workers, and seamen) and 1,000 police allowed it to take place peacefully, those who attended were attacked while returning home and at least 150 people were injured.[102]

In reviewing a show of Shahn's work at the Downtown Gallery in November 1949, Charles Corwin of the *Daily Worker* commented on the importance of the painting *Nocturne*. Corwin first described Shahn as "one of our finest artists and one of our best social painters," able to portray the truth and meaning of particular situations, such as mining disasters or racial discrimination, "by bringing together the most contrasting and unexpected elements of reality." *Nocturne* struck Corwin as a typical example of this ability:

> Here Shahn pictures two husky men singing with open-mouthed gusto against a background of delicately patterned leaves and tree branches. The park bench, the working class garb, and the singers' bridgework are as real as today's headlines. Most of us keep them in mental pigeonholes widely separated from poetry and what we usually call beauty. Yet Shahn, in combining them, restores a wholeness which is lacking in our lives, where beauty is linked only with the refined and aristocratic.[103]

Corwin was impressed, therefore, with what he saw as Shahn's celebration of the details of working-class life—the garb, the bridge-
work—and his recognition of the poetry and beauty to be found in
these details. The one aspect of Shahn's work that Corwin took exception to, however, was the artist's increased interest in the elaboration
of the paint surface for its own sake, which seemed to contradict rather
than reinforce the stark reality of his vision. "His painting has become
richer in texture," stated Corwin, "yet especially in his variegated
backgrounds does it set up discordant notes, dissipating the simple
and taut expression of the theme."[104]

Shahn was obviously not immune to the effects of the intense formal
experimentations that were going on all around him, and neither was
he totally resistant to them. He would allow his backgrounds to act
more and more as areas for such formal experimentation. The fore-
grounds of his paintings remained reserved, however, for what he
would constantly refer to as humanistic content, content that consisted of forms immediately recognizable to the human eye, no matter
how distorted or abstracted. Corwin, in keeping with CPUSA cultural
policy, was concerned primarily with this humanistic element, with
the narrative, celebratory content of a work of art. The further Shahn
moved away from descriptive detail, the more ambiguity he allowed
into his work, the less acceptable it became to Corwin.

Hess also felt that *Nocturne* was an important example of Shahn's
new looser, more painterly manner, but he viewed this development
in a more positive light than Corwin. Hess's response to the social
commentary in the artist's work was also different from Corwin's.
Whereas Corwin noted Shahn's ability to reveal the concrete reality of
a mine disaster through attention to minute and often contrasting details, Hess found that the best of Shahn's work displayed evidence of
"an ability to dislocate a private, insignificant fragment from the com-
monplace and to endow it, for the spectator, with the hallucinatory
magic of symbol and form."[105] The CPUSA vied with the establishment art world, therefore, in trying to determine the meaning of
Shahn's work, to locate its significance in both political and aesthetic
terms. Corwin admired the working-class content, Hess the manner
in which Shahn articulated this content, embuing it with symbolic dimensions. Each spoke to a different audience, using the language of
that audience to make his case for the importance of Shahn's work.

While Hess may have found Shahn's more painterly manner a step
in the right direction in the development of Shahn's work, a consider-

able distance still separated Shahn from the more radical formal experimentations of the time. This distance is epitomized in the contrast between Hess' article on Shahn's *Nocturne* and a piece on Jackson Pollock that appeared a few months later in *Life* magazine. Whereas Shahn, according to Hess, worked with meticulous care, pushing his brush slowly across the surface, measuring the exact amount of pigment for his paints, Pollock scrawled the paint on with a stick, scooped it with a trowel, or poured it straight out of the can. "In with it all he mixes sand, broken glass, nails, screws or other foreign matter lying around. Cigaret ashes and an occasional dead bee sometimes get in the picture inadvertently."[106] While Shahn's content was derived from his surroundings, Pollock's painting "had a life of its own," and any lifelike images that happened to appear on his canvases were "cheerfully" rubbed out. Pollock's giant canvases were tacked to the floor; Shahn's medium-sized boards rested on a work table.

Despite their radical differences, and despite the fact that the *Life* article is less respectful of Pollock's work than Hess' piece is of *Nocturne*, both artists are presented as having achieved success. Pollock's paintings hung in five American museums and forty private collections. His work had "stirred up a fuss in Italy," and in Paris he was "fast becoming the most talked-of and controversial U.S. painter."[107] Shahn's paintings, when brought to his dealer, the Downtown Gallery, were often "sold almost immediately, for Shahn is one of the most sought-after American artists, both by museums and private collectors."[108] The two artists would continue to attract their own coteries of supporters well into the fifties, with disagreements between the two groups regarding the relative value of nonobjective and figurative painting persisting unabated.

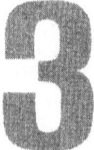

DEFENDING CIVIL LIBERTIES AT HOME
AND THE AMERICAN IMAGE ABROAD

> Whoever can predict the course of art during the
> coming fifty years will be a valuable citizen, for he will
> be able to predict also the course of human affairs—
> whether we will have war or peace, whether we will
> live under civilian conditions or military, under
> dictatorship or democracy. He will be able to tell us
> whether the individual will still be free and sovereign.
> —BEN SHAHN
> "The Future of the Creative Arts," 1952

Signs of an Epoch

In her review of an exhibition of Shahn's work in 1949 at the Down-town Gallery, Emily Genauer found that Shahn's bitterness was begin-ning to be "leavened with wit and an arresting and almost desperate 'Let us be gay' attitude." While *Summertime* (Figure 27) was "a tour de force of capricious pattern . . . suffusing everything in the midst of these colorful arabesques with a sunny freshness and gaiety," the man's face was "as grim and unhappy as ever." "Perhaps Shahn is too," sug-gested Genauer, "and this is the whole point of his picture—that it is impossible today truly to give oneself up to joy."[1]

At fifty-one, Shahn had reason to be content, if not joyous. He had been honored with a retrospective at MOMA and, in 1949, with two medals for his graphic work.[2] In 1950 his paintings appeared in major group exhibitions at the Whitney, the Metropolitan, MOMA, and the Carnegie Institute[3] and sold almost as soon as they were finished for sums ranging from $450 to $2,000.[4] That same year he was once again listed in *Art News'* annual selection of best one-person exhibitions[5] and was described elsewhere as one of the most successful artists in the United States and one of the few who were able to earn a living at painting alone.[6] He had also made his first television appearance on WJZ-TV in February 1949 and had continued with his college and mu-seum lectures.[7]

Yet no one who was at all informed about the events of the past two years and who had any degree of foresight could feel optimistic at the thought of what lay ahead. Shahn had predicted to his friend Bud Still-man, in the summer of 1949, that with the judicial condemnations of

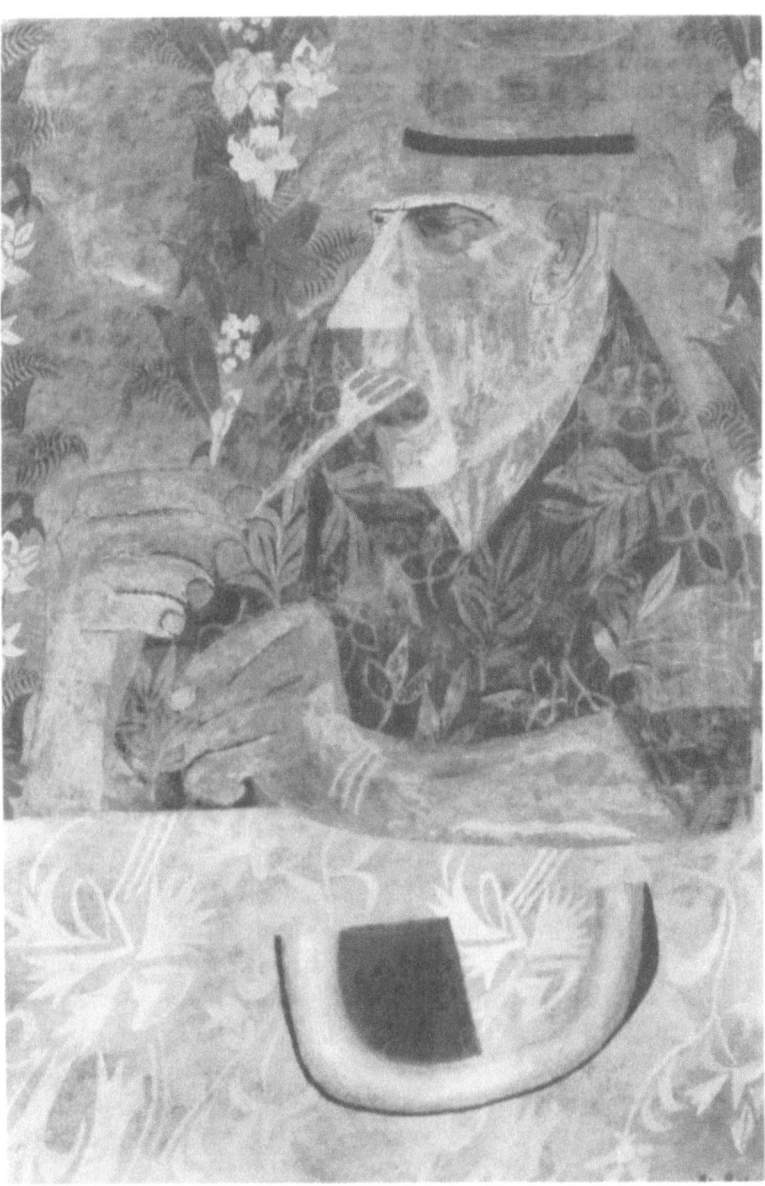

FIGURE 27

Ben Shahn, *Summertime*, 1949
Tempera
39¾ × 27″
Collection: Addison Gallery of American
Art, Phillips Academy, Andover, Mass.

Alger Hiss, the Communist 11, and Judith Coplon, America was going to enter quietly into its own brand of national socialism.[8] Truman's announcement on January 31, 1950, that he had given the go-ahead for the production of the hydrogen bomb and Albert Einstein's televised report that the "annihilation of any life on earth has been brought within the range of technical possibilities" created an even greater sense of horror and foreboding in a country already anxious about the direction in which it was headed.[9] Add to this Senator Joseph McCarthy's claim, on February 9, 1950, in Wheeling, West Virginia, that the State Department was full of communists and the subsequent escalation of the search for "subversives," and it is little wonder that it took another five years and a highly publicized trial between McCarthy and the United States Army before Shahn was certain that his prediction would not come true.

The fifties began, therefore, with a new emphasis on the threat of communism, a new need to search even deeper into the souls and the files of government employees in order to exorcise the tiniest shadow of anti-Americanism. There was also a new sense of manifest destiny, a renewed belief in America's role as preserver of the "free world." When Truman ordered American air and naval units into Korea on June 27 and committed ground troops three days later, it was this role that he called upon to justify his actions. World order had to be maintained, and military power was the only way to deal with the threat of communism.

After North Korean troops crossed the 38th parallel on June 25, Truman had little difficulty getting congressional approval for military intervention in Korea or for nearly tripling his defense budget, giving added impetus to the arms race. The first successful thermonuclear test was completed at Eniwetok Island in the Pacific in March 1952 and the first atomic-powered submarine launched that same year, part of a defense budget that had expanded from $10 billion in 1950 to $60 billion in 1952.[10] In 1951 it was estimated that the United States had between 750 and 1,000 atomic bombs while the Soviet Union might have as many as 200.[11]

What was the reaction of the American public to this increased militarization, to the proliferation of atomic weapons and the use of American forces to fight a war that appeared to have little to do with the country's own immediate interests or safety? How did it attempt to deal with the anxiety and fear that such developments must surely have engendered? One response was the wide availability, by Novem-

ber 1950, of bomb shelter plans. Another was the appearance of the
first official government publication dealing with the effects of an
atomic bomb, *You Can Survive*. This pamphlet was only a small part
of the American government's attempt to teach the American people
to "love the bomb," a feeling that was necessary in order for the arms
race to continue. But not everyone could be convinced that atomic
warfare was not harmful, at least to Americans, or that military intervention was necessary to save Europe or Southeast Asia from communism. The peace movement continued to grow, with new groups
springing up throughout the country. In October 1950 Shahn joined in
the establishment of one such group, the New Jersey Committee for
Peaceful Alternatives.[12]

Shahn also painted *Epoch* in 1950 (Figure 28), a work both humorous and grim. The smiling faces of the cyclists with their "yes" and
"no" signs raised high are countered by the pale, tight-lipped visage of
the man balanced so precariously on their heads, pants crumpled
about his knees. The fear and confusion of 1950 are here conveyed
with symbols, ones with a particularly down-home quality, suggesting
fairgrounds and circus acrobats. This may be, as Soby suggests, "Everyman, balancing precariously between the opposites of consent and dissent which exist in this epoch, as they have in nearly all others."[13] But
it is also Everyman in the simple dark suit of Shahn's workers, Everyman whose balancing act will not last, who must choose between the
two alternatives offered him by the cyclists and act on this choice via
one of the most important means offered him in the United States—
the vote. For the curtained enclosure behind the figures is not a circus
tent or concession stand but a voting booth. It closely resembles the
structures included in a painting of voting booths Shahn had executed
a short time earlier for Container Corporation. In a letter to Edward
Warwick of the advertising agency N. W. Ayer and Son, Shahn commented on this painting:

> . . . I think of the voting booth as the most succinct pictorial statement
> about democracy. Where the voting booth is present government cannot
> for long pursue ends other than those of the public good. . . . The sug-
> gestion of war and destruction behind one booth is intended to indicate
> how serious a responsibility the vote is. The uninformed vote, the emo-
> tionally partisan vote, the intimidated vote may lead to disaster.[14]

Shahn has not included the suggestion of war and destruction in *Epoch*, but he has intimated another misuse of the voting process, one

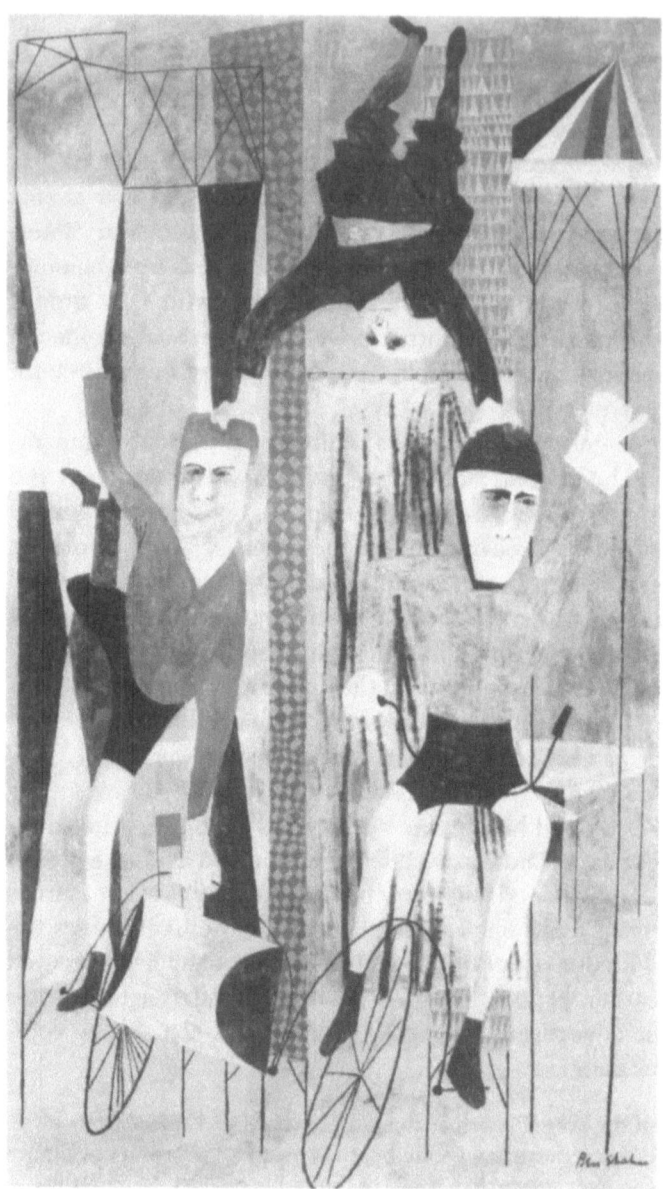

FIGURE 28

Ben Shahn, *Epoch*, 1950
Tempera
52 × 31″
Collection: Philadelphia Museum of Art;
Purchased: Bloomfield Moore Fund

that was equally applicable to 1950—its transformation into a charade or a circus, a transformation that boded ill for the future of the nation.[15]

Shahn had always believed in the power of the electoral process. His most politically charged work had been executed in the context of election campaigns. It was not always possible, however, to present the choices in terms of the evils of the Republican businessman and the benefits of the Democratic New Dealer. For one thing, anticommunism had blurred the issues. Shahn does not refer to Republicans or Democrats or anti-communism in his painting. It is, as he meant it to be, a symbolic portrayal of the element of decision and choice in people's lives, though inspired by the events of 1950. Two years later, however, Shahn would create posters for the Democratic Party in the 1952 presidential campaign that would exhibit the particularity of his earlier CIO-PAC works.

Humanism and Art

As a member of the American Continental Congress for World Peace, Shahn realized the benefits of, and need for, international organizations in an era when few countries could escape the influence or attention of the United States and the Soviet Union. He willingly served, therefore, on the Visual Arts Panel of the United Nations Educational, Scientific, and Cultural Organization (UNESCO), founded in 1946 and committed to world peace. The preamble to UNESCO's constitution stated that "since wars begin in the minds of men, it is in the minds of men that the defenses of peace must be constructed."[16] In 1950 Shahn, Grace McCann Morley, and Edward Steichen were part of a smaller committee set up "to study the problem of how the Visual Arts can contribute to the dissemination of information on the Universal Declaration of Human Rights."[17] Thus Shahn continued at an international level the work he had begun the year before at the conference on the Bill of Rights in New York.

Human rights. Humanism. Shahn would devote many hours to defining these two concepts and contribute many dollars to causes he believed were supportive of them, from the Southern Conference Educational Fund to the American Labor Party.[18] In a talk at the State University of Iowa on April 20, 1950, he reiterated the hope expressed the year before at Smith College that there would be a resurgence of humanism among artists. At the most basic level, this would mean a renewed attention to the objects and activities of people's daily lives. In his own work, while he often used symbols, they had to be sharply observed and "of the most usual and ordinary sort and directly out of the daily, contemporary life of human beings." Such symbols would then be assured of having "that unmistakable stamp of human personality that only the real, individual object can have."[19] One only has to think of the crumpled pants of the upturned figure in *Epoch* to know what Shahn meant here.

Shahn also defined humanist art in terms of its opposite, abstract or nonobjective art. "Of our fine art, there are two main streams," stated Shahn, "one humanistic, necessarily asking the question, 'to what end?', greatly concerned with the implications of man's way of life; the other, the abstract and non-objective, absorbed in its own plastic problems, and not involved with the human prospect." Abstract art was aligned with science, sharing its emphasis on "know-how," appropriating much of the time-space terminology of physics, ignoring the human implications of its actions. Humanistic art necessarily evaluates things "according to their human ends."[20]

Art critic Carol Seeley, writing in 1950 on the nature of abstract painting, also connected abstract art with the twentieth-century obsession with science. "Our vision," she stated, "has become a space-time concept; we think naturally in terms of micro-organisms and the penetrations of outer space." This was not the rational science of the nineteenth century concerned with objective reality, a science whose artistic counterparts were the works of Winslow Homer and Thomas Eakins:

> Today the objective reality of the material world has receded; mass has disappeared, become fields of energy. The conflict is no longer between man and his environment; everything is possible to man. The conflict is now inside the mind of man. . . . [Nonobjective art] has produced a metaphor, a brilliant metaphor, on the indifferent universe.[21]

Yet Seeley was not as rigid in her connection of science and abstract art as was Shahn, nor did she find nonobjective art as devoid of human concerns. According to Seeley:

> The compulsion behind this art, we can see now, is less that of a physical and concrete ideal, in comparison with our more literal past, but in becoming abstract is more spiritual, insubstantial, trying to find itself as part of an ordered system. For the artist is not like the scientist, who tells us how hot the material is; he must accept the ultimate question and say what hot is.[22]

If Seeley's analogy were to be applied to Shahn, it would read as follows: if scientists tell us "how hot the material is" and nonobjective artists attempt to convey "what hot is," Shahn asks "what are the social consequences of that heat?" His painting *The Blind Botanist* (1954; Figure 29), depicting a blind man gripping a large thorny plant, prompts the viewer to question the nature of scientific endeavors. Shahn wrote of this painting that his intent was "to express a curious quality of irrational hope that man seems to carry around with him," and to suggest the unpredictability of the vocations that men and women pursue.[23] His Lucky Dragon series of 1960–1961 is a particularly powerful depiction of the tragedies and human consequences of nuclear research. In this series of paintings Shahn traces the fate of the crew members of the Japanese fishing boat (the *Lucky Dragon*) that, six years earlier, had wandered close to the Bikini Atoll where the United States was testing its new hydrogen bomb.

Others also entered into the debate over just how humanist abstract and nonobjective art was. In March 1950 MOMA, the Institute of Contemporary Art (ICA) in Boston, and the Whitney Museum jointly issued "A Statement on Modern Art." In this statement the three museums reaffirmed, among other things, their belief in

> the humanistic value of modern art even though it may not adhere to academic humanism with its insistence on the human figure as the central element of art . . . We recognize the humanistic value of abstract art, as an expression of thought and emotion and the basic human aspirations toward freedom and order. In these ways modern art contributes to the dignity of man.[24]

The museums' statement was not simply a response to artists like Shahn, who claimed that only an art whose subject matter was derived from the perceived reality of daily life could be described as humanistic. It was a response, as well, to the attacks of Dondero and other right-wing politicians on modern art as depraved and inhuman. "We also reject," continued its authors, "the assumption that art which is esthetically an innovation must somehow be socially or politically subversive, and therefore un-American."[25] The ICA was particularly committed to supporting what it perceived as the humanistic values of modern art and was less willing than others to dismiss as somehow outmoded or irrelevant artists who made claims for a revival or continuation of such values in the postwar world.[26]

The same month that MOMA, the Whitney, and the ICA issued

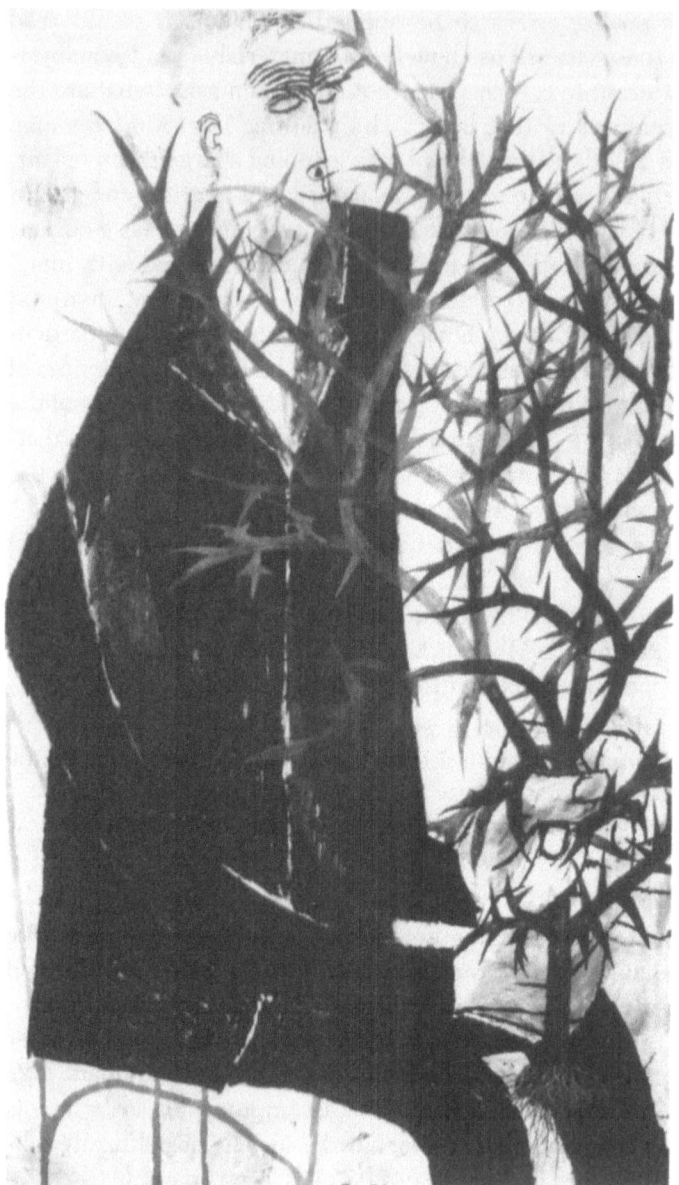

FIGURE 29
Ben Shahn, *The Blind Botanist*, 1954
Tempera on masonite
52 × 31"
Courtesy Wichita Art Museum; the
Roland P. Murdock Collection

their statement, a group of artists, who willingly accepted the label "humanist," met at Del Pezzo Restaurant in New York City in response to a postcard from Raphael Soyer. They included Henry Varnum Poor, Soyer, Yasuo Kuniyoshi, Edward Hopper, Shahn, Leon Kroll, and Isabel Bishop. In this and subsequent meetings over the next few years the group discussed current developments within the art world and the tendencies of museums and critics "to surrender all the values that we felt were permanent . . . making of our profession a thing of cults and fads, and obscurity and snobbery."[27] In particular, they were concerned about MOMA's championing of abstract and nonobjective art. While they relayed this concern to the museum's directors, both in person and in writing, they were simply told that the museum did not see itself as giving undue attention to nonobjective art.[28]

The group grew in numbers as word of its activities spread, and in 1953 it published the first of three issues of *Reality*, a journal committed to the promotion of "human qualities" in painting. Articles such as "Humanism in Art" by Honoré Sharrer, "Man Is the Center" by Jack Levine, and "Drawing and Tradition" by George Biddle filled the journal's pages. By this time, however, Shahn had stopped attending meetings, and he was not among the forty-six artists listed along with the statement of principles in the first issue of the journal. According to Bernarda Bryson Shahn, he felt that the group was too exclusive and that, while the issues they talked about at the early informal meetings were important, they were not the basis for an official organization. Raphael Soyer felt, however, that Shahn's departure was influenced by a combination of his close relationship with MOMA and the museum's criticism of the group.[29]

Shahn's withdrawal from the *Reality* group did not mean that his commitment to a humanist art lessened or that he was unwilling to voice his opinions in art journals on this issue. The first issue of *Reality* included, in fact, excerpts from his *Paragraphs on Art*, a pamphlet published by Spiral Press in 1952. The pamphlet contained short paragraphs gathered from speeches Shahn had made at various times and places over the past few years. The sections quoted in *Reality* included Shahn's call for "a resurgence of the humanities, a rebirth of spirit."[30] But a central element in Shahn's concept of a humanist aesthetics was also the ability of a work of art to communicate with, or be meaningful to, individuals outside of the art world, and he subsequently channeled much of his energy in this direction.

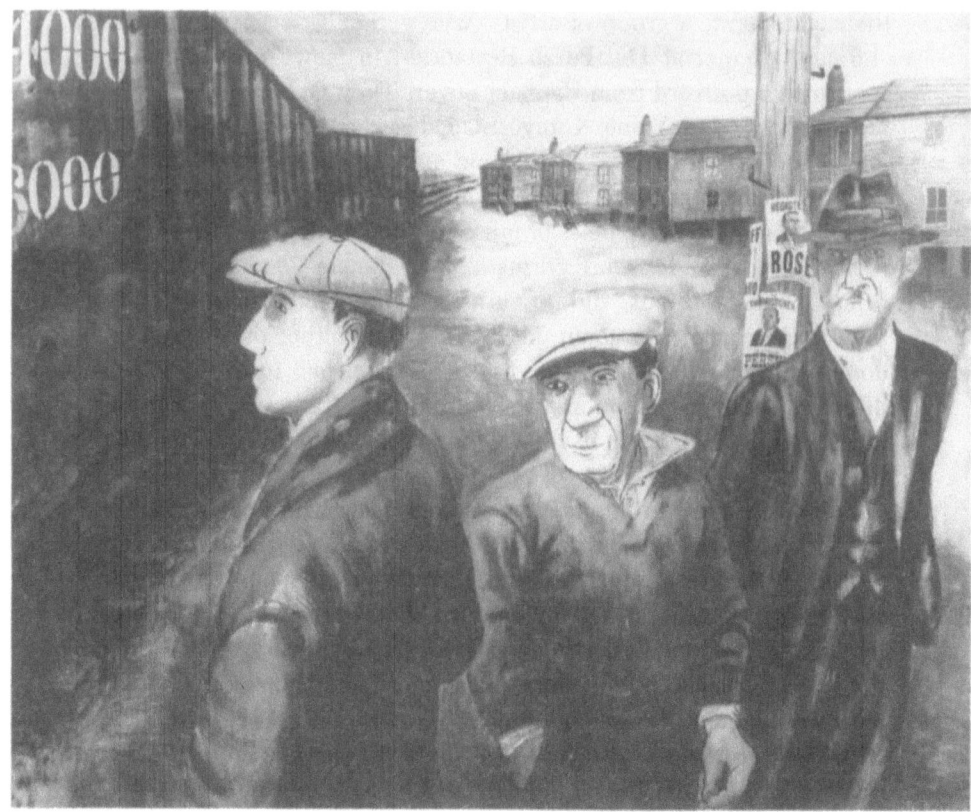

FIGURE 30
Ben Shahn, *Scotts Run, West Virginia,*
1937
Tempera on cardboard
22¼ × 27⅞″
Collection of Whitney Museum of
American Art, New York; Purchase
38.11
Photographer: Geoffrey Clements

Shahn's correspondence reveals one instance where such communicative attempts on his part met with particular success. At the end of 1950 Dr. Lorin E. Kerr, area medical advisor for the United Mine Workers of America office in Morgantown, West Virginia, wrote Shahn asking if a color reproduction of *Scotts Run, West Virginia* (1937; Figure 30) existed that would be suitable for framing and hanging in the office. Shahn's negative reply prompted Kerr to express his disappointment that there were no reproductions of paintings of coal miners and coal mining communities that showed "our people in the conditions under which they live." He was particularly disappointed at the unavailability of Shahn's work, as Scotts Run was only a short distance from Morgantown. "I know that if it is possible to locate such reproductions," Kerr stated, "there are at least a half dozen similar offices which would be interested in the same reproductions as well as a number of our district officers who would like to have the reproductions either for their homes or for their offices."[31]

Shahn was also contacted at the beginning of 1951 about another project involving the decoration of union halls. Irving Richter, the head of Organizational Services Company of Detroit, wrote to Shahn on January 16 stating how happy he was that Shahn was interested in giving him some advice on his latest undertaking. Shahn had worked with Richter on the UAW-CIO exhibition in January 1947 when Richter was the national legislative representative for the union. Richter had been a member of both the AFL and the CIO in the thirties and forties, and had edited *News Flash,* a bimonthly labor legislative letter. He had also been contributing editor of *Ammunition,* the monthly magazine of the UAW-CIO, and had written various pamphlets on labor legislation.

Richter wanted Shahn's help in producing a series of three large panels that he could sell to unions to be hung in union halls and used at conventions. The project had been prompted by the upcoming 250th anniversary of Detroit. According to Richter, the birthday celebrations were being organized by the city's large stores with no labor participation. He wanted to "offer labor a chance to participate to the extent of putting up in their halls the official insignia but on a picture which shows labor, not Ford and GM, as the builders of Detroit." By removing the insignia, the same panel could be used nationally.[32]

This birthday panel would be the first in the series, depicting both black and white settlers and native Indians engaged in farming, logging, and hunting, as well as the first factories. The second would show the various strike and legislative activities of union members and would include a portrait of Franklin D. Roosevelt, who was "the only non-controversial labor hero" in both the AFL and the CIO locals. The third panel would show labor looking toward the future, with perhaps Shahn's drawing of the hand of labor holding the ballot and a general theme of peace and plenty.

What Richter wanted from Shahn were some ideas with regard to content, materials, and presentation, and perhaps even some finished work. The image of a bricklayer that Shahn had produced for the January 1951 cover of *Fortune* was, according to Richter, "a perfect example of the great Shahn touch—which may have escaped a few PAC brass hats, but which I know I can sell to AFL business agents as well as Reutherites, Stalinites, Trotskyites, Peoples Partyites and Democrats."[33] It was this appeal of the "Shahn touch" to all of the various factions of the labor movement that Richter hoped to parallel in his project, for only by establishing a nonpolitical base in a number of unions could it be a success.

Richter's choice of Shahn indicates that Shahn's reputation as an artist interested in the concerns of labor was still strong in 1951. Shahn's willingness to help indicates that this reputation was not unwarranted. Yet Richter approached him as the representative of a private firm, not of a union, which may have been an indication of the lack of interest on the part of unions themselves in assuming the role of art patron that Walter Abell had once defined so enthusiastically for them. This lack of interest was, indeed, evident to Richter, who commented on the "crying need" for some sort of meaningful visual imagery in union halls across the country.[34]

Portrait of the Artist as an American Liberal

The ability to communicate depends, of course, on the accessibility of an artist's work. In Shahn's case, his paintings and drawings were available for viewing in numerous major museums and in the pages of national magazines. This accessibility was further enhanced by the publication, in 1951, of Selden Rodman's book *Portrait of the Artist as an American, Ben Shahn: A Biography with Pictures*. While Soby's monograph on Shahn for MOMA and the numerous articles in both art journals and mass circulation magazines like *Look* had offered information on Shahn and his work to a broader audience, this was the first full-length study of the artist to appear.

Like Soby before him, Rodman emphasized Shahn's complex and paradoxical nature—the fact that he was popular with both labor organizations and big business, that he defended the primacy of content at the same time as he engaged in formal experimentation, that he was both political and spiritual. Rodman attempted to explain such seeming paradoxes by examining Shahn's past, by searching for the sources of many images and political beliefs in Shahn's early years in Lithuania and Brooklyn.

Rodman also made persistent claims regarding Shahn's Americanness and stressed that the artist had been less inspired by radical doctrines than was often assumed. In fact, Rodman spent considerable time pointing out the exact nature of Shahn's associations with leftist groups in the past. For example, Shahn's signed contributions to the Artists' Union's publication *Art Front*, whose staff contained a number of communists, included, according to Rodman, only two drawings—a collective caricature entitled "The Committee of 100—Count 'Em!" in the November 1934 issue and a wash caricature of Jonas Lie, then president of the National Academy of Design, in the April 1935 number. By the mid-thirties both Shahn and his wife had ended any dealings they might have had with communists. Rodman quotes Shahn: "I was fed up with factional bickerings from the start, but in the early editorial meetings when the Communists fought my efforts to broaden the sheet I'd debate with them until five in the morning."[35]

While Rodman's concern with verifying Shahn's Americanness and his distance from communism is understandable in light of the reactionary political climate of the early fifties, it also appears to be connected to the author's own political past. At the beginning of the book Rodman describes himself as having been involved, in the thirties, in editing "a political magazine exploring American alternatives to Marxism." His work in the foreign nationalities branch of the Office of Strategic Services during the war was followed by two studies of popular painting and the supervision of the mural decoration of a cathedral by folk artists in Haiti. Rodman was attracted to Shahn's work because of its similarity to that of these self-taught Haitian artists, though the attraction was not unqualified. Sometimes he had been repelled by the insistent propaganda of Shahn's painting, its "Marxian emphasis on the hard lot of the 'workers' or the callous vulgarity of the 'bourgeoisie.'"[36]

Yet Rodman ultimately overcame these reservations and presented Shahn as his own American alternative to Marxism. Shahn was an artist concerned with poverty, oppression, and injustice who worked through distinctly American channels—the New Deal, the CIO, the OWI, the civil rights movement—to combat these conditions and who produced an art readily distinguishable from both the socialist realist canvases of "vulgar Marxists" and the escapist fantasies of Europeanized abstractionists.

In responding to Shahn's suggestions regarding final changes in the manuscript, Rodman jokingly commented that the book was "now tidied up, politically speaking, the way you wanted it, and if you're now mistaken for a good 'liberal,' or even an anti-Stalinist that Clement Greenberg could approve of, don't blame me!"[37] Two years after the publication of Rodman's book Shahn would, in fact, outline in more detail his vision of the role of the liberal in American society.[38] In the meantime, in a lecture at Harvard in April 1951, he argued that a connection existed between the rise of abstract art after the war and the right-wing attacks on New Deal liberalism:

> I shall now unabashedly align the change in the art landscape with the
> change in the political atmosphere. . . . Repudiation was indeed in the
> air. The Congress was busily vanquishing the ghost of the New Deal,
> the Reign of Committees had begun. Relations between the recent allies,
> the United States and Russia, chilled, provoked by mutual intransigence.
> Liberalism was in bad odor, both for its New Deal leanings, and for
> its indulgence of Communism. Suspicion, accusation and renuncia-
> tion grew.[39]

In addition, artists were investigated by government agents and questioned regarding their friends and activities.

> You may disagree with me that such a political atmosphere can have any
> effect upon the esthetic content of art, to stimulate the trend toward ab-
> straction, or toward anything else. I believe that it has. Abstract painting,
> is, politically speaking, about the most non-committal statement that can
> be made in art. . . . Abstract art had left its political banners far behind,
> and has for many years gone its way, "disengaged."[40]

Artists who believed in the liberalism and social-reform policies of the New Deal, therefore, had to resist this move toward abstraction on political as well as aesthetic grounds. They had to remain, according to Shahn, "engaged," committed to more than formalistic experimentation.

In his final presentation of 1951 at the Niagara Convocation in Buffalo, New York, Shahn issued the following challenge to his audience:

. . . if either art or society is to survive the coming half-century, it will be necessary for us to re-assess our values. The time is past due for us to decide whether we are a moral people, or merely a comfortable people, whether we place our own convenience above the life-struggle of backward nations, whether we place the sanctity of enterprise above the debasement of our public. If it falls to the lot of artists and poets to ask these questions, then the more honorable their role. It is not the survival of art alone that is at issue, but the survival of the free individual and a civilized society.[41]

Shahn's somewhat apocalyptic language may appear exaggerated today, but the end of 1951 was for many an apocalyptic moment. For a year and a half American armed forces had participated in the systematic destruction of the small nation of Korea.[42] This destruction and the misery and suffering it caused were fully reported by the press throughout the war. The head of the Far Eastern Bomber Command, Major General Emmett O'Donnell, Jr., felt confident enough of the extent of the destruction by the end of the first year of war to publicly declare that "the entire, almost the entire Korean Peninsula is just a terrible mess. Everything is destroyed. There is nothing standing worthy of the name."[43]

At home, the damage being inflicted was more psychological than physical. Bomb shelters continued to be dug in back yards and the loyalty-security mania that had been set off by McCarthy's Wheeling speech and the passage of the McCarran Internal Security Act later in 1950 inspired such popular anti-communist thrillers as Mickey Spillane's *One Lonely Night*. It also produced the arrests of Julius and Ethel Rosenberg. Their trial on charges of conspiracy to commit espionage began March 6, 1951, and ended later that month with a verdict of guilty.

In the art world, Alfred Frankfurter noted in December 1951 that "hardly a week elapses between outbursts of amateur criticism by councilmen and cabinet ministers, congressional representatives and commissars."[44] One particularly brash incident had occurred the previous month, when Los Angeles city councilmen accused a municipally sponsored art exhibition of containing "communist" art. The painting *First Surge of the Sea* by Rex Brandt was especially singled out as sporting the hammer and sickle on the sail of the boat in the foreground. The artist explained, at the city council meeting to which a number of artists and paintings were dragged, that the symbol was

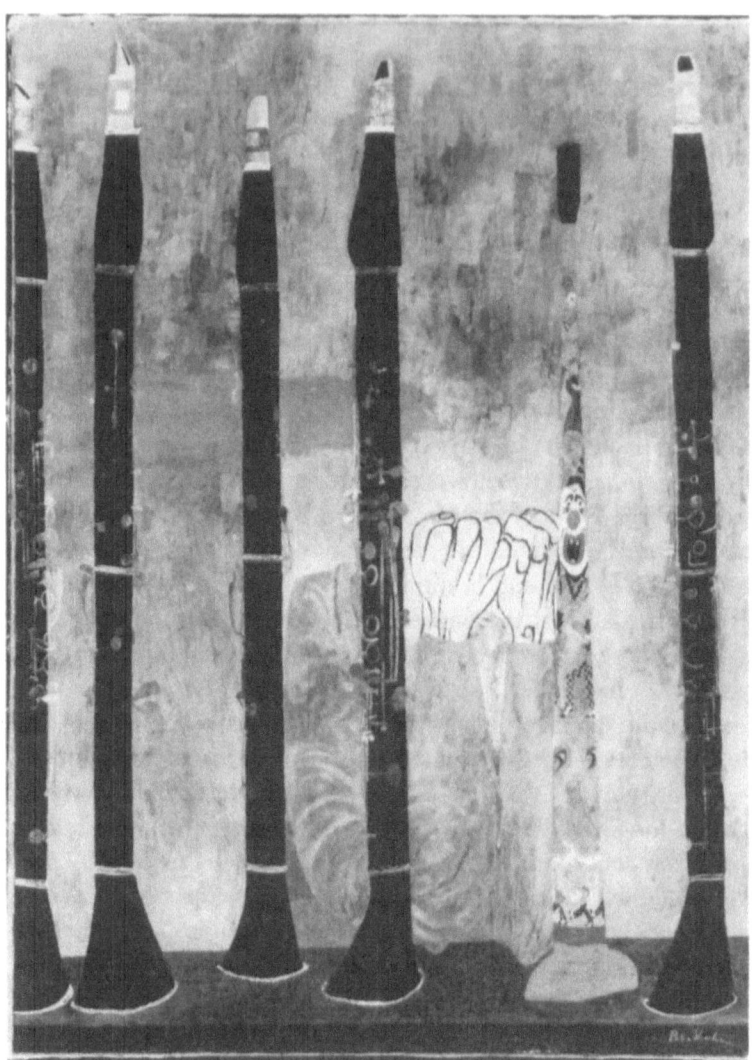

FIGURE 31

Ben Shahn, *Composition with Clarinets
and Tin Horn*, 1951
Tempera on panel
48 × 36″
Collection: Detroit Institute of Arts; Gift
of the Founders Society, Friends of
Modern Art Fund, Accession No. 51.85
© The Detroit Institute of Arts, Founders Society Purchase, Friends of Modern Art Fund

an "I" and a "C," the standard marking and abbreviation for Island Clipper Class.[45]

Shahn conveyed the mood of farce and tragedy of 1951 in his painting *Composition with Clarinets and Tin Horn* (1951; Figure 31). Stylistically, it retains the sharply detailed and particularized objects from everyday life of his earlier work in the foreground, while the background gives way to a textured overlaying of paint. The power of the painting, however, lies in its incongruities—the brightly painted horn among the solemn black clarinets, the flame emerging from the mouthpiece of one of the latter instruments, the absence of any indication of the figure's head. The large face of the clown halfway down the horn acts almost as a surrogate head, with its enormous smiling mouth and bright red nose. Yet any sense of gaity introduced by this face is immediately countered by the overwhelming mood of tension and pain created by the flaming mouthpiece, the clenched hands, and the long red section of paint that cuts into the area where the figure's head should be. The figure is, in fact, imprisoned between the closed background, with its red gash, and the line of instruments, reminiscent of the prison bars in a drawing Shahn made for a *New York Times* ad earlier that year.[46]

Two years later Shahn used the language of symbol and allegory to create allusions to contemporary moral and political dilemmas in a work entitled *Second Allegory* (1953; Figure 32). While a confrontation of sorts is taking place in the painting, the identity of the participants is unclear. There is no telltale white shirt, unbuttoned at the neck, to indicate the class of the individual on the ground, no distinct facial features to particularize him. And the arm descending from the fiery wreath—is it the oppressive presence of the atomic bomb, suggested by the molecular-like structures above the figure's raised knee, or the intervening hand of a divine being, or the accusing finger of Senator Joseph McCarthy? All three interpretations would have been plausible in 1953.

The sense of uncertainty that marks *Second Allegory* is heightened by the appearance of a new formal element in Shahn's work, a change in the manner in which he manipulated the painted surface. Around the hands and feet of the reclining figure in particular, one can discern Shahn's use of "palimpsest," the markings or traces left upon a picture as it is reworked. "The feeling-about for form," stated Shahn, "is a vital part of a picture; it has a dimension, almost a time dimension."[47] By leaving the traces of his structuring of the image visible within the im-

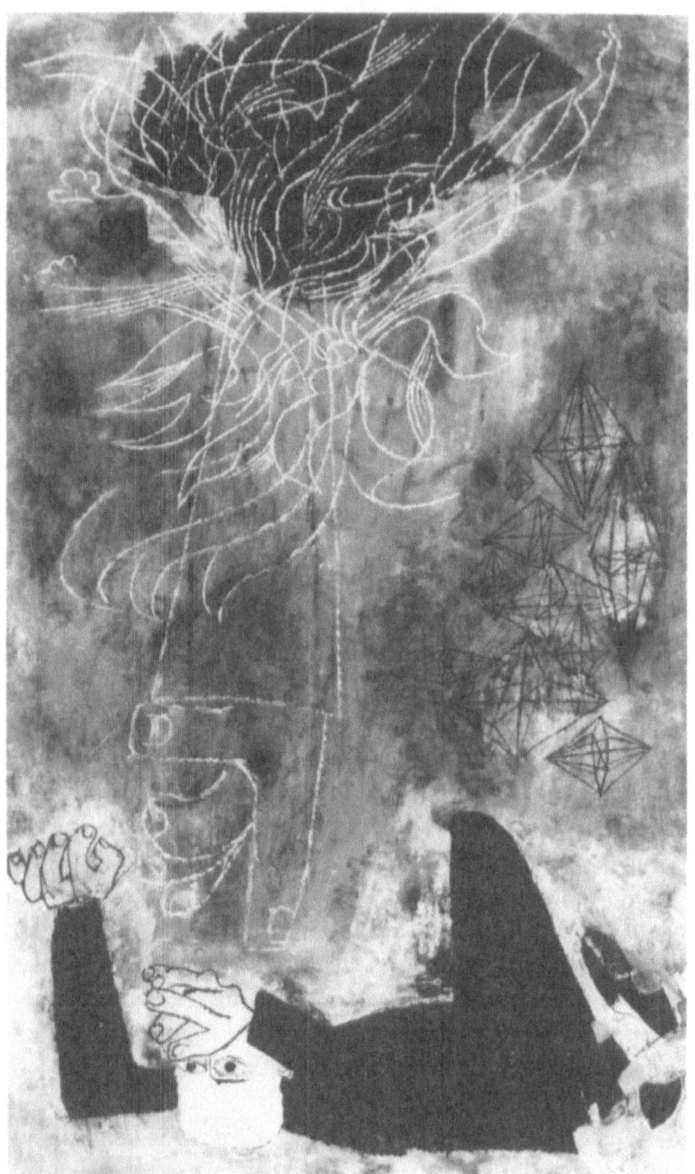

FIGURE 32

Ben Shahn, *Second Allegory*, 1953
Tempera on masonite
53⅜ × 31⅜"
Collection: Krannert Art Museum, University of Illinois

age itself, Shahn provided a sense of process, of shifting ideas, of the artist thinking and acting out the work. This allowed another level of engagement by the viewer.

Shahn developed his use of palimpsest during the summer of 1951, while in residence at Black Mountain College. Founded in 1933 as an alternative educational institution owned and administered by the faculty and kept small to provide close student-teacher relations, the college attracted many of the better-known abstract artists in the forties and fifties, including De Kooning, Motherwell, and Franz Kline. While it is quite clear Shahn was aware of the formal experimentations of these artists and others like them prior to 1951, his stay at Black Mountain would have placed him in much closer proximity to both the creation of such new work and the opinions of its practitioners. He even admitted in a talk at the college that he "like[d] to look at a great deal of abstract art, and . . . at some non-objective art," although he added that he knew he was "in a stronghold of anti-humanists."[48]

While Shahn allowed the viewer room to maneuver in investigating and assigning meaning to the various forms and marks within his work, he also wanted to encourage the transfer of this heightened perception to a contemplation or consciousness of larger social issues. To this end he supplemented his painted messages with lectures and articles, addressing large groups of people about the nature of his work and the socially important role of art and thus providing a framework within which his paintings could be viewed. He wanted his work to provide an antidote to the increasing dislocation and mechanization of life in the United States, to remind people of basic human values that seemed to have disappeared from sight. "It is the mission of art," he claimed at the end of 1951, "to remind man from time to time that he is human, and the time is ripe, just now, today, for such a reminder."[49]

Attack and Counterattack

It was only a matter of time before Shahn's public criticisms of Dondero and McCarthy caught the attention of the two politicians and their helpers. Carey McWilliams of the *Nation* noted in the first weeks of 1952 that "it has become clear—if it was not always clear—that literally no American is beyond the reach of witch-hunters or the vicious activities of informers." Even Henry Luce, related McWilliams, had been threatened by McCarthy for publishing a story critical of the senator in *Time*.[50] This national situation was the result not only of McCarthy's increased power and influence within the Senate, but also of the close cooperation between the senator and J. Edgar Hoover, head of the FBI, who provided McCarthy with information from FBI files.[51] Hoover had also set up a vast network of informers to gather new information on "suspected communists," a network that appeared, according to McWilliams, to include individuals within the White House itself.

Hoover and McCarthy were aided in their gathering of information by countless private citizens who became self-appointed guardians of American institutions against "subversives." In the area of radio and television, such private informers were particularly influential. The most powerful of these groups was American Business Consultants, set up in 1947 by three ex-FBI agents (Ted Kirkpatrick, Jack G. Keenan, and Ken Bierly) and financed by the businessman Alfred Kohlberg. American Business Consultants published a regular newsletter, *Counterattack,* edited by Frank McNamara, that listed individuals suspected of communist associations. Companies wishing to maintain a healthy image and avoid public accusation of harboring "Reds" would pay $24 a year for the newsletter or hire American Business Consultants to check out prospective employees. In addition, in June 1950, three days before the beginning of the Korean War, the company published *Red Channels: The Report of Communist Influence in Radio and Television.* The 151 actors, directors, and writers listed in its 213 pages soon found it impossible to find work in the industry.[52]

But actors, directors, and writers were not the only individuals of interest to the producers of *Counterattack* and *Red Channels.* The July 25, 1952, issue of the newsletter contained a lengthy denunciation of Shahn. What had prompted the attack was a full-page ad executed by Shahn for CBS that appeared the first week of July promoting the network's coverage of the Republican and Democratic conventions. It consisted of a maze of television antennae, with the CBS eye in the center. Below the eye were four black rectangles, positioned one below the other like street signs, containing the words "See the 1952 Republican Convention, CBS Television Network." Beneath the drawing was the statement that all CBS coverage of the conventions was sponsored by Westinghouse, including the Democratic Convention on July 21.[53]

Counterattack opened its July 25 issue with the statement: "BIG BUSINESS HELPS ENEMY OF REPUBLICAN AND DEMOCRATIC PARTIES TO CAPITALIZE ON THEIR CONVENTIONS."[54] Shahn was "the enemy" for a number of reasons. He had executed art work, claimed

Counterattack, for three communist publications: *Masses and Mainstream, Morning Freiheit,* and *Jewish Life.* He had supported several "communist-backed" events in 1949, including the Waldorf Peace Conference, the American Continental Congress for World Peace and the Bill of Rights Conference, and was a member of the National Council of the Arts, Sciences and Professions. He had illustrated the cover of the *Nation's* recent special issue on civil liberties, and had mocked the Republican and Democratic parties with his Truman and Dewey poster for Henry Wallace's campaign. *Counterattack* readers were urged to write to CBS and Westinghouse and "ask them if they can justify their firms' carelessness in helping to finance a leading, continual supporter of Communist Party causes."[55]

Shahn was, indeed, guilty of the actions *Counterattack* outlined. Whether these actions were subversive is, of course, another question. While communists were certainly actively involved in the peace movement, so too were a number of non-communist Americans. Shahn's cover drawing for a cultural supplement to the November 1948 issue of *Jewish Life* consisted of a version of the head of the fire beast from his painting *Allegory.* In *Masses and Mainstream* his drawings were used from August 1948 to January 1949 to illustrate stories about the elderly, the chicken farmers of southern New Jersey, Marxist ethics, and industrial accidents. On one occasion, three drawings appeared on their own.[56] The images themselves were far from controversial—a mine building, a farmer, a miner, a uniformed officer singing "Silent Night." Nor were the articles themselves particularly threatening to American moral values or national security. Their appearance in a communist publication was enough, however, to brand them suspect.

There is a possibility that Shahn did not, in fact, authorize the use of his drawings in *Masses and Mainstream.* His work was often considered public property by members of the left and reproduced indiscriminately from previous publications.[57] The totally unrelated juxtaposition of a drawing of an officer singing "Silent Night" and a discussion of Marxist ethics and morals suggests that the use of Shahn's image in this instance may have been unauthorized. In fact, Shahn had issued a serigraph version of *Silent Night* in 1949 that later appeared in pirated editions.[58]

Authorized or not, Shahn's images did appear in leftist publications as well as in ads for CBS. CBS' public response to *Counterattack's* charges appeared in the newsletter's August 8 issue in the form of a letter from the president of the network, J. L. Van Volenburg. Van Volenburg praised Shahn as "universally recognized as one of the greatest living painters" and claimed the ad was meant to build "maximum audiences" for conventions and to help "a free people reach independent decisions on the basis of what they have seen with their own eyes."[59] Yet *Counterattack*'s charges had their desired effect. The July 21 *New York Times* ad for CBS coverage of the Democratic Convention did not contain an illustration by Shahn, and William Golden, the network's art director and a close friend of Shahn's, was told by his superiors to cease commissioning work from the artist.[60]

CBS actions in Shahn's case were not unusual. The network had, in fact, hired American Business Consultants in 1950 after *Counterattack* had labeled CBS one of the worst supporters of "Communist fronters." In December of that year all network employees were required to sign a loyalty statement based on the Attorney General's list as of October 30, 1950. Among the performers blacklisted from CBS programs were the lyricist Oscar Hammerstein, the comedian Jack Gilford, and the choreographer Jerome Robbins.[61]

CBS blacklisting of Shahn lasted until the middle of the decade. Edward R. Murrow, however, commissioned a number of illustrations from Shahn to advertise the programs he produced for CBS throughout the fifties. As an independent producer who bought his air time from the network, he could hire whomever he desired without the approval of CBS executives.[62] Leo Lionni, art director for *Fortune*, also continued to employ Shahn, refusing to be intimidated by *Counterattack*'s blacklist. Indeed, according to Shahn, when Lionni heard about the newsletter's charges, he immediately called Shahn and commissioned a drawing.[63] Lionni's actions were undoubtedly supported by Henry Luce, who had, himself, sent a letter to Jack G. Keenan, then president of American Business Consultants, in response to an attack on *Life* by *Counterattack*. "We have not as yet," stated Luce, "engaged or organized a private F.B.I. to check up on all painters, sculptors or other artists to give them a loyalty clearance before any of our Art Directors give them any assignments."[64]

American Business Consultants was not the only organization interested in documenting Shahn's activities in the early fifties. While he had had to contend with FBI agents in Roosevelt in the late 1940s, it was only in the middle of 1951 that the agency began to take a real interest in Shahn; over half of his FBI file covers the years 1951 to

1953.[65] It is probable that McCarthy's rise to prominence and the escalation of the Korean War were important factors in the emphasis on these three years in Shahn's file. Shahn had made his opposition to McCarthy and his supporters public by signing a petition sent to President Truman in 1952 demanding that he grant amnesty to the CPUSA leaders convicted under the Smith Act.[66] In addition, he designed and illustrated the program booklet for the 1953 off-Broadway production of *The World of Sholom Aleichem,* which provided employment for some of the many people blacklisted as a result of HUAC's and American Business Consultants' investigations. The play was a critical success and was restaged later that same year, with a new set of drawings by Shahn.[67] Shahn was also not averse to criticizing American foreign policy in his numerous lectures throughout the country. It is not surprising, therefore, that at a time when dissidents of any kind were being kept under close watch, Shahn came to the attention of the FBI.

Shahn's file was classified "Security Matter—C"—suspected communist. The earliest document in it is dated November 25, 1940, and refers to Shahn's employment with the RA/FSA. The main point of the document was that Shahn and an individual employed by the Rural Electrification Administration "used to argue furiously at times about Communism and each characterized the other as being a soap-box Communist." It was also noted that the other individual had access to maps of all the power plants and high-tension electric plants throughout the country and "used to take a month to a month and a half leave without pay every year to make a trip to Europe."

It is somewhat surprising that an account of an earlier encounter between Shahn and the FBI while he was painting his Jersey Homesteads mural was not included here. Someone in the area had reported at the time that Shahn was painting propaganda in the town's community center, a charge in keeping with attacks that had already been directed at Jersey Homesteads. Shahn's experience as an assistant to Diego Rivera on the Rockefeller Center mural in 1933 may also have added to the fears that Shahn might include "subversive" images or personages in his mural. In order to ensure, therefore, that Shahn did not paint propaganda in Jersey Homesteads, an FBI agent was sent over. After a period of surveillance, however, the agent became convinced that there was nothing "communistic" about the artist's intentions or his work.[68]

The only other document predating 1951 is a background check on

OWI employees prepared for the House Committee on Appropriations dated July 29, 1943. It simply contains a short job description and the dates of Shahn's employment. As was indicated in Chapter 1, Shahn's tenure with the OWI was brief and stormy. When the bureau was first set up in the fall of 1942, with Shahn on its staff, its offices were located in the Social Security Building, where Shahn had just completed his murals. Hank Brennan, former art director of *Fortune*, headed the graphics bureau, while David Stone Martin, Shahn, and approximately a dozen other artists made up the working staff.

In the beginning they spent a great deal of time talking about how they were going to "win the war with posters."[69] Thomas D. Mabry, acting chief of the bureau, set out the three major themes war posters should address: (1) The Issue—why we fight, whom we fight, how we fight; (2) Our Allies—who they are, what their characteristics are; (3) How We Can Win—the means with which we fight, how the civilian can help through work and sacrifice. He added that special topical posters would have to be created occasionally, dealing with such themes as "Don't Talk."[70] But it seems that such topical posters gained precedence over the other categories, forcing Shahn to comment that "the only idea we never had to fight for was KEEP QUIET: THE ENEMY IS LISTENING."[71]

Shahn's own posters were either "too violent," like *This Is Nazi Brutality*, or "not appealing enough," like *We French Workers Warn You . . . Defeat Means Slavery, Starvation, Death*. Another reason why the latter poster might have proven inappropriate is the flyer attached to the wall behind the crowd of figures. It contains the Official Vichy Decree, compelling French workers, male and female, to engage in any form of work which served "the interests of the nation." Many on the OWI staff in North Africa had already been charged by certain government officials with being too critical of the Vichy government in France and its North African representative, Admiral Jean Louis François Darlan, a Nazi collaborator who had worked with Rommel's Afrika Korps against the British in Libya.[72] The United States government supported the Vichy regime, and those who voiced their displeasure with the OWI staff in North Africa certainly would not have taken kindly to the association of the edicts of the Vichy government with "defeat, slavery, starvation, and death."

By early 1943 the situation within the graphics bureau had become unbearable, not only for Shahn and the other artists on the staff, but for Brennan as well. According to Brennan, the recent reorganization of the bureau had placed in positions of control individuals better suited to the world of commercial advertising than the world of wartime propaganda. Having neither the talent nor the stomach for the kind of material being produced by the division, Brennan submitted his resignation.[73] He was succeeded by Price Gilbert, a naval officer and former Coca-Cola vice-president. Some thought that Gilbert had been picked by Gardner Cowles, Jr., director of the domestic branch of the OWI, to clear out the "radicals" and tone things down.[74] To indicate their displeasure at the change in personnel, Shahn and a number of other artists took a poster depicting soldiers with raised bayonets and replaced the guns with Coca-Cola bottles, inserting the captions "Try Our Four Delicious Freedoms" and "The Cause That Refreshes."[75] Gilbert was equally disapproving of Shahn's work, arguing that his Nazi brutality poster was too unattractive for display.[76]

It appears that Gilbert's attempts to clear out the "radicals" were unsuccessful, and so the House Committee on Appropriations, having requested the FBI background check on OWI employees, solved Gilbert's problems for him. In July 1943 Elmer Davis informed Shahn that, because of a cut in 1944 appropriations for the OWI, it had been necessary to discontinue the functions performed by Shahn's office.[77]

The first lengthy report on Shahn in his FBI file was submitted October 3, 1951. Its primary focus was his "communist activity." According to the author of the report (who was not identified), communism was a vital issue in Roosevelt, New Jersey, after World War II, when large numbers of professional people, "all of whom have remained intimate with Ben Shahn," began to settle there. It was further noted that "This group is a tightly knit organization which has continually backed Communist projects; further that they have been active in the World Peace Petition sponsored by Moscow, and have attempted to have the same endorsed by the community as a whole through legislative process." In addition, the group had circulated various leaflets advocating an end to the Korean War and had espoused the cause of the "Trenton Six," six local black men who had been convicted and sentenced to death for the murder of a Trenton, New Jersey, storekeeper.

Shahn was further cited for his membership in, or support of, organizations designated by the Attorney General or the House Special Committee on Un-American Activities as communist or communist-front: the Civil Rights Congress, the International Workers Order, and the Southern Conference for Human Welfare. Shahn's "communist activity" in the realm of art included "a tendency to play up the lower class" in his paintings. In addition, his work had appeared in a communist paper, the *Daily Worker.*

While the author of the report notes that Shahn had denied being a communist and that it was not known whether he had actually been a member of the Communist Party, his support of "pro-communist activities" was enough reason to continue the investigation. The identification of such activities and the organizations sponsoring them seems to have been the focus of much energy on the part of the agents assigned to Shahn. Included among the organizations and activities named were the American Artists' Congress, the Cultural and Scientific Conference for World Peace of 1949, the Artists' Union, the CIO-PAC 1944 presidential campaign, the Morning Freiheit Association, Inc., publisher of *Jewish Life,* Henry Wallace's 1948 presidential campaign, and the National Council of the Arts, Sciences and Professions (NCASP). That he was a registered Democrat and a fan of Franklin D. Roosevelt was also noted.

Shahn's involvement in the peace movement appears to have been of particular interest to the FBI in the early fifties. In addition to his support of the above-mentioned Cultural and Scientific Conference for World Peace of 1949 and his call for an end to the Korean War, Shahn was identified as a member of the New Jersey Committee for Peaceful Alternatives. This committee was founded in October 1950 in Princeton by approximately forty-five New Jersey citizens. According to an FBI report of August 4, 1952, Shahn was among those who helped organize this meeting and was one of the sponsors of a peace convocation organized by the committee on March 8, 1952, at Rutgers University. A subsequent report added that he had also painted peace Christmas cards which were sold by the committee that year. The FBI considered the New Jersey Committee for Peaceful Alternatives a communist front organization.

On February 27, 1953, Shahn and his wife, Bernarda, were interviewed by FBI agent "SA" and an unidentified companion. The agency hoped that the Shahns would provide them with information about Communist Party activities in the New Jersey area. Their hopes were not realized. While "SA" noted that both interviewees were "very courteous" and "talked freely," they refused to name anyone they considered to be communist. Ben Shahn admitted that he might have belonged to seven or eight organizations cited by the Attorney General as subversive, but stated that he had never been a member of the Communist Party. He added that "he was interested in peace and would offer his assistance to any group that he thought was working for a good cause."

"SA" advised that the Shahns be interviewed again in the near future. This advice was not heeded, however, and on August 19, 1953, it was recommended that Shahn not be placed on the Security Index list. His file was subsequently closed, although it was reopened a number of times over the next thirteen years, primarily in the context of name checks requested by various government agencies.[78]

Civil Liberties and the Liberal Community

While *Counterattack* and the FBI were busy leafing through leftist periodicals or attending Shahn's lectures in search of evidence of his lack of patriotism, Shahn was busying himself with yet another political campaign—the presidential election of 1952. It is not difficult to understand why Shahn was drawn to the Democratic candidate, Adlai Stevenson. Stevenson has been described as "a thoroughly civilized man, sensitive, reasonable, gracious, humorous, urbane, and a man of true style, . . . a civil idealist who was most earnest and high-minded, raising both the intellectual level and the moral tone of our political debate."[79] Like most liberals of the time, however, he was forced to prove his patriotism by publicly declaring his opposition to communism, although he also sharply criticized McCarthy, something too few politicians were doing openly in 1952.

Shahn attended the 1952 Democratic Convention in Chicago and made drawings of its proceedings.[80] He also designed at least two works for Stevenson's campaign. The first was a print of a shoe with a hole in it, undoubtedly inspired by a newspaper photograph of the candidate that highlighted a hole in the sole of his shoe. The print was sold to raise money for campaign funds. The second work was a broadside entitled *Watch Out for the Man on a White Horse!* (Figure 33). Published by the Volunteers for Stevenson, Roosevelt, New Jersey, it depicted Republican candidate Eisenhower astride a somewhat shaky political horse that carried the names of, among others, Senators Taft and McCarthy in the front and vice-presidential candidate Richard M. Nixon bringing up the rear.

In addition to these two published works, Shahn produced designs for two flyers or ads that were never printed. Each contained, along with the faint outlines of bodies, two paragraphs at the bottom of the page. The first paragraph referred to the Holocaust, the second to

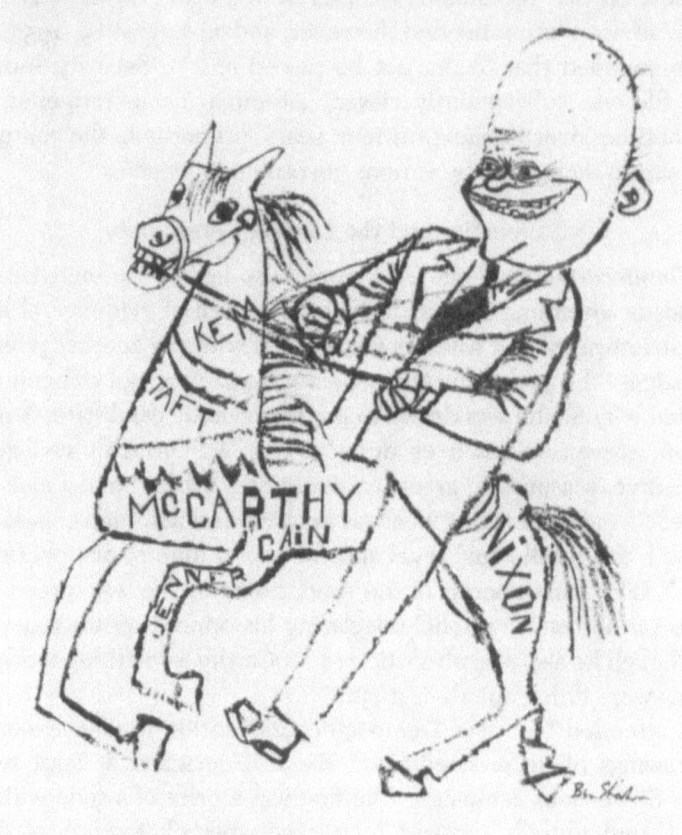

FIGURE 33

Ben Shahn, *Watch Out for the Man on a White Horse!*, 1952
Offset
14⁷⁄₁₆ × 10″
New Jersey State Museum Collection, Trenton; Gift of Bernarda Bryson Shahn
Photographer: Elton Pope-Lance

Eisenhower's willingness to rearm Germany and to let "bygones be bygones." Questioning the sincerity or longevity of Eisenhower's response to the atrocities carried out by Nazi Germany during World War II, however, was probably viewed as politically unsound in 1952, particularly in light of the public furor that had been created the previous year by Truman's removal of General Douglas MacArthur from his post as commander of the United Nations military forces in Korea.[81]

One of the central issues of Stevenson's campaign was the defense of civil liberties. In addition to criticizing McCarthy (he chose an American Legion Convention for his initial anti-McCarthy speech), he campaigned actively, in both the North and the South, for civil rights for blacks. Shahn was also deeply concerned with the discrimination faced by blacks in the United States and supported organizations such as the Southern Conference Educational Fund (SCEF) in their efforts to combat this discrimination. One SCEF project for which Shahn provided a number of drawings was a pamphlet on racial discrimination in southern hospitals entitled *The Untouchables*. Twenty-five thousand copies were distributed in the fall of 1952, and the full text, with drawings, appeared in the October issue of the SCEF publication *The Southern Patriot*. Shahn also joined a number of others in expressing outrage, via an open letter organized by the National Council of the Arts, Sciences and Professions in 1952, at the bombing and death of Harry T. Moore, state coordinator in Florida for the National Association for the Advancement of Colored People (NAACP).[82] The September 27 issue of the *Nation* carried a testimonial to Moore, for which Shahn provided a portrait drawing.[83]

During the 1948 Wallace campaign Shahn had executed numerous drawings for articles in the *New Republic*. In 1952 his work appeared, instead, in the *Nation*. For example, Shahn designed two *Nation* covers during the summer months.[84] The first was for the June 28 special issue on civil liberties (Figure 34). Carey McWilliams, the editorial director, sent Shahn a tentative table of contents on May 22 and asked if he could suggest ideas for layout and art work. "It occurs to me," McWilliams added, "that the cover presents an interesting opportunity. I doubt that we will print the contents on the cover; therefore the entire cover might be used to dramatize the central theme of the supplement—namely the impact of the witch hunt on the civil liberties of the American people."[85]

Shahn chose to dramatize the theme of civil liberties with a familiar image—the Statue of Liberty. But his treatment of the image was not the more familiar kind. He did not present a full-length portrayal of the statue or a close-up of the torch. He also rejected one of his preliminary sketches of Liberty with her arm, torch in hand, thrown across her face, her eyes closed. Shahn had used this gesture of pathos and defeat at least twice previously, once in *Sing Sorrow*, a painting of 1946, and a second time in one of the Hickman drawings. In 1952, however, he chose a more confrontational pose, depicting the face and part of the arm bearing the torch from a position close to and directly below the statue. Thus, the image appears to loom before the viewer, both protective and ominous. The torch is also missing, the statue's right arm abruptly truncated above the elbow. This is not a reassuring picture of a national symbol of freedom, but an ambiguous and questioning one. The lettering on the cover reinforces this ambiguity. The Statue of Liberty does, indeed, represent "The Nation," yet in a land that spawns and nourishes a man like McCarthy, "How Free Is Free?"[86]

Shahn's second design for the *Nation* appeared on the cover of the August 23 issue and commemorated the twenty-fifth anniversary of the execution of the Italian-American anarchists Nicola Sacco and Bartolomeo Vanzetti (Figure 35). Charged with the robbery and murder of a paymaster and a guard in 1920, the two men were convicted after a trial in which the evidence was far from conclusive. Their fate was sealed, however, by Judge Webster Thayer's anti-foreigner, anti-anarchist biases, which he made no attempt to hide. Also working against the two men was the Red-scare atmosphere stirred up by Attorney General A. Mitchell Palmer's roundups of "subversives" in the early twenties. The appeal process went on until 1927, when Sacco and Vanzetti were finally executed in the electric chair after the Lowell Committee had determined that "racial feeling" had not influenced the trial. Since 1912 Lowell had been the national vice-president of the Immigration Restriction League, an organization founded in 1894 to encourage the admittance of only "good" immigrants—i.e., those from northern and western Europe—into the United States.[87]

Shahn's line drawing of the two figures on the *Nation* cover is based on a gouache he produced in 1931–1932 as part of his Sacco and Vanzetti series (Figure 36). In composing the works in this series, Shahn relied heavily on newspaper accounts and photographs for ideas and images. In 1952, he translated one of these images back into this mass-media context. In so doing, he simplified the figures to basic outlines,

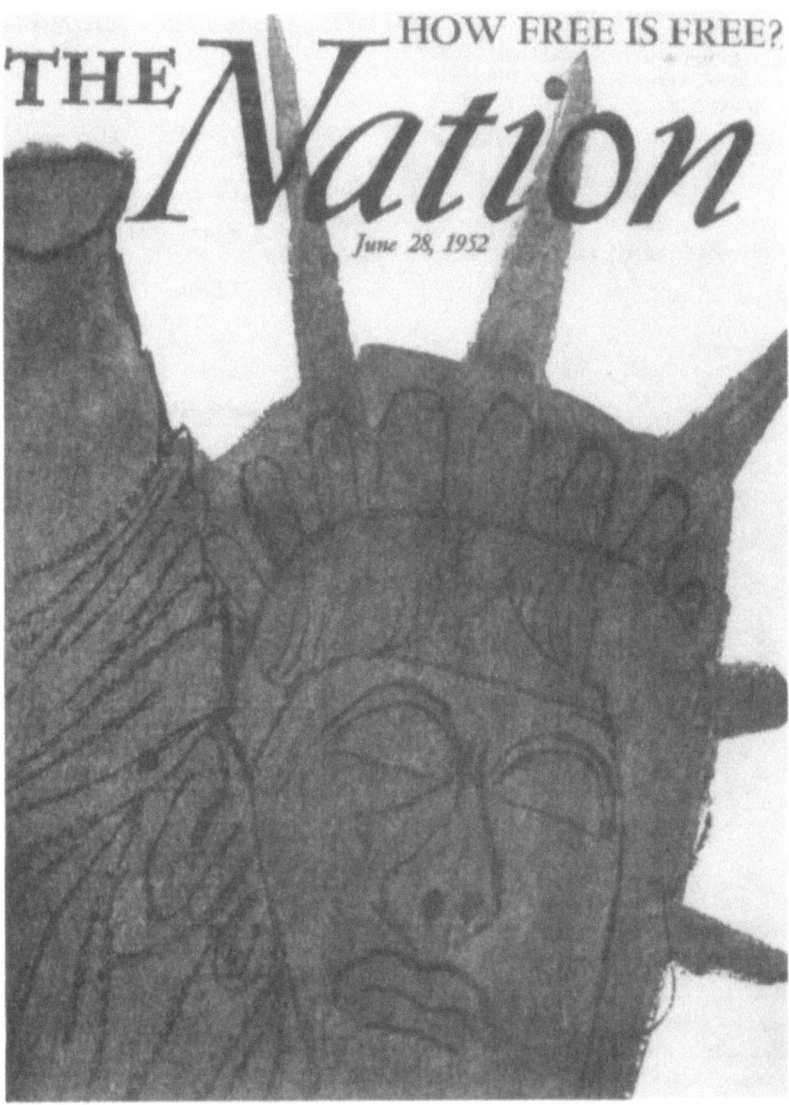

FIGURE 34
Ben Shahn, Cover for *Nation*, June 28,
1952
Photographer: Stephen Cahill

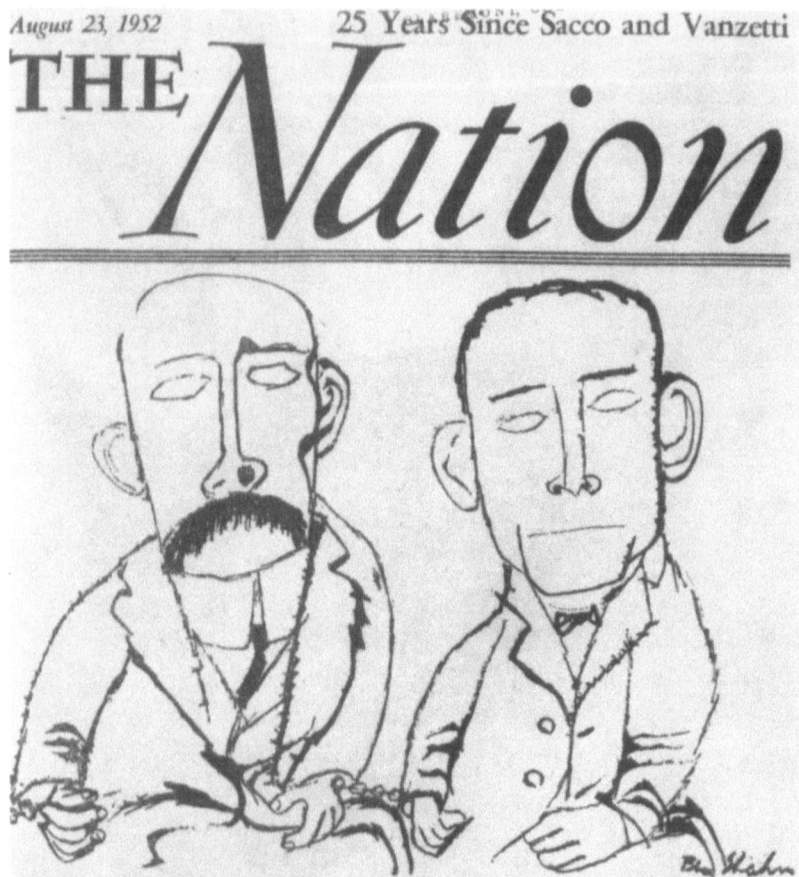

FIGURE 35

Ben Shahn, Cover for *Nation*, August
23, 1952
Photographer: Stephen Cahill

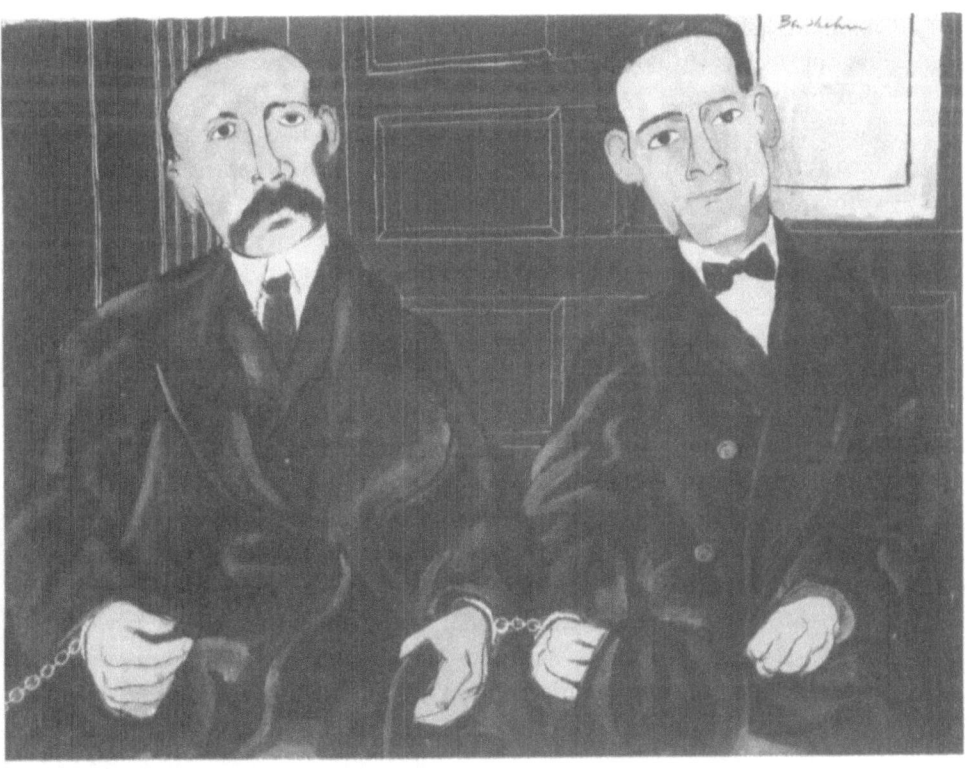

FIGURE 36

Ben Shahn, *Bartolomeo Vanzetti and Nicola Sacco;* from the Sacco-Vanzetti series of 23 paintings, 1931–1932
Tempera on paper over composition board
10½ × 14½"
Collection, The Museum of Modern Art, New York; Gift of Abby Aldrich Rockefeller

removing all background detail and three-dimensionality and increasing their cartoon-like quality. Beneath the two men he inserted a
shakily-written text by Vanzetti based on a transcription made during
the trial by reporter Philip Strong. Shahn has retained not only the
incorrect grammar, but the misspellings that convey the accent of the
author. Again, as in his earlier cover, Shahn is creating contrasts and
ambiguities—between the eloquence of the statement and its awk-
ward grammatical construction, between a seemingly unsophisticated
drawing and a very finely balanced composition, between the simplicity of the two figures and the complexity of the historical moment
in which they were caught.[88]

Those who contributed to the *Nation,* whether as artists, editors, or
writers, often found themselves heavily criticized by others within the
liberal community. For example, in September 1951 Arthur M. Schlesinger, Jr., of the ADA used his *New York Post* column, "History of the
Week," to mock a letter that proposed a civil liberties conference because it was signed by "Thomas Emerson of the Progressive Party,
Carey McWilliams of *The Nation,* and Stringfellow Barr of the solve-
the-Russian-problem-by-giving-them-money school." Schlesinger continued: "None of these gentlemen is a Communist, but none objects
very much to Communism. They are the typhoid Marys of the left,
bearing the germs of infection even if not suffering obviously from the
disease."[89]

Emerson, McWilliams, and Barr undoubtedly found Schlesinger
and the ADA equally distasteful and joined with others that year to
form their own organization, the Emergency Civil Liberties Committee (ECLC). According to the historian (and current editor of the
Nation) Victor Navasky, ECLC members "were non-Communist lib-
ertarians who vigorously fought domestic repression but refused to
advertise their reservations about Communism, believing that such
rhetoric at the time would be self-serving and at the expense of the
civil liberties of those under attack in this country."[90] Ready, willing,
and able to defend the rights of communists and noncommunists alike,
the ECLC gained the substantial financial backing of the philosopher-
philanthropist Corliss Lamont in 1953.

The conference that Emerson, McWilliams, and Barr proposed at
the end of 1951 came to pass in January 1953. Among its sponsors
were Albert Einstein, Frank Lloyd Wright, and Shahn. Having contributed time and energy to the Progressive Party campaigns in the
past and to the *Nation* in the immediate present, it is no surprise that

Shahn was involved in the activities of the ECLC. A number of the committee's founders, including Clark Foreman, Carey McWilliams, and I. F. Stone, were also personal friends of Shahn.[91]

The announcement of the upcoming conference prompted another anti-communist liberal organization, the American Congress for Cultural Freedom (ACCF), to join with certain members of the ADA in condemning the ECLC as communist-dominated and dangerous, despite the fact that there was no proof the ECLC was a communist front (it was not even included on the Attorney General's list). Shahn received a telegram in the middle of January from George S. Counts, chairman of the ACCF, expressing concern that Shahn was involved in a communist front that had no sincere interest in defending liberty in the United States or elsewhere. Counts urged Shahn to reconsider his participation in the January 30–31 conference.[92]

Shahn did not heed Counts' advice, and instead delivered his talk, "The Artist and the Politicians," in the session on freedom of the arts.[93] While ECLC members may have attempted to avoid advertising their reservations about communism, Shahn did not follow suit. "The liberal of today," stated Shahn, "—the altruist—the humanitarian—any citizen who feels his responsibility toward the public good—finds himself caught midway between two malignant forces."[94] To the right of the liberal stood "the force of reaction," which opposed reform and progress and often utilized calumny and slander. To the left of the liberal stood the "Communist contingent," which continually misappropriated the liberal's words, acts, and intentions and, in so doing, "thoroughly demoralized the great American liberal tradition." Together, these two forces constituted an "unholy team":

> The accusation of Communism is the most powerful scourge that has fallen into the hands of reaction since heresy ceased to be a public crime. And the liberal might better be able to silence this charge were it not for a constant and unwelcome espousal of his works by Communist groups and press—plus the uneasy fear that perhaps the charge may be true.[95]

To make matters worse, those who accused groups of being dominated or influenced by communists were often indifferent to, or ignorant of, "the real nature of Communism, or to the kind of threat that it actually is." They used the word, instead, to attack anything they did not like or any move toward reform. Thus, for Shahn the greater threat to civil liberties in the United States in 1953 was the accusation of communism rather than communism itself. He devoted over three-quarters

of his speech, in fact, to exposing the debilitating effects of such accusations in the realm of art.

"By far the most sinister attack against art—against the arts—,"
stated Shahn, "comes by way of a subrosa magazine called *Counterattack*." While he did not cite his own case, he pointed out that not
only radio commentators or performers were blacklisted as a result of
this magazine's accusations, but writers and artists as well. The effect
of this blacklisting was even more destructive for artists because they
did not receive the publicity that well-known performers received
when they were dropped. "When the artist or writer is dropped very
few people know about it." This lack of publicity made it even more
difficult for such individuals to obtain a fair trial and judgment or to
gain public sympathy. In fact, the artists themselves were often unaware that they had been attacked by the magazine until told by
a friend.[96]

Shahn also cited the various pronouncements by Dondero in Congress on the communist nature of all modern art, the cancellation
of the State Department exhibition, and the attempts of the Los Angeles City Council to remove numerous modern canvases from a city-
sponsored art exhibition.[97] Thus, "throughout the country, people of
the basest ignorance are sitting in judgment upon art, upon the universities, upon the very meaning of thinking itself." Such investigations and suppression damaged not only American culture, but the
country's reputation abroad. According to Shahn, the ultimate victory
or defeat in the struggle with communism would be a victory or defeat
of ideas:

> Our idea is Democracy. And I believe that it is the most appealing idea
> that the world has yet known. But if we, by official acts of suppression,
> play the hypocrite toward our own beliefs, strangle our own liberties,
> then we can hardly hope to win the world's unqualified confidence.[98]

For Shahn, the time was ripe for a reassertion of democracy. It was
time to take a stand, not simply as a matter of self-interest, but of
"much needed, and much wanting, patriotism." Thus, the fight against
McCarthyism and the forces of reaction within the United States was
not simply in the interests of individual reputations, but of the reputation of the country as a whole.

While Shahn's sentiments were in keeping with the general objectives of ECLC, he did not identify himself personally with the committee. In the last paragraph of his talk he distinguished between the

ECLC, formed to "stand by, to invoke, when necessary, those laws that were written to protect freedom," and "the rest of us," who were "resolved to confront intimidation, and the half-legalized infringement of our liberties with some stubborn resistance."[99] In a letter to Alfred Barr shortly after the conference, Shahn also indicated that he had originally shared some of Barr's doubts about whether the ECLC was being "used" by communists. But he had been convinced that it was not and that it was a "completely honorable" grouping. "I believe that, at long last," he added, "liberals are toughening up on that score, and that while it is essential to protect civil liberties, no matter whose they may be, it is equally essential to prevent the incursions of our old friends the professional manipulators, into liberal organizations."[100]

Shahn's attempt to define for himself a liberal political position immune to infiltration from the far left and Red-baiting from the right was accompanied by an effort to develop an artistic language equally resistant to political categorization. To a certain degree he was successful. While the art critics for the *Daily Worker* praised his work as being concerned with the working class, they were almost always critical of what they saw as his preoccupation with formal concerns and his unwillingness to portray the struggle of this class in a positive light.[101] As the figures in his paintings became more schematized and the historical events they referred to less obvious (e.g., *Epoch, Second Allegory*), the interest of communist art critics diminished. And while Dondero continued to cite Shahn as a "communist dupe," his reasons were more often Shahn's past political affiliations than the particular style or content of his work, although Dondero was certainly no admirer of Shahn's artistic achievements.[102]

"With works of Art their armies meet,
And War shall sink beneath thy feet."[103]

As Shahn indicated in his ECLC talk, the reactionary political climate in the United States was of concern not only to many American citizens, but also to American allies abroad. In fact, the rise of McCarthy and the Cold War created the need for a new kind of international propaganda campaign, one in which art played a significant part.

Blanche Wiesen Cook, in her book on Eisenhower, notes that during his presidency "a massive program of psychological warfare unprecedented in scope and intensity" was developed to help protect American interests throughout the world from war and social upheaval:

All the structures required to introduce and defend the American Century were redesigned and implemented. The United States' business and commerce, U.S. fashions in literature, entertainment, dress and architecture, all accompanied the penetration of the United States' worldwide military and political presence.[104]

American art was also "redesigned," in a manner of speaking, to introduce and defend the American Century. This is not to say that artists followed the dictates of businessmen or politicians to paint or act a certain way. The work they produced came from their own aesthetic and political commitments and beliefs. Yet such work inspired a body of writing that associated modern art—both representational and nonobjective—with key aspects of the new Cold War ideology. The United States was free, individualistic, aggressive, liberated—and so, too, was the art it produced. Political dissent was allowed in all forms in America—written, verbal, pictorial. This was to be the message sent abroad through radio broadcasts, dance performances, and art exhibitions. This was the message designed to win the hearts and minds of Europe.

And why was it so important to win the hearts and minds of Europe, to convince Europeans that Americans were not the materialistic barbarians so many Europeans seemed to think they were? In the immediate postwar era the American government was concerned that another depression would ensue if the country's economy could not be expanded, or at least maintained at its wartime production level.[105] The Truman administration felt that such an expansion was possible only if there existed "an expanding world economy based on the liberal principles of private enterprise, nondiscrimination, and reduced barriers to trade."[106]

Europe played an important role in this expanding world economy, both as a marketplace for American products and as a buffer against the westward spread of communism. American economic and political goals required sympathetic governments in Western Europe. But immediately after the war such governments were threatened by strong left-wing and nationalist forces in the four major Western European nations—Britain, France, Germany, and Italy. In the spring of 1947 the Truman administration was very much aware of the fact that "the primary, immediate threat to America's interests was the emergence of assorted brands of socialism and capitalist nationalism in Europe."[107] Through a combination of political and economic pressures, both overt and covert, the American government managed to help ensure that at least the communist element in these countries was effectively prevented from gaining control.[108]

But the single-mindedness with which American interests were pursued in Europe created a growing climate of animosity toward the United States. The diffusion of this animosity was one of the major reasons for the inauguration, at the beginning of the decade, of Truman's "campaign of truth." On April 20, 1950, a little over two months after McCarthy had begun his campaign of "untruth," Truman addressed the American Society of Newspaper Editors on the need for a campaign of truth to counteract the negative image of the United States in Europe. This image was not the result of American actions, claimed Truman, but of either ignorance or communist propaganda. "Our task," he stated, "is to present the truth to the millions of people who are uninformed or misinformed or unconvinced."[109]

The year 1950 marked, in fact, a shift in the nature of government information programs abroad. Immediately after World War II such programs, of which cultural activities were a part, avoided the notions of propaganda or psychological warfare due to a general public mistrust of their use during peacetime.[110] The specter of communist domination promoted by Truman had, by the late 1940s, resulted in the acceptance of a more aggressive information program. Initially an attempt was made to separate informational and cultural activities, the latter being defined as those activities relating to education, science, and art. While the former were recognized as being closely involved in "politics," cultural activities were to be "nonpolitical," i.e., they were to be "kept clear of propaganda."[111] To maintain this separation, private agencies and state and local governments were to be responsible, as much as possible, for the dissemination of cultural activities. The role of the federal government, and particularly the State Department, was to be "a strictly secondary one, limited to stimulus, facilitation and coordination."[112]

With the first atomic explosion by the Russians and the defeat of Chiang Kai-shek in 1949, followed by the Korean War in 1950, the separation of cultural and informational activities no longer appeared necessary or desirable to the federal government. Instead, both were included, along with military and economic programs, in government plans for national defense, set out by the National Security Council and approved by Truman on October 18, 1951.[113] In September 1951 two staff members of the Bureau of the Budget in Washington drew up a report containing the following observation:

> The objectives of so-called information and cultural activities are the same. . . . The value of international cultural interchange is to win respect for the cultural achievements of our free society where that respect is necessary to inspire cooperation with us in world affairs. In such a situation, cultural activities are an indispensable tool of propaganda. [114]

The previous November overseas libraries had been renamed "information centers," indicating a more politically oriented role for the films, exhibits, and lectures contained within their walls. [115]

In June 1951 Eloise Spaeth, speaking to members of the American Federation of Arts on the need for government-funded art exhibitions abroad, acknowledged the importance of culture in any "campaign of truth" meant to improve a country's international reputation. "Everyone in the State Department with whom I have spoken," she stated, "knows only too well how our prestige suffers by our not having a strong consistent program geared to show the world that other facet of American life—the part that is the heart and soul of any people— their creative life." [116] The attitude of many major European art critics, museum personnel, and collectors toward American culture in the late forties and early fifties was, in fact, far from laudatory. In 1949 Soby lamented that the most effective propaganda charge being used against the United States by Europeans at that time was that America was

> a rich, vast, powerful nation, but a nation not deeply concerned with the arts or with related spiritual values. On the political front, we are accused of "dollar diplomacy"; on the cultural front, the American movie is cited in its worst examples as an indication of our materialism. [117]

The finest writers, musicians, actors, painters, and sculptors needed to be sent abroad in order to show Europeans what the United States was "really like."

Shahn agreed with Soby on this point. In his 1951 Ohio State University talk he quoted from a recent survey of European opinions undertaken by *Fortune*. The French Catholic author François Mauriac had stated: "It is not what separates the United States and the Soviet Union that should frighten us, but what they have in common . . . man is treated as a means and no longer as an end." "Why they should not be originally creative is puzzling," noted the British writer V. S. Pritchett. "It is possible that the lack of the organic sense, the conviction that man is a machine . . . turns them into technicians and cuts them off from the chaos, the accidents and intuitions of the creative process."[118] While Shahn did not mention it in his talk, he himself had received a letter from the British art critic Elkan Allen the year before expressing disappointment in what he had seen of recent American art. "While there is no doubt of the technical excellence of American artists," Allen wrote, "a certain inhumanity chills me."[119]

Such opinions were, in Shahn's view, the result of misunderstanding and ignorance, which, in turn, were the result of the constant emphasis on such things as the number of automobiles and washers Americans owned in the propaganda beamed across the world. Shahn reiterated the concerns expressed by Eloise Spaeth that same year:

> It is quite clear that we do not have the complete confidence of our new allies. They mistrust our ability to respect and understand their culture and their way of life. If they continue to believe that we are a nation of unregenerate Philistines, we cannot expect them to feel warm friendship for us, or to place faith in our leadership.[120]

The government needed, therefore, to "pay some official homage to art." This could best be done, in Shahn's mind, by establishing some sort of ministry of fine arts as part of the administrative branch of the government. Not only could such a ministry encourage the arts at home and promote a broad comprehension of American art and ideals abroad, but it would even "supply expert opinion to the Congress in order to forestall inept and uninformed acts."[121] Of course, Shahn did not envision government-sponsored modern art exhibitions as a substitute for government action in the areas of social reform or world peace or as a smokescreen for questionable exploits at home and abroad. Shahn wanted the American government to assume responsibility, as it had in the 1930s, for the well-being of the country's artists and for the uncensored exchange of artistic ideas and products at an international level.

One European who shared the views of Shahn, Soby, and Spaeth was the British poet and critic Stephen Spender. Forced to choose between aligning themselves with either the United States or the Soviet Union, Europeans were most concerned, according to Spender, with which political system would allow them to maintain their European way of life and culture, which would be most conducive to the existence of spiritual freedom. Many Europeans were not convinced that the United States was the best choice. They often felt that this country was interested only in expanding its own political and economic influence and not in preserving European civilization and liberty. Yet, "where American policy finds dubious allies and half-hearted friends, American freedom of expression in its greatest achievements has an authenticity which can win the most vital European thought today."[122] America needed to send the best of its intellectuals over to Europe to impress upon Europeans America's concern for spiritual and cultural freedom.

Another factor that further complicated the debate over America's culture, or lack of it, was the Russian peace offensive. This offensive included cultural as well as political overtures toward noncommunist countries, which contributed to an improved image of the Soviet Union in Europe. In 1953 the Italian journalist Guido Piovene commented: "I am writing these lines during the Russian 'peace offensive.' . . . All over Europe the students and athletes of Soviet Russia invariably draw public applause." This did not mean that Europe wished to fall under Russian domination. "But Soviet Russia has spoken of peace without demanding capitulation," stated Piovene, "and this is quite enough to arouse a popular response." As for the United States, many "cultivated people" in Europe feared that it might "shatter a precarious peace by making demands the satisfaction of which seems to us unimportant."[123]

Lewis Galantiere, critic, author, and policy advisor to Radio Free Europe, also pointed out the danger that the Soviet Union's peace campaign posed for the United States. By improving its public image, the Soviet Union was driving a wedge between Europe and the United States, thus facilitating the installment of communism on the Atlantic shores of Europe. The attainment of this grand Soviet objective was made easier by three factors: American isolationism, which argued against involvement in European affairs; European isolationism, which claimed that a refusal to align with the United States would convince Moscow to "keep its hands off"; and "the reluctance of Europeans in general, and of the opinion-creating intellectuals in particular, to see in the United States a leader worth following."[124]

While the United States could do little to stop this Soviet peace offensive, it could increase its own efforts to convince Europeans that it was a leader worth following, to show them the high quality of American culture, and to constantly contrast it with the low quality of Soviet culture. In order to do so, examples of American culture had to be sent abroad. Of course, the State Department exhibition fiasco of 1947 and the congressional tirades of Dondero had made the open support of modern art by the American government extremely difficult. The promotion of modern art abroad, therefore, became primarily the responsibility of private agencies, though often with indirect funding from the federal government.[125]

This shift in emphasis from public to private support occurred at all levels of informational activities. While the reorganization of these activities in 1953 under the United States Information Agency (USIA) resulted in general cutbacks in funding, the only agency activity to receive an increase was the Office of Private Cooperation, whose budget was doubled. The rationale behind such a move is found in the USIA's first *Review of Operations:* "We are convinced that the maximum of business and other non-governmental actions and services must be marshalled behind the Government's information program. This has been demonstrated to be one of the most effective ways to strengthen the entire program."[126] MOMA was the main private institution to promote American modern art abroad. Its assumption of this task was due to a genuine belief in both the aesthetic qualities of this art and the need for a strong cultural propaganda offensive to counter the accusations of barbarism and materialism that were being directed at the United States.[127]

The bulk of the museum's promotion of modern art was carried out through its International Circulating Exhibitions Program, begun in 1952 with a five-year grant of $625,000 from the Rockefeller Brothers Fund. According to Russell Lynes, the purpose of this program was "to let it be known especially in Europe that America was not the cultural backwater that the Russians, during that tense period called 'the cold war,' were trying to demonstrate that it was."[128] In the absence of government-organized exhibitions of modern art abroad, MOMA's shows came to represent not simply its own tastes, but those of the country as a whole. This was particularly true for such exhibitions as the Venice Biennial, where all the pavilions except that of the United States were government-owned. MOMA had been responsible for organizing the Venice shows since the late forties and in 1953 actually bought the pavilion with money from the Rockefeller Brothers Fund.[129]

The museum also cooperated with the State Department in certain cultural projects. In February 1950 Betty Chamberlain of MOMA wrote to Shahn asking for a copy of the talk he had given that month at the museum because "the State Department's recording machine gave out of tape in the middle and they lost a paragraph or two while changing."[130] This tape may have been part of a general gathering of materials on modern art for circulation abroad. Of course, such material was often strictly censored, as was the case with an article written by John Baur of the Whitney Museum on contemporary American sculpture. The State Department had requested the article in 1952 for publication in Europe but refused to allow Baur to include William Zorach's *Victory* as one of the illustrations. Zorach had been cited earlier by Dondero as having been a member of the John Reed Club.[131]

Shahn had also received a letter in October 1951 from Howard Flyn, chief of the State Department's International Press and Publications Division, requesting eight-by-ten-inch photographs of Shahn at work and of *Nocturne*. The photographs were to accompany a reprint of Hess' article "Ben Shahn Paints a Picture" that was to be circulated abroad to approximately one hundred United States Information Service (USIS) posts in more than seventy-five countries. Such reprints from American magazines, newspapers, and other publications were supplied to the foreign press as part of the State Department's overseas information program, "to give people of other countries a true picture of the United States and of the American way of life."[132] Shahn sent the photographs, but the article may not have passed the State Department censors, for when Shahn was nominated the following year by a committee of leading American museum officials as the painter "most worthy to be represented in an important foreign exhibition," the nomination was vetoed by a spokesperson for the State Department.[133]

Shahn was also not averse to publicly criticizing State Department actions. For example, early in 1951 he designed an ad to protest, among other things, the denial of passports to American citizens and visas to foreigners because of their political opinions. The previous summer the painter Rockwell Kent and the singer Paul Robeson had been denied the validation of their passports. Kent had, according to the State Department, violated passport regulations on a trip abroad earlier that year by visiting Moscow with a delegation representing the World Committee of Peace Partisans. This organization had been cited by the State Department as "communist-line." Robeson had also been active in the peace movement and had repeatedly condemned the Marshall Plan, the NATO pact, and American involvement in Korea.[134]

Shahn's drawing for the ad that appeared in the *New York Times*— an intense face behind prison bars—referred to the paragraph beneath it, relating the story of Ralph Waldo Emerson's visit to Henry David Thoreau after he had been put in jail for not paying his taxes.

"What are you doing in there?" asked Emerson. "What are you doing out there?" responded Thoreau. The rest of the ad protested the judging, convicting, and firing of artists solely on the charges of professional informers; the jailing of writers for refusing to betray their political beliefs; and the firing of scholars as a result of the imposition of loyalty oaths which had nothing to do with their competence as teachers. The ad, whose sponsors included Arthur Miller and Mark Van Doren, did not solicit financial contributions or call for people to join any organization:

> We only ask you to raise your voice for freedom. The voices of bigotry and aggressive intimidation are loud and raucous throughout the country today. If the voices of decency and courage remain silent, the right of everyone to live and work in peace and freedom may be lost.[135]

Another government agency concerned with the export of American culture abroad was the Central Intelligence Agency (CIA). Thomas W. Braden, who served as an executive secretary of MOMA for a brief period in the late forties, took over in 1951 as supervisor of the CIA's cultural activities, a post he held until 1954.[136] Braden later admitted he had used private organizations and foundations as fronts for the furtherance of official government policies.[137] One such organization was the Congress for Cultural Freedom, founded in 1950 by Michael Josselson, formerly an officer in the Office of Strategic Services, and Melvin J. Lasky, a veteran of the American Information Services and former editor of *Der Monat*, a magazine sponsored by the United States High Commission in Germany.[138] The Congress held its first conference in West Berlin in 1950 and another in India the following year. Both conferences were responses to the Soviet peace offensive and were meant to establish the Western anti-communist nations as the keepers of the peace and to convince non-aligned nations of the "immorality of neutralism."[139]

Braden was also supportive of the export of modern cultural expressions and, backed by the money available to him through the various paper organizations set up by the CIA, was able to circumvent congressional censorship.[140] He may well have shared some of the same objectives as Porter McCray, head of MOMA's International Circulating Exhibitions Program, who also had a background in government employment. McCray had worked for the Office of Inter-American Affairs during the war and served in the Marshall Plan's exhibitions sections in Paris in 1951.[141]

While the CIA was working covertly through foundations to achieve many of its goals, both cultural and political, private enterprise made a more open use of foundations for cultural projects. In 1951 Shahn received a letter from James Laughlin, a consultant to the Ford Foundation on a project involving the establishment of an international magazine. "The Foundation asked me to prepare a pilot issue for them," he wrote, "and of course I chose you for the artist to be represented in it, because I consider you the best we have."[142] A detailed proposal for the magazine outlines its purpose: "To promote peace by increasing respect for America's non-materialistic achievements among intellectuals abroad." This respect had been destroyed, according to the proposal, by the preponderance of Hollywood movies and popular magazines in foreign countries as opposed to higher-quality art works and magazines. The latter were unavailable largely because of currency restrictions.[143]

It was proposed that the new magazine be published in six languages—English, French, Italian, German, Spanish, and Russian—and focus on literary criticism, poetry, creative prose, short plays, and philosophical speculation, with collateral emphasis on the arts. Science should be avoided, as well as propaganda for the "American Way," and only historical theory of the "non-controversial kind" should be included. There would be a series of guest editors chosen for their "liveliness of mind rather than their academic respectability." The accent would not necessarily be on the "latest" thing, but more importantly on the most perceptive and "best." The Ford Foundation would fund the magazine for three years, its continuance to depend on its success in fulfilling its purpose rather than on its profit margin.[144]

In the pilot issue of the new magazine, *Perspectives, USA*, which appeared in January 1952, American art was represented by Ben Shahn. The article on Shahn was written by Selden Rodman and was, in fact, a series of excerpts from Rodman's biography of the artist published the previous fall. Almost all of the excerpts were quotes from interviews with Shahn, and these were followed by eight color reproductions of his work. The majority of the works were produced between 1948 and 1950. The "best" and most perceptive American art in 1952, therefore, was, according to *Perspectives, USA*, a figurative modern art that addressed the daily reality of individuals, contemporary political events, and spiritual concerns; that was respectful of the achievements of past artists; that was painted only according to the dictates of the artist's own conscience; and that was able to fuse "idea with matter" and "emotion with form."[145] This was the kind of art that Laughlin and the Ford Foundation thought would best improve the reputation of the United States in the minds of European intellectuals.

The pilot issue was obviously a success, for in the fall of 1952 the first regular issue of the magazine appeared, in English, French, Italian, and German. And, once more, American painting was represented by Shahn. The article about Shahn was written, again, by Selden Rodman, but this time it contained fewer direct quotes and more biographical commentary by Rodman. The general tenor of the article, however, was the same. Shahn was a man of paradoxes, more interested in life than in art, having little use for the escapism of non-representational art yet also rejecting the "prosaic idiom" of the American regionalists, preferring the works of such European masters as Paul Klee and Picasso.

> A political man who has worked out of deep conviction for the Congress of Industrial Organizations (CIO) and Henry Wallace's ill-fated Progressive Party, Shahn calls himself a "mystic" and acknowledges that the greatest painting of the past was inspired by religious sentiment. Painter of the "hard-boiled," the exploited, the misplaced, and the lost, Shahn is himself intellectual, well integrated, social, something of a gourmet, and connoisseur of expensive gadgets. Creator of the most "American" of images, he is more critical of his country's "materialism," political backwardness and local prejudices than any Paris Existentialist on a six-months' shopping tour of native blight.[146]

In his presentation of Shahn, Rodman managed to counter, in one fell swoop, almost all of the major criticisms leveled at American culture by Europeans. American artists were intellectuals, gourmets, and connoisseurs, not uncivilized barbarians. They were concerned with both spiritual and political matters, and could criticize the faults of excess materialism along with the best of the Parisian existentialists. Shahn was also imbued with "a hatred of militarism and oppressive rule," surely evidence that the American presence in Europe was not motivated solely by "dollar diplomacy."

The tone of Rodman's presentation of Shahn was also conciliatory. Rather than insisting on the formal superiority of American over European art, Rodman presented Shahn in an anecdotal, friendly manner, stressing his appreciation of past European art and telling stories of his early days in Brooklyn. Rodman aimed to convince his readers of the humaneness of Shahn's art in terms that Europeans, intellectuals and non-intellectuals alike, could understand. Rather than offending them with brash protestations of American superiority, he called upon their political sympathies and upon a spirituality that was not connected to any specific organized religion. "Shahn is not a religious man himself," stated Rodman, "but he insists that growth from here on out in America lies in the direction of a greater fulfillment of the human spirit."[147] Thus Rodman answered Spender's doubts about America's interest in safeguarding spiritual freedom not only in the United States, but in Europe as well. The general success of this type of appeal in improving America's cultural image abroad will become even more evident in examining Shahn's exhibit at the 1954 Venice Biennial.

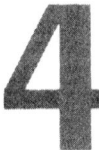

AN AMERICAN IN VENICE

The arts of a country should be so integrated into the
life of a country that any comprehensive exhibition
going forth would act as a mirror. The stranger should
be able to look into it and see reflected there the
vitality, the creativity, the spiritual force of the
country—yes, the confusion, diversity and materialism
also.   —ELOISE SPAETH
Hindustan Times, 1953

The Slaying of the Dragon

While 1953 marked, in many ways, the height of domestic repression
during the Cold War, with McCarthy firmly ensconced as chair of the
Senate Committee on Government Operations and its Permanent
Subcommittee on Investigations, it also marked the beginning of the
demise of this repression. On March 6, two months after McCarthy
assumed his Senate chair, Joseph Stalin died. The new Soviet leadership stepped up the peace offensive begun four years earlier, calling
for a new era of "peaceful coexistence." Georgi Malenkov, Stalin's successor as Chairman of the Council of Ministers and Secretary of the
Communist Central Committee, announced to party officials that
there were no outstanding disputes with the West that could not "be
decided by peaceful means, on the basis of mutual understanding by
interested countries." As evidence of this change in policy, the Soviet
government allowed Russians married to foreigners to leave the country, reestablished diplomatic relations with Greece and Israel, and
agreed to an end to the Korean War.[1]

While these new developments did not have an immediate effect
on either domestic or foreign policy initiatives in the United States,
they set the groundwork for the easing of Cold War tensions and the
Geneva Conference of 1955, the first meeting between American and
Soviet leaders since the wartime alliance. At the same time, the increasingly irresponsible behavior of McCarthy, particularly his interference in the area of foreign policy, was proving more and more prob-
lematic for the Eisenhower administration. After a trip around the
world in 1953, Adlai Stevenson commented that "in all countries they
know of him, and in all tongues they speak of him." McCarthy had
come to represent all that was evil in American foreign policy and in

American life in general. The *London Times* commented that "the fears and suspicions which center around the personality of Senator McCarthy are now real enough to count as an essential factor in policy-making for the West."[2] According to the historian Richard H. Rovere, American foreign policy in 1952–1953 "became largely a matter of assuring allies and potential allies that McCarthy really wasn't running the show in Washington, despite contrary appearances."[3]

Part of these assurances would be made through cultural exchanges between the United States and Europe, in which the presence of painters or writers or musicians cited by McCarthy or his cohorts would provide proof that freedom of expression still existed in America. Of course, the majority of these exchanges would be carried out under the auspices of private organizations, but the assurances were there nonetheless. Exactly how cultural promotions functioned in this manner will become apparent in examining the exhibition of Shahn's painting that was sent to Venice in 1954.

While Europeans were being treated to this display of American painting in Venice in the summer of 1954, those back home were watching a display of another sort. McCarthy had finally gone too far by attacking the United States Army, in particular General R. W. Zwicker and Secretary of the Army Robert Stevens. The hearings that resulted from these accusations were broadcast over network television and proved to be McCarthy's demise. While the blacklists and repression did not end immediately with the censure of McCarthy by the Senate later that year, the charge of "communism" no longer held the same guarantee of disgrace for the accused or of publicity for the accuser.

The Army-McCarthy hearings were not the first time that the Republican senator had appeared on national television. On March 9, 1954, Edward R. Murrow had devoted one episode of his *See It Now* documentary series on CBS to McCarthy. Through a combination of film clips of McCarthy's various public appearances and a commentary of factual information about the various accusations he had made, Murrow succeeded in exposing the methods and the character of the senator. That CBS was willing to air Murrow's show was an indication of the beginning of the decline of the senator's power and of the tactic of Red-baiting in general. The response to the show was, according to CBS reports, overwhelmingly favorable, with calls to the station fifteen to one against the senator in San Francisco and New York, and two to one in Chicago.[4]

Shahn had done work for Murrow just prior to the McCarthy program, designing an ad for a *See It Now* episode on the New York Philharmonic that aired the week before the McCarthy show.[5] Shahn had, in fact, been asked to design an ad for the McCarthy program as well, but had been out of town at the time so was unable to comply.[6] He was moved by the program, however, and executed two drawings which he sent to Murrow and Fred Friendly, the program's director. One was of "David Slaying Goliath" and the other of "St. George Killing the Dragon," with the slayer in both instances bearing the features of Murrow and the slayed those of McCarthy.[7]

Shahn did execute illustrations in conjunction with the Army-McCarthy hearings, although for the *Nation* rather than CBS.[8] They consisted of portrait sketches of the main characters in the hearings—Secretary of the Army Stevens, the Army's counsel Joseph Welch, McCarthy, David Schine, and others. The hearings lasted thirty-six days, with over two million words of testimony. While the findings were inconclusive, Joseph McCarthy definitely emerged the loser. A Senate investigation into the nature of his activities as a senator followed, resulting in a vote in December 1954 to censure him for "conduct . . . unbecoming a member of the United States Senate." While he remained a United States senator until his death three years later, his power and influence were at an end.

During the course of the Army-McCarthy hearings two of McCarthy's assistants came under particular scrutiny—Roy M. Cohn, the chief counsel for McCarthy's committee, and G. David Schine, who carried the somewhat vague title of "chief consultant." During the spring of 1953 they had traveled throughout Europe "upbraiding American diplomats supposedly soft on communism, attacking United States Information Service libraries for exhibiting the work of such 'radicals' as Mark Twain and Theodore Dreiser, and provoking the wrath of the European press."[9] Their activities thoroughly demoralized American government employees in Europe and made many Europeans question even more seriously the ability of the American president and his administration to control McCarthy. The Italian journalist Guido Piovene commented in 1953:

> The excesses of a McCarthy, the ridiculous arbitrary visa requirements, and the exclusion of certain writers and actors have done more harm to the reputation of the United States in Europe than the withdrawal of a few divisions of troops or a few million dollars. . . . Europeans must not get the idea that American civilization, upon which they base so much of

their hope for the future, is introverted, calculating, narrow and obtuse, with no antennae for capturing ideas other than its own.[10]

The American government could not simply dismiss these statements as "communist propaganda." Piovene's words appeared in a collection of essays edited by James Burnham and entitled *What Europe Thinks of America*. The authors were Europeans selected by Burnham in a process, outlined at length in his introduction, that reflected his own history as an ex-Trotskyite who avidly denounced his 1930s communist affiliations in the 1950s:

> I invited as contributors only proved friends of the West and the United States. I deliberately excluded communists, fellow travellers and neutralists. . . . Most of the contributors . . . are not merely noncommunist but anti-communist; they are all nonsocialist and I think that all or almost all are anti-socialist.[11]

With such criticisms coming from those considered friends of the West, the need for reassurances from both government and private sources in the United States became crucial. This was particularly so in Italy, where the centrist American-backed government of Alcide De Gasperi was battling a resurgent right of its own. Piovene had also voiced reservations concerning the unreasonableness of American demands on the Soviet Union and had warned of the success of the latter in gaining support in Europe through its peace offensive. It was in this particular political climate, therefore, that the 1954 Venice Biennial was held and that the responses to Shahn's work were formulated.

Italy, the United States, and Cultural Propaganda

In 1953 H. Stuart Hughes, an American historian of Western and Central Europe and chief of the research staff of the Office of Strategic Services for a year in Italy during World War II, wrote a book entitled *The United States and Italy*. In his first page of text, Hughes listed the major capacities in which Italy appeared in American foreign policy in 1953:

> as one of the four great powers of Western Europe—indispensable partner, first in the European Recovery Program, now in the Atlantic Alliance; as a friend in one World War and an enemy in the next—forgiven and reaccepted into the democratic fraternity, but still unaccountably excluded from the United Nations; as the territorial headquarters of the

Catholic Church, the birthplace of modern fascism, and the home of the largest Communist party in the non-Communist world.[12]

By supporting De Gasperi's Christian Democrat Party and its anti-communist platform in the 1948 elections, in large part through Marshall Plan funding, the American government helped ensure this party's victory over left-wing forces, though the Communist Party emerged as the major opposition party.[13] This victory, however, was not without its drawbacks. As Hughes pointed out, it brought into power a Christian Democrat Party composed of two distinct forces: one which stood for "personal liberty and the Western democratic tradition," i.e., De Gasperi and his pro-American followers; and another which maintained its allegiance to a fascist nationalism and which rejected American interference in the Italian economy.[14]

The Christian Democrat Party was similar, therefore, to the American Republican Party, which was made up of both moderates like Eisenhower and reactionaries like McCarthy. The effectiveness of the right-wing forces in both parties lay in their commitment to anticommunism. They were able, through charges of official "softness" toward communism, to limit the actions of more moderate party leaders.[15] By 1953 these reactionary movements, rather than communism, posed the biggest threat to the American government's interests in Italy. McCarthyism eroded the American democratic image and limited, through Congress, aid to Europe, while Italian neo-fascism threatened the effectiveness of the North Atlantic Treaty Organization (NATO) and the achievement of an economically united Europe. It was, in fact, De Gasperi's unwillingness to align himself with neo-fascist parties that brought about his defeat in the summer elections of 1953.[16]

De Gasperi's immediate successor within the Christian Democrat Party was Giuseppe Pella, who attempted to meet "the wishes of both the economic and clerical Right."[17] Though he was replaced in February 1954 by Antonio Scelba, a Christian Democrat of more centrist leanings, right-wing elements within and outside of the party continued to exert pressure on the government.[18]

Such shifts in the power structure of the Italian government were, according to Hughes, "very much an American problem."[19] He suggested that one of the ways to help keep the centrist faction of the Christian Democrat Party in power was to improve the American image that this faction supported. The main governmental agency assigned this task during Eisenhower's administration was the USIA. In Western Europe the agency's program was designed

> to promote greater understanding of, and support for, NATO and related collective security measures; to encourage the will to move forward toward unification; to expose the Soviet myth and reduce Soviet influence; and to present to this highly literate area a convincing and inspiring picture of America and its policies, both internal and international.[20]

The last of these four considerations provides a clue as to the form much American propaganda was to take in Europe, the key phrase being "highly literate." The American government acknowledged the need in the U.S. propaganda offensive for "the classification of different countries on the basis of their strategic importance to the United States campaign; the selection in each country of target groups; and the choice of the most effective materials and media for reaching those groups."[21] The techniques used to appeal to a highly literate European audience would necessarily have to avoid, as the USIA put it, "strident and propagandistic material," which would create suspicion rather than cooperation.[22]

The first few years of Truman's "campaign of truth" had, in fact, created such a suspicion. The emphasis of this campaign on urgent and unilateral propaganda to combat communism was seen by many in the newly reorganized USIA as having been "too direct, too shrill, too polemical and, in a sense, too patronizing." While a policy of "vigorous and careful guidance" was required, the program should be "honest, calm and moderate, and intellectually mature, and . . . should be directed toward the fundamental attitudes and values of foreign peoples."[23]

The "fine" or "high" arts were particularly suited to this new program, as such arts were generally considered exempt from political concerns or at least from blatant political propaganda. Messages regarding the American way of life could be conveyed directly through the content of the works or indirectly through their styles. Of course, the USIA was not yet free to sponsor exhibitions or displays of the more modern versions of these arts, and would not be until the end of the decade. Private institutions like MOMA continued, therefore, to send exhibitions of modern art abroad and to represent American interests at such international contemporary art exhibitions as the Venice Biennial.

The Venice Biennial

The Venice Biennial was not simply a showcase for individual artistic talent, but an important arena for the presentation of national ideologies and cultural achievements. Art critic Lawrence Alloway has compared it to the great exhibitions of the nineteenth century. Just as these exhibitions broached issues particularly relevant to the expanding industrial societies of that century—"free trade, division of labor, increase in means of communication, the stimulus of competition"—the post–World War II Venice Biennials embodied contemporary social and political concerns.[24] One of the most important of these concerns in the early fifties was the Cold War. Bernard Denvir, in his review of the 1954 Biennial for the British magazine *The Artist,* wrote: "As this year saw the participation of a number of Iron Curtain countries, one almost inevitably began viewing the Biennale in terms of cultural 'blocs.'"[25] R. H. Hubbard, critic for *Canadian Art,* also noted that "jury day brought out this cleavage between the communist and non-communist worlds," with the Iron Curtain countries voting "for no one but the 'social realists' and when these were eliminated they would turn in blank ballots."[26]

In the decade after World War II, attendance at the Biennials ranged from 150,000 to 216,471. The size and variety of these crowds made the Biennial "a significant factor in the spreading of knowledge and shaping of taste"[27] and therefore increased the importance of national identity and prestige in the individual exhibitions. The role of the exhibits at the Venice Biennials as "temporary emblems of national dignity"[28] was further emphasized by the government sponsorship of each of the pavilions. This was true of all save one, however—that of the United States, which had been overseen by MOMA since the late forties and which, as mentioned earlier, was purchased by the museum in 1953.

Denvir remarked that the purchase of the pavilion by MOMA marked "the beginning of a new era of American art at Venice," for the pavilion was now part of MOMA's "Rockefeller-financed programme of effecting closer cultural contacts between Europe and the U.S.A."[29] The absence of U.S. government-sponsored exhibitions of modern art both at Venice and elsewhere throughout Europe further increased the sense that MOMA's exhibitions represented not merely the museum's tastes, but the tastes of the United States as a whole. At least one American critic condemned MOMA's "dictatorial powers" in this respect. F. Taubes, an avid supporter of traditional as opposed to modern art, pointed out in his review of the 1954 Biennial that "these shapers of the 'official' taste in art are the ones who arrange international shows and thus they are in the position to misrepresent us abroad."[30]

Many, however, felt the pavilion was better off in private hands than in the control of a government whose hands were continually tied when it came to modern art. Alfred H. Barr, Jr., expressed this sentiment clearly in his article in *La Biennale di Venezia:* "Private ownership of the American pavilion will ensure, the Museum feels, a progressive spirit that is free from censure."[31] Denvir voiced a similar view when he commented that "at the [1954] Biennale at least, artistic conservatism and Communism go hand in hand, whilst free enterprise is linked to the more adventurous forms of artistic explorations."[32]

MOMA's choice of Shahn may, in fact, have been partly prompted by the State Department's veto of a government-sponsored Shahn exhibition a few years earlier.[33] The official theme of the Biennial—surrealism—was probably another factor. Shahn was associated with the American art movement known as magic realism, which took up the surrealist notions of detailed, in some cases almost photographic, realism and bizarre or fantastic imagery. Shahn had been well represented in MOMA's 1943 exhibition "American Realists and Magic Realists."

Yet neither Shahn's censure by the State Department nor the surrealist aspects of his work emerged as major themes in the promotional literature and reviews surrounding the exhibition. Instead, Shahn was cited time and again for his defense of the poor and oppressed and his championing of humanist politics and aesthetics. This was in sharp contrast to the literature on de Kooning, which dealt primarily with aesthetic issues. A brief look at the response to de Kooning's exhibit prior to examining Shahn's will help us understand better the particular success of the latter.

We have already seen how the political and economic ascendancy of the United States after World War II was accompanied, in the minds of many, by an artistic ascendancy. Greenberg's pronouncements with regard to the latter are summarized in a question he both asked and answered at a 1953 symposium. "Do I mean that the new American abstract painting is superior on the whole to the French? I do."[34]

The reaction to de Kooning's work at the 1954 Venice Biennial, however, was not quite so favorable. According to a press analysis compiled by MOMA, reproductions of de Kooning's work appeared "only in the more advanced periodicals," and the only magazine to request material on him for an article was the Italian "avant-garde publication *Spazio*."[35] In general, the response was either neutral or unfavorable. Critics, especially in the French press, tended to focus on the failure of the artist's work to maintain the advanced character that had been its strong point three or four years earlier.[36] Phrases such as "too facile," "boring," and "lacking in freshness" pointedly conveyed this attitude.[37] G. Mario Marini, in the Roman current art events periodical *Notiziario d'Arte*, commented: "For de Kooning we will not use much paper, not because he isn't an artist worthy of serious consideration, but because in him form and content present problems identical to those that we find in almost a hundred other European painters."[38] De Kooning had lost his edge, therefore, on innovation.

If de Kooning failed to convince the European art world of American inventiveness, he succeeded, at least, in convincing it of another American attribute—aggressiveness. His *Woman* series evoked a particularly negative response from European reviewers, Alain Jouffroy describing it as "horrible" and "violent" in *Beaux-Arts*,[39] and Marini as "disproportionate, contorted, mutilated, unrecognizably transformed [and] repulsive" in *Notiziario d'Arte*.[40] In a summary of the press reaction to the exhibition as a whole, MOMA noted that "as in the United States, de Kooning's *Woman* series fascinated and outraged many critics. Some found their expressionism boring, others distasteful, others questioned their intense ferocity."[41]

Barr included a statement by de Kooning in his *La Biennale di Venezia* article in which the artist described his art as "not peaceful," "enveloped in the melodrama of vulgarity," and "uncomfortable."[42] It was, unfortunately, an accurate description of many Europeans' view of the United States in 1954. While de Kooning's paintings could well have suggested some of the positive aspects of American aggression—the expression of individualism and freedom—the European art world appears to have focused primarily on the negative connotations. His art failed, therefore, to win for the United States the respect and good feeling that was in such short supply.

Promotional Literature and Press Reaction

In order to arrive at a complete understanding of Shahn's reception in Venice, we need to examine the promotional literature and press reaction surrounding his exhibition. The major pieces of promotional literature produced for the Biennial by MOMA were its own special catalogue and the article by Alfred H. Barr, Jr., on the American exhibition for the Biennial publication *La Biennale di Venezia*.[43] Shahn's essay "The Artist and the Politician," which appeared in translation in the November/December 1953 issue of the Italian art journal *Sele Arte*, can also be considered a type of promotional literature.

As much as a year prior to the actual Biennial, galleries would arrange special shows throughout Europe of any of their artists included in the upcoming exhibition at Venice and write articles on them for various European magazines with an eye to the major prizes awarded at the Biennial.[44] Shahn's article "The Artist and the Politicians" is not typical of this type of promotional literature in that it records his political sentiments rather than his artistic views or achievements and was probably not arranged through Shahn's gallery. Still, it served to familiarize the Italian art public with an aspect of Shahn's work that would receive much attention in MOMA's promotional literature.

In "The Artist and the Politicians" Shahn presented himself as the consummate social liberal, a man who criticized both the far right and the far left yet maintained a concern for civil liberties that distinguished him from the anti-communist liberals in the United States who belonged to such organizations as the ADA. His criticism of the debilitating effects of charges of communism issued by the right was particularly meaningful in Italy. Many Italians were relying on the United States to help in combatting rising neo-fascism in their own country, and the appearance, therefore, of a similar reactionary climate in America was of great concern. This concern was highlighted in the commentary by Carlo Ragghianti, editor of *Sele Arte*, that preceded Shahn's article:

> The article attacks one point that involves us directly. America as an ideal and a potential of liberty is too important for the whole world, as well as for culture, for us to remain indifferent to the grave complications that Ben Shahn points out and which confirm so much other information that we constantly read in American newspapers and magazines . . . [The] work of the free American artist found among us a deep and anxious echo and represented an opportune and fruitful admonition.[45]

Shahn helped ease this anxiety by publicly condemning McCarthyism, proof that it had yet to stifle free speech in the United States. What Ragghianti found most consoling about Shahn's article was not its content, however, but the fact that it had been published by *Art News*, "one of the greatest, most accepted and diffused American magazines," rather than by a "small club magazine." The wide circulation this magazine enjoyed would allow the American public, like the readers of *Sele Arte,* to "find again and defend the traditional positions of liberty, which are at the base of the 'ideal of America.'"[46] While the reputation Ragghianti claimed for *Art News* was obviously exaggerated, this magazine's status as an art, rather than a political, journal was important, for it meant that it was viewed as a conveyor of nonpartisan, artistic "truth" rather than of partisan political opinion.

Shahn had complained in his article that, in America, "people of the basest ignorance are sitting in judgment upon art."[47] Ragghianti found that a similar situation had developed in December 1952 in Italy, when right-wing Italian senators criticized the selection of prizes and purchases by the public administration and national gallery at the 26th Venice Biennial. These senators had described the works in question as "grotesque objects that could not possibly, in any way, be considered expressions of art, and that were contrary to every aesthetic sense and that were loathsome and derisive to the sound and balanced aesthetic taste of the Italian people."[48] The works attacked included both the modern painting and sculpture of Mario Radice and Alberto Viani and the social realist canvases of Carlo Levi and Renato Guttuso. In Italy, as in the United States, therefore, members of the right were attacking government art policy. Shahn's labeling of such attacks as "tragic buffoonery" placed him among the defenders of modern art, an art that represented, for many, a vital part of progressive, liberal culture and that Shahn had earlier described as "one of the few remaining outposts of free speech."[49]

The essay on Shahn that appeared in both the official Biennial catalogue and the smaller one published by MOMA was written by James Thrall Soby.[50] Soby focused on two major themes: Shahn's respect for Italy and his concern for the oppressed, particularly the laboring classes. Shahn's proclaimed love of Italy was obviously of help in winning the good will of the Italian people. In a letter to Shahn before the Biennial opened, Soby referred to the significance of this love: "I won't make a big point of this, of course, but a few statements might help the Italians to understand that even though we were officially enemies, we grieved for them nevertheless."[51] Soby's devotion of almost half of his piece to Shahn's feelings for Italy suggests that a big point was, in fact, being made.

Soby related at length an incident from Shahn's past in which an Italian barber explained to the young Shahn why the peasants returned to their homes beneath the still-smoking Mount Etna: "When you have planted so much in one place, you have to go back to it." In addition to admiring this perseverance in the face of disaster, Shahn was also fascinated by Italy's superb visual heritage, and the dignity and grace of the people. "Like most artists," Shahn is quoted as saying, "I look upon Italy as 'the home place.'" In his grief over the disasters of war, Shahn had made a number of paintings "in which Italian children, unquenchably imaginative, explore the new ruins of ancient buildings." One of these paintings, *Italian Landscape* (1944), was present at the Biennial.

Shahn's concern for the oppressed and the working class was, according to Soby, the result of his upbringing in the "poorer sections of Brooklyn," where he was forced by "local toughs" to make sidewalk sketches. A rejection of art-for-art's-sake and an acceptance of, in Soby's words, "narrative commentary on the life and social issues of his time" resulted in two series of pictures—the first on Sacco and Vanzetti, the second on the labor leader Tom Mooney. What Soby did not mention is that these series touched on two important issues in Italy in the first half of the twentieth century—the American government's attitude toward Italian immigrants and the position of organized labor as the stronghold of the Italian Communist Party.

In the first two decades of the twentieth century, Italians were allowed into the United States with few restrictions. The decade from 1901 to 1911 alone saw the influx of over a million and a half Italian immigrants. By 1920, however, growing xenophobia had changed Americans' attitudes toward immigration. The subsequent quota acts of 1921 and 1924 cut off virtually all new immigration to the United States.[52] Resentment over this, as well as over the persecution of Italian immigrants such as Sacco and Vanzetti, was still present in Italy in the 1950s. In 1953 Vittorio Zincone, editor of *Giornale dell'Emilia* of Bologna and an active member of the Liberal Party, commented on "the disappointment of the popular classes with the America that went back on its assumed promise of redistributing the wealth through migration."[53] The American immigration quota for Italians in 1953 was actually lower than that of 1924.[54]

Organized labor constituted the core of Communist electoral and organizational strength in Italy and accounted for a large share of the two and a half million members that made the Italian Communist Party the largest in the non-communist world.[55] The American-backed attempt by De Gasperi to purge communists from Italian unions in the late forties added to the animosity already exhibited toward the

United States by many Italian workers and union leaders.[56] Soby presented Shahn as a critic of American actions in the 1920s toward Italian immigrants and as a supporter of the causes of labor in Italy and in the United States, with one major qualification: "[Shahn's] sympathies always have been with the oppressed, though he has vigorously repudiated the cure for their ills proposed by Communism."[57]

In addition to the essays in the Biennial and MOMA catalogues and Shahn's article in *Sele Arte*, Alfred H. Barr, Jr., MOMA's Director of Museum Collections, produced an article on the American exhibition for the journal *La Biennale di Venezia*. In it he reiterated many of the themes that appeared in the writings of both Soby and Shahn. Shahn's "profound, passionate interest in the human condition" was revealed in his Sacco and Vanzetti series, represented at the 1954 Biennial by a portrait of the prisoners, *Bartolomeo Vanzetti and Nicola Sacco* (Figure 36).[58] But rather than emphasize the fact that the victims were Italian immigrants or labor organizers, Barr took a different tack. Instead, he quoted the artist as follows: "Ever since I could remember I'd always wished I'd been lucky enough to be alive when something big was happening, like the Crucifixion. And suddenly I realized I was living through another crucifixion. Here was something to paint!"[59] Equating Sacco and Vanzetti with Christ held obvious advantages in Italy, where the bulk of the population, including many of those voting for the Communist Party, were practicing Catholics. Shahn's words deified, in fact, two Italian immigrants who had been condemned to die by the Pontius Pilate of the American justice system, Judge Webster Thayer.

Barr went on to comment on Shahn's work for the CIO and the OWI and his murals dealing with the subjects of work and social well-being. Italy was a country of high unemployment, high political consciousness, and a low standard of living.[60] In dealing with politics, labor, and social well-being, Shahn was addressing issues of immediate relevance to the majority of the Italian population. But after connecting Shahn with these issues, Barr, like Soby and like Shahn himself, added the same qualifier: "But Shahn is not a social realist in a communist sense." He went on to quote Shahn as condemning "the formulae of commissars," the "exaggerated generals and extremely idealized proletariat" and the "lack of conviction" evident in Soviet art. It was an art in which, according to Shahn, "the search for truth has for the time been arrested."[61]

Barr, seemingly anticipating the criticism that McCarthyism had greatly hampered the search for truth in the United States, acknowledged that Shahn's searchings had, on occasion, brought him "into conflict with orthodox conservatives in the United States as well as with orthodox radicals." These conflicts had not, however, hampered Shahn's success:

> He has received five government commissions for murals, sixty of his works are found in thirty American museums, and many others are included in wealthy private collections. He designs covers for American businessmen's periodicals and participates in conferences in American universities. The prestige of Shahn is very great, both as an artist and as a champion of freedom without compromise. [62]

The three pieces of writing discussed above contributed to the reinforcement of a very specific image of Ben Shahn. He was a defender of individualism and democracy, in politics and in art, and a sharp critic of social injustice. He supported organized labor, though not the Communist Party, and produced a realistic art that rivaled communist socialist realism in terms of socially relevant content, yet remained decidedly "modern" and individualistic. Was this, in fact, how Shahn was perceived by the European, and particularly the Italian, press?

MOMA's International Program Report on the 1954 Biennial exhibition included the following passage:

> Ben Shahn . . . proved to be a chief focus of interest at the Biennale. He was awarded the top purchase prize, offered by the Museo de Arte Moderna of Sao Paulo, Brazil . . . numerous illustrations of his work . . . appeared in newspapers and periodicals. . . . [A] number of museums and galleries throughout Europe . . . requested the Museum to arrange a show of Shahn's work for them following the close of the Biennale. [63]

Another request for Shahn's work was made by the Italian Minister of Fine Arts, who wished to explore the possibility of a one-man show sponsored by the Italian government. This was, according to the director of the American pavilion, H. Lester Cooke, an "impressive compliment" as "the only other living non-Italian artists who have been honoured by the Government this way are Picasso, Matisse and Rouault." [64]

The summary of European press reaction referred to earlier in the discussion of de Kooning's work accompanied the above report. It appears, according to the information contained within this summary, that Shahn more than met the expectations of MOMA's organizers, and that the response to his work reflected the concerns of the museum's promotional literature:

Shahn's personal version of realism and his recognizable content appeared unique and refreshingly unhackneyed. Moreover, his understanding of poverty and tragedy and his sympathy with the oppressed struck an immediate responsive chord with the Europeans because of their own war and post-war experience. To the Italians, especially, Shahn's use of Italian subject matter made his work even more sympathetic, and he appeared to them as an understanding friend.[65]

The connection between Shahn as an artist and Shahn as an official representative of the United States was also accomplished:

One of the most striking and possibly surprising aspects of Shahn's appeal was the fascination that he exerted as a distinctly "American" painter of "American" subjects. In spite of his European birth and his kinship with certain European painters, Shahn was regarded as entirely representative of the United States in his psychology, subject matter and pictorial means.[66]

This appeal as a distinctively American painter was noted by Lisa Licitra Ponti in her article on Shahn for the art magazine *Domus*. She saw a "lightly satirical observation of the 'real' in American customs" in Shahn's work that was "truly wonderful."[67] Franco Catania provided a more detailed observation in the *Corriere de Sicilia:*

This Lithuanian-born Jew paints precisely the myth of America—the America of Washington, of Ford, of gangsters; of the America that grew so rapidly out of the courage, the simplicity and the struggles of the early pioneers. . . . The painting of Ben Shahn is one of the most sincere, alive and original documents in contemporary American art.[68]

Shahn's works were also, according to Catania, "born out of a human and poetic experience which can be clarified not inappropriately by evoking the name of Chaplin."[69] Evoking this name in Europe in 1954 would have brought to mind a much-publicized incident of the previous year, when Charlie Chaplin had refused to return to the United States after being harassed by the FBI and the Internal Revenue Service because of his political opinions.[70] Shahn, like Chaplin, condemned these developments in the United States and offered reassurances that such deviations from the tradition of democracy were, in fact, being dealt with. The Army-McCarthy hearings, which ended two days before the Biennial opened, helped drive these reassurances home.

Shahn's sympathy for the poor and oppressed was of a distinct kind. Catania described his work as containing "an affectionate attachment for the world of poor people, for the disinherited, for the oppressed, whom he always represented in an aura of redemption, expressing pained sensibility in the face of injustice."[71] Pilon Ugo, the sixty-year-old Italian guard at the American pavilion and one of the poor about whom Shahn painted, wrote to the artist: "Your paintings constitute that which is most loved and most beautiful in the struggling life of poor populations."[72] According to Cooke, the pavilion's director, Shahn was able to represent the poverty, suffering, and dignity of Italians "with a sincerity and understanding which every visitor to the American pavilion can see and understand."[73]

Shahn did not present the harsher or more dismal aspects of poverty, as did many Italian communist artists. "There are other painters here in Italy," commented a factory worker from Bologna in talking of Shahn's work, "who like to remind us of our poverty. Carlo Levi and the Communists, for example, but they show us as though we were ox-like actors in a third-class opera. We know a good painting when we see it and we know when someone is sincere."[74]

MOMA's press review stated, in fact, that Shahn's sympathy with the poor and oppressed "created a special problem for Communist writers, for although they found his subject matter acceptable to them, his style and nationality were not."[75] His condemnation of the Communist Party also made his acceptance difficult. The communist newspaper *L'Ora* of Palermo dealt with the issue by reproducing Shahn's painting *Liberation* (1945; Figure 37), along with two social realist paintings, in an article by Maria Poma that discussed the prize-winners at the Biennial. Not unexpectedly, Poma condemned the "avant-garde tendencies" at the exhibition. But she also, without mentioning any names, spoke disparagingly of noncommunist "social realist" artists, commenting that "their social realism is still like a seed sown on arid ground, without realism or tradition, and has not yet been translated into formal terms, thus is 'social' only in the widest and most basic sense of the word."[76] Communist readers familiar with the party line on art may well have taken Shahn's painting as an example of this "arid" social realism, even though Shahn himself was not named.

Social realism in Italy in the early 1950s was not the same, however, as socialist realism in the Soviet Union. Just as the Italian Communist Party under Palmiro Togliatti maintained a certain independence from the Soviet Communist Party, so too did Italian communist artists distance themselves from Soviet communist artists. The realism of Renato Guttuso and Carlo Levi was much less exact and naturalistic than that of such Soviet artists as S. A. Grigoriev and F. Reshetnikov. And while the paintings of the Italian artists remained within the party dictates of peasants and workers, they presented, on the whole, a much gloomier and more static picture of the life of the lower classes than that described by Russian socialist realists.

The 1953 Annual All Soviet Union art show, for example, was dominated by academic paintings with moralistic themes—*The Return, Discussion of a "D," Fresh Number of the Shop Paper*—showing healthy Russian workers acting to improve their lot by encouraging such virtues as faithfulness and intelligence.[77] The works of Levi and Guttuso at the 1954 Biennial, on the other hand, tended to provide simple portraits of the Italian peasants in all their roughness and poverty—*Three Laborers* (1953) by Levi—or depressing examples of the decadence of Western habits and art—Guttuso's *Roman Boogie-Woogie* (1953). In 1955 John Berger, the leftist British art critic, wrote of Guttuso:

> Guttuso deals with the very elements (heat, dust, the soil) which the common Italian people work with every day of their lives. . . . The Italian character of Guttuso's paintings does not belong to the Italy of the "cultured" tourist—and this must be allowed for. Rawness comes before mellowness, effort before elegance, labour before a meal—and Guttuso does not disguise such facts.[78]

While the paintings of these Italian artists may have been less idealistic than the Russian canvases, they were also less appealing to those whom they depicted. An art that simply reminded Italian workers of their poverty in an aesthetically unpleasing manner ran the risk of being rejected by these workers and of creating a dissatisfaction that might work against communist aims, or at least against the positive reception of communist art.

The success Levi and Guttuso enjoyed in Italy indicates that not all Italians were offended by the style and content of their paintings, particularly not those who were responsible for the exhibition and sale of art works. The two artists also gained a certain degree of acceptance outside of Italy. Just how acceptable they actually were to noncommunist audiences is indicated by an article in the November 30, 1953, issue of *Time* magazine, in which Guttuso is praised as "one of Italy's most talented artists." This talent was described as the result of his unwillingness to fit his artistic conscience "into the tight jacket of Red discipline." It was an unwillingness which allowed him, in *The Dying*

Hero, to rise "above the level of flat political posters with his geometric handling of pillow and sheets, skillfully done in shades of off-white against a violently contrasting red drapery." What was important, and what made Guttuso's work acceptable, was not that his canvases were filled with "miners, child laborers, peasants, and decadent rich folks sunning at Capri," but that he had broken with "Red discipline" by rejecting the academic style of Soviet socialist realism for a "less rigid, more flexible" style.[79]

While *L'Ora* had dealt indirectly with Shahn's work at the Biennial, the communist weekly *Il Contemporaneo* of Rome carried a front-page article by Gian Paolo Paoli titled "Shahn in the Cellar," which was accompanied by a reproduction of *Handball* and which criticized the organizers of the American exhibition for not publicly exhibiting certain of Shahn's posters dealing with the subjects of peace and labor.[80] MOMA, in its press review, explained that "the posters were listed in the catalog and were shown on request though not hung, since it was thought preferable to devote the limited wall space at the pavilion to showing paintings and drawings rather than graphic works."[81] But another reason was given to Paoli: "[The curator], with an austere look, told me that those catalogue numbers corresponded to posters not exhibited for 'reasons of public order,' which however could be shown as requested."[82]

There were eight posters in all: *We Demand the National Textile Act* (1935), *This Is Nazi Brutality, We French Workers Warn You, For Full Employment after the War: Register/Vote, Break Reaction's Grip: Register/Vote, We Want Peace: Register/Vote, For All These Rights We've Just Begun to Fight: Register/Vote,* and *Warning! Inflation Means Depression: Register/Vote.* How these works could have been conceived of as "a threat to public order" can be understood only by once again reviewing the particular issues in the forefront of Italian politics at this time—the rise of a reactionary party reminiscent of its precursor led by Mussolini and the increase in the Communist Party's power due to the backing of organized labor. Unemployment, inflation, and the threat of another war were also sensitive subjects in Italy in 1954. Shahn's posters contained powerful images calling for action in all of these areas.

It is unlikely that riots would have broken out in the American pavilion had the posters been hung. But it would have been next to impossible for the Italian public to have viewed these works without being reminded of the reactionary climate, unemployment, and inflation in their own country and, more important, to have seen the solution to their problems in organized labor, which in Italy meant the Communist Party.

Paoli found that these posters by Shahn constituted an image of the United States that was dear to most Italians—an anti-fascist America—and that to keep them secluded in a back room, especially after having listed them in the Biennial catalogue, was a "grave insult" to both logic and culture. He also suggested that their seclusion was the result of the museum's fear of encountering the prohibitions of the American State Department. Paoli ended his article by pointing out that this whole incident had cast doubt on the reliability of America's "religion of freedom."[83]

Why the museum sent these posters in the first place, knowing that there would be no room to show them and that the subject matter would be controversial, is uncertain. Perhaps it wanted to exploit the full range of Shahn's appeal, or perhaps it was unaware of the full extent of the controversy these posters might arouse until after their arrival in Italy. It was easy enough, however, to categorize them as less important than Shahn's paintings and remove them from public view.

A Broad Appeal: *Liberation* and *The Red Stairway*

In his official summary report, H. Lester Cooke observed that European criticism tended to be divided horizontally by national boundaries and vertically by national opinion and political orientation. "It can often be said in advance what a French left-wing writer, for example, will say about a non-objective Italian painter." Shahn had fared well at the hands of this critical hierarchy "because his paintings cannot be docketed into any of the categories of modern art."[84] MOMA's press review commented further on this quality in Shahn's work: "An interesting phenomenon is that each writer seemed to find a different and highly personal basis for admiration. Some dwelt on the content of Shahn's paintings, others on purely formal aspects of his art; some stressed his lyricism, others his satire."[85] Thus, in Italy as in the United States, Shahn succeeded in creating an art that resisted a single political or aesthetic categorization and that was accessible to a broad range of people. Exactly how he did so can be discovered by examining the various stylistic and thematic references in two of his works, *Liberation* (Figure 37) and *The Red Stairway* (1944; Figure 38).

One of the measures of Shahn's popularity in Italy was the appearance of illustrations of his works in all types of publications, from the

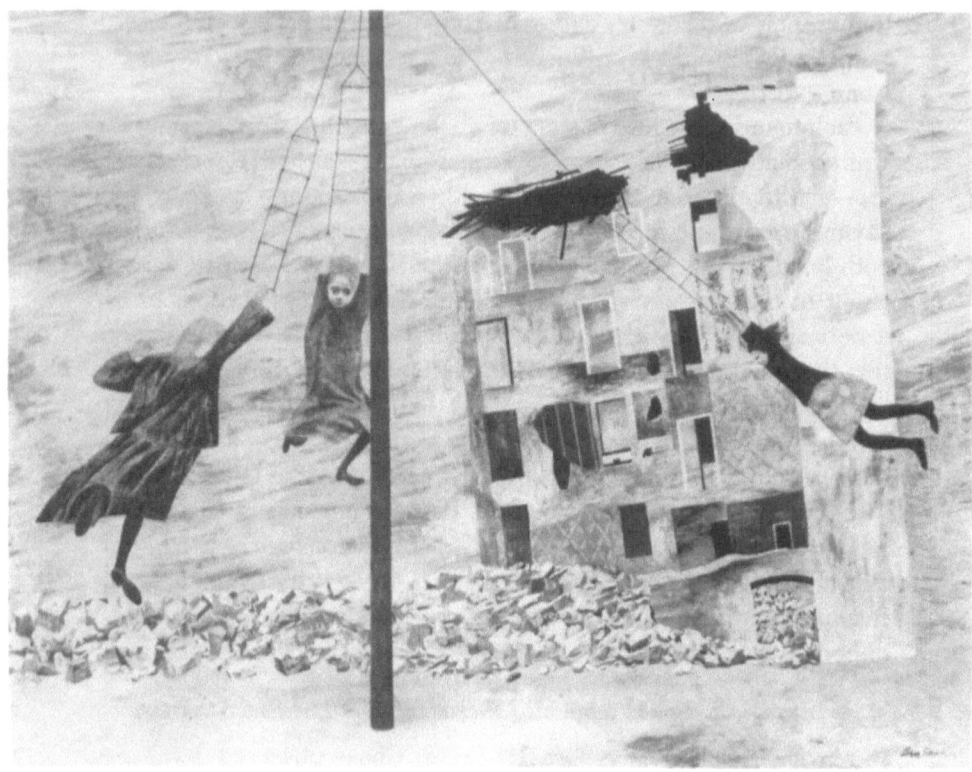

FIGURE 37
Ben Shahn, *Liberation*, 1945
Tempera on cardboard, mounted on
composition board
29¾ × 40"
Collection, The Museum of Modern
Art, New York; James Thrall Soby
Bequest

liberal art magazine *Domus* to the communist weekly *Il Contempo-raneo*. According to MOMA, *Liberation* was the universal favorite, with *The Red Stairway* a close second, followed by *Italian Landscape*, *Father and Child* (1946), *Spring*, and *Summertime*. Shahn's post-1949 works were the least popular. Cooke wrote that this may have been because of their esoteric nature or the fact that they lacked "the passionate conviction of the earlier paintings."[86]

Passionate conviction was not lacking, apparently, in *Liberation*. Its popularity in Italy was due in large part to its subject matter—the joy felt at the end of World War II. Yet *Liberation* is not all joy and play.

The central child whirls about with a certain maniacal intensity, while the child on the right appears much too small for comfort or safety. Indeed, their frozen postures, combined with the sweeping diagonal brushstrokes of the agitated blue-gray sky, suggest that the world is spinning around the children rather than the children around the pole, that they are caught helplessly in the center of a man-made maelstrom. The contrasts between the bright patches of wallpaper and the blackened remnants of the ceiling, the neatly preserved cornice and the pile of rubble, add further to the sense of uncertainty and ambiguity in the painting. The only truly stable element, to which our eye continually returns, is the bright red pole placed slightly to the left of center.

Shahn's intention in creating this sense of ambiguity in his work is revealed in a 1944 interview with John D. Morse:

> But most important is always to have a play back and forth, back and forth. Between the big and the little, the light and the dark, the smiling and the sad, the serious and the comic. . . . My type of social painting makes people smile. The height of the reaction is when the emotions of anger, sympathy, and humor all work at the same time. That's what I try to do—play one against the other, trying to keep a balance.[87]

Shahn achieved his desired balance in *Liberation* and in so doing presented a combination of anger, sympathy, and humor proper for a postwar painting of Italy. Too much humor or joy would have suggested an insensitivity to the actual sufferings of the people, too much anger or sadness an unwanted reminder of the reality of these sufferings, many of which were still present in 1954. Too much joy could also have suggested the idealism of fascist art and its attendant nationalist sentiments, too much anger the dogmatism of certain leftist art. In playing off one against the other, Shahn prevented the viewer from being preoccupied with either extreme, and created instead a more general feeling of pathos, of awe and contemplation.

Pilon Ugo, the Italian guard, confirmed this quality in Shahn's paintings and their effect on the visitors to the exhibition:

> Your paintings hanging from the walls of these halls are admired by everyone, are like an invitation to a prayer and the visitors are the best proof of it; they come by themselves, in groups, and on their tiptoes they come close to them. They observe them with attention, they contemplate them in the most dead silence, collected almost as mute as at a Pilgrimage.[88]

Marini also noted in his article in *Notiziario d'Arte:*

> Shahn has been a revelation for us. He spoke to us, he impressed us, he
> attracted us again. . . . We have encountered in him a delicacy and a
> virile energy, bitter and sometimes ironical, intimate and extrovert, rich
> with a richness of content and imagery.[89]

In *Liberation*, Shahn attempted to portray a certain "truth" about
the events surrounding World War II. The validity of this truth in the
art world, however, often depended upon a recognizably modern
style. This modern style in *Liberation* distinguished it from the art of
socialist or social realists, who might have dealt with the same topic
but, because of their manner of presentation, would have been labeled propagandists rather than bearers of truth. "Ben Shahn," commented the German critic Heinz Keller in 1954, "appears to succeed
in doing what 'Social Realism' futilely attempts: the revival of subject
matter in a legitimately modern form."[90]

While an art's claim to truth often relied on its position on the "cutting edge" of the modernist revolution (since outmoded styles con-
noted outmoded truths), this claim also relied on a connection with
the old masters or with the "universal" truths found in all art of all
ages. Though not in the absolute forefront of formal developments,
Shahn revealed his modern roots in *Liberation*'s collage-like building
interior, bright, flat colors, and distorted perspective. "No one," stated
the head of a Rome art gallery, "wants to return to the academic style
of 1880 like the communists do. [Shahn] has found a style which
is wide enough in range to allow him to say what he wants, and he
still is as contemporary as avant-garde abstractionism."[91] The two-
dimensionality, simple forms, precise outlines, and use of tempera in
Shahn's work also aligned him with the past masters of fourteenth- and
fifteenth-century Italian art. "In the art of Ben Shahn," claimed an article in *Corriere Militare,* "one can find again that state of grace of
fifteenth-century painting which gave a complete and penetrating picture of its time."[92]

Liberation, then, contained a mixture of references to war, destruction, reconstruction, children, fifteenth-century Italian painters and
the churches where their works were found, and modern art. Such
references would have appealed, accordingly, to an Italian viewer's
persistence and fortitude, hatred of war, sense of home and family,
cultural pride, religious beliefs, and tastes for modern, but not *too*
modern, art. And whichever of these references were perceived, once

the associations surrounding them had run their course, the viewer would have been left with the realization that the source of these familiar and predominantly reassuring feelings was the work of an American.

The Red Stairway, like *Liberation*, deals with the destruction caused by World War II. A one-legged man climbs a bright red stairway which is propped against the remaining wall of a bombed-out building. Behind the wall to the left is a pile of rubble surrounded by a network of rafters. To the right of the stairway a desolate, rocky landscape stretches back to the horizon and is occupied, in the foreground, by a lone figure bent under the load of a basket of stones. His shirt is similar in color and texture to the stone that he carries and that surrounds him.

Again, we find the same ambiguity that characterized *Liberation*. What is the meaning of this stairway that acts as a bridge between the two figures and that leads them, along with the eye of the viewer, in endless circles? Are the rafters remnants of the old building or the beginnings of a new one? Is the stone carrier rising out of the earth or sinking into it? Who is this cripple ascending the stairway, and is he a sign of hope or of futility?

A year after *The Red Stairway* was painted, it appeared, along with a number of other war paintings by Shahn, in the December 1945 issue of *Fortune*.[93] It was described as having had its genesis in Shahn's memory of the eruption of Mount Etna and the persistence of the Italian people in returning to their destroyed homes. It embodied, therefore, aspects of that persevering, home-loving image of Italy so aptly presented by Soby in his essay on Shahn in the MOMA Biennial catalogue. *Fortune* also commented on the manner in which Shahn dealt with the subject of war in this painting:

> The most penetrating war art has not depicted battle action. How could it? Battle action in war painting is like the sex act in the literature of love; artists have learned that literalism is the worse part of esthetic valor.[94]

In 1951 Rodman described Shahn's series of war paintings in a similar manner:

> The impression conveyed by these ten pictures may be summed up in the word "pathos." The war is seen not in terms of action or battle or masses or ideals. It is seen in terms of desolation, homelessness, loneliness, civilian starvation and the individual sufferer.[95]

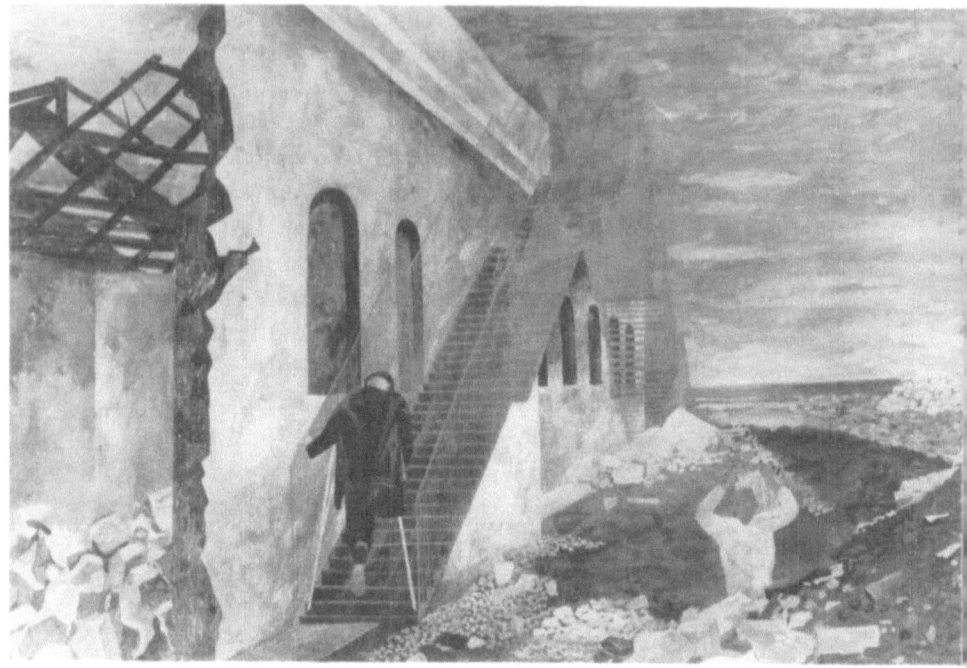

FIGURE 38
Ben Shahn, *The Red Stairway*, 1944
Tempera on masonite
16 × 23⁵⁄₁₆″
Collection: The Saint Louis Art Museum; Purchase

And Cooke concurred with both Rodman and *Fortune* when he wrote in 1954:

> Described in words or painted by a lesser artist, the theme would be either sentimental or propagandistic. With the lyrical vision of Shahn it is neither, but is a simple description of the seemingly futile endeavour of the dispossessed people, stated with compassion and poetic sincerity.[96]

Shahn's paintings provided an alternative, therefore, to the literal depictions of battle action (abstract art would provide another). His anonymous figures, symbolism, and sense of pathos found favor with an audience unwilling to allow the more gruesome realities of war to invade the domain of art.

Ambiguity is evident in the style, as well as the content, of *The Red Stairway*. In the area below the rafters Shahn has utilized Cézanne's "passage" technique to create confusion as to the actual shape and consistency of the form being depicted. Whether this area is supposed to represent stone, sky, or earth is also uncertain, for it combines the textures and colors of all three as portrayed elsewhere in the painting. A further play back and forth between flatness and depth is found in the manner in which the sharply receding plane of the main wall is brought up short by the large red patch halfway down its length, which represents the underside of the staircase.

There are also references in the painting to earlier Italian art. The sharply angled wall marked by a series of arched windows and the macabre atmosphere carry reminders of the work of Giorgio De Chirico, particularly a painting such as his *Melancholy and Mystery of a Street* (1914). The influence of fourteenth- and fifteenth-century Italian artists is found in a number of elements—the simple massive figures, plain walls, arched windows, and general sense of narrative found in the works of Giotto and Duccio. The broken, jagged end of the wall was also a device used by both Leonardo da Vinci and Sandro Botticelli to divide up space in their depictions of *The Adoration of the Magi* in the Uffizi (c. 1481 and early 1470s, respectively). The rafters in Shahn's painting can also be found in another version of *The Adoration of the Magi* (1482) by Botticelli, where a similar network of beams covers the figures of Mary, Joseph, and Jesus.

Thus Shahn has drawn upon a lengthy artistic tradition in his construction of *The Red Stairway*, one that stretches from the realism of fourteenth-century Italians to the modernism of Cézanne and the surrealism of De Chirico. He has provided his viewers with a broad spectrum of not only thematic, but also stylistic, references through which they can attach meaning to the work. As with *Liberation*, no one person would have perceived all of the associations contained within the borders of the canvas. But the very presence of such an extensive range of interpretive possibilities allowed for a greater degree of positive response to the work.

The Museum of Modern Art chose to send to Venice two painters described by Barr in *La Biennale di Venezia* as having not only radically different personalities, but also radically different styles.[97] In the promotional literature their differences were further emphasized. De Kooning was discussed almost solely in terms of his art and his position in the avant-garde of the art world, Shahn in terms of his politics and his relationship to Italy. There was a difference in the tenor of these discussions as well. The descriptions of de Kooning's art were more specialized, filled with phrases such as "juxtapositions of organic and inorganic phenomena" and "suggestive and associative ambiguity."[98] Shahn, on the other hand, was described in an informal, almost chatty, manner, a manner used to relate anecdotes from his childhood, his concern for the poor and oppressed, and the nature of his vast acceptance and financial success in the United States. Thus, the writing about Shahn, like the work he produced, was made more accessible to a wider audience.

While de Kooning's paintings may have been intended as proof to the avant-garde of the European art world that the United States was in the forefront of contemporary artistic developments, they were not a total success. Indeed, whatever successes de Kooning's art might have enjoyed in the more advanced European art circles were more than offset by the negative impression the aggressiveness and violence of this art made on the more general viewing public. Marini commented that while he had observed de Kooning's work with true interest, he would "not dare say with any sense of identification."[99]

It was with this public that Shahn's work found exceptional favor, a public composed of industrial workers, intellectuals, liberal and conservative art critics, and a few slightly reluctant communist writers. A Roman lawyer made the following observation:

> We often think of Americans as rich, friendly, but slightly irresponsible children, who have not experienced enough hardship to be adult in our sense of the word. It comes as a surprise, therefore, and in a way it is flattering, to see an American painter with such a deep understanding of life here in Italy . . . Shahn sees things from the inside; we feel he is one of us.[100]

In spite of all their differences, there was one common factor that united de Kooning and Shahn at Venice in 1954: they were both representatives of freedom and individualism in the United States—de Kooning the freedom to be aesthetically unconventional, Shahn the freedom to include politically meaningful, and often controversial, subject matter in his art and to openly voice political dissent. How Shahn chose to exercise his freedom formed the basis of his popularity in Italy in 1954, a popularity that remains to this day.

CONCLUSION

Twenty years have passed since the group that so
suddenly discovered a conscience were the Alger boys
of the New Day. For all the hue and cry, most of their
names are all but forgotten . . . Out of all the list, it
is chiefly the name of Ben Shahn which endures.
                                        —RUDI BLESH
                               Modern Art USA, 1956

The material in the preceding chapters may come as a bit of a surprise
to those accustomed to locating Ben Shahn in the 1930s. Shahn has, in
a sense, been the victim of a linear art historical tradition that allows
an artist only one appearance at front-center on the stage of art history, the late forties and early fifties being reserved for abstract expressionism. Shahn's continued association with the 1930s is also due
to his persistence in portraying and discussing, in his painting and
writing, aspects of the 1930s New Deal Era that had fallen into disrepute in avant-garde art circles by the end of the forties—socially
relevant content, recognizable form, and active political engagement.

These issues had not fallen into disrepute, however, with many outside of such circles. It was Shahn's willingness to express, visually and
verbally, his concern regarding the move to the right in the world of
politics and the move toward total abstraction in the world of art that
contributed to the size and loyalty of his following. This following included members of labor unions, civil rights organizations, and community and religious groups, as well as artists, critics, and museum
officials.

Of course, Shahn's visual language underwent certain changes during the late forties and early fifties. While unwilling to abandon recognizable content altogether in his painting, he turned from documenting specific historical incidents to recording "universal experiences."
The symbolic portrayal of such experiences—anger, discord, death—
would, he felt, have a particular aesthetic as well as political effect. By
avoiding connections to specific events, these images could extend
their meaning over time and place. They would also be less likely to
fall prey to attacks from the right, for during this period in American
history, depictions of social ills in a figurative style were invariably associated with communism. And this charge of communism was, ac-

cording to Shahn, more of a threat to freedom in the United States than communism itself, for it tied the hands of non-communist liberals attempting to carry out social reform measures within the two-party system.

Shahn's move from the particular to the universal in his paintings did little to diminish his reputation as a social critic, someone who not only attempted to express his convictions in his paintings, but also executed posters, prints, and newspaper ads calling for an end to nuclear testing, the war in Vietnam, and racial discrimination.[1] Even in what can be termed his religious works, Shahn often drew upon images and texts that expressed his moral and political concerns. For example, he completed several prints and drawings based on the writings of Martin Luther. In one such print, *Credo* (1960), he included the quote:

> I have the right to believe freely, to be a slave to no man's authority. If this be heresy so be it. It is still the truth. To go against conscience is neither right nor safe. I cannot . . . will not . . . recant. Here I stand. No man can command my conscience.

Drawn from Luther's statement in defense of his beliefs at the Diet of Worms in 1521, it was also a fitting testimonial to the end of a decade of HUAC hearings.

In Europe, Shahn became representative not only of artistic and political freedom in the United States, but also of the responsible use of this freedom. The continued effectiveness of his work in this respect is evident in his increased popularity throughout Western Europe after 1954. In February 1956 Shahn traveled to London (his first trip to Europe since the 1920s) under the sponsorship of MOMA and the USIA to deliver a lecture at the Institute of Contemporary Art entitled "Realism Reconsidered."[2] Douglas Glass of the *London Sunday Times* described him at this time as "one of the most gentle and pugnacious artists alive, a quiet-speaking man of peace invariably involved in battle," a "liberal radical" who was in England to "speak out in favor of his own kind of realism, and against what he considers to be the essential sterility of abstract or non-objective painting."[3]

That same year the Norwegian art journal *Kunsten Idag* ran an article on Shahn by Ole Henrik Moe in which Moe described Shahn as a "militant humanist . . . a doughty champion in the service of human rights." "Through the most shattering actuality and over-mechanized dehumanisation of life he seeks to make contact with something in the past which will provide hope for the future," stated Moe, hope that a more humane attitude would prevail between individuals and nations.[4]

This hope for a more humane relationship between countries such as the United States and the Soviet Union was fulfilled, to a certain extent, by the Geneva Conference of 1955 and the subsequent easing of the Cold War. In 1956 Eisenhower also signed the International Cultural Exchange and Trade Fair Participation Act which led, two years later, to an agreement between the United States and the Soviet Union to exchange national exhibitions "devoted to the demonstration of the development of science, technology, and culture."[5]

This exchange, the first of its kind ever undertaken in American-Soviet relations, took place in the summer of 1959, with the American exhibition in Moscow and the Soviet exhibition in New York City. Its success, according to the director of the USIA, George V. Allen, was undeniable. Approximately three million Soviet citizens visited the American exhibition in Sokolniki Park and even more were reached by Vice President Nixon, whose address at the opening of the exhibition was carried over Soviet radio and television and reported in the Soviet press. Nixon spoke, stated Allen, "of freedom and democracy and the basis for peace,"[6] thus providing evidence of the American government's willingness to negotiate with the Soviet Union for world peace.

Not everyone in the United States, however, viewed the Soviet-American exchange in a positive light. Eugene W. Castle, "Roving Editor" for the right-wing publication *American Mercury,* claimed the Kremlin had "scored massive propaganda victories within the United States and throughout the world" during 1959 "under the fraudulent umbrella of 'Cultural Exchange.'" Such cultural exchanges did not encourage world peace but were, instead, "Communist-inspired schemes to entice the American people out of their anti-Communism. Any further journeying by Americans into this treacherous terrain will surely lead us to Armageddon." In referring to the "American" paintings exhibited at Sokolniki Park, Castle lamented the fact that "in at least one department, notorious Communists, who are outspoken disbelievers in the American way of life, had their works displayed."[7]

Two such "notorious Communists" were Philip Evergood and Shahn, who were called before HUAC by its chair, Francis E. Walter, on July 1, 1959, to justify the inclusion of their work (Evergood's *Street Corner* [1936] and Shahn's *Parable* [1958]) in the Moscow show and to answer questions regarding their alleged communist affiliations. Both artists refused to answer the latter questions, invoking the first, fifth, ninth, and tenth amendments of the Bill of Rights.[8] They also prepared statements in which they condemned the actions of the committee and argued for the value of art works in helping attain world peace and understanding. "Whatever its temporary successes at home," stated Shahn, "the *world* effect of the Un-American Activities Committee has been more than once to turn us into an international laughing-stock, to lose us respect and friendship on every hand, to earn us the reputation of being a Philistine nation—which we are not."[9] Shahn had also made his opinion of HUAC public earlier that year by signing a petition to Congress published in the *Washington Post* on January 7 calling for an end to the committee.[10] His *Credo* print of 1960 was undoubtedly executed with his committee hearing, and HUAC in general, in mind.

HUAC failed to stop the exhibition from being hung or to obtain the removal of the offending paintings.[11] In fact, Eisenhower chose the very day the committee was interrogating Shahn and Evergood to announce at a press conference his refusal to censor the art exhibition, even though he did not particularly like certain of the works included, such as Jack Levine's satiric portrayal of military generals in *Welcome Home* (1946).[12]

Eisenhower's decision had been confirmed the day before at a Legislative Leadership Meeting, where he pointed out "the impracticability of attempting now to censor the selections."[13] Eisenhower was highly aware, throughout his two terms as president, of the importance of public opinion abroad. It was not enough to gain a people's support through physical force; their minds had to be "won" as well.[14] He did, however, attempt to soothe the critics of the American art exhibition in Moscow by indicating that the next time a government-sanctioned art exhibition occurred, he would like to see to it that the selection committee contained one or two people who "are not too certain exactly what art is but . . . know what we like and what America likes."[15] What Eisenhower, himself, liked was basically the same kind of art Francis E. Walter liked—naturalistic painting with little or no social commentary. His favorite artist in the Moscow show was Andrew Wyeth; hanging on his office wall was a painting of ducks.[16] While he did not impose his artistic tastes on the exhibition that opened in Moscow on July 25, a number of eighteenth- and nineteenth-century paintings by such artists as Mary Cassatt, John Singleton

Copley, and Gilbert Stuart were added to the original group in order to ensure that "what America likes" was adequately represented.

Shahn brought with him to the HUAC hearing a copy of the May 1959 issue of *Amerika*, the Russian-language magazine distributed in the Soviet Union by the USIA.[17] It contained a reprint of a lecture he had presented at Harvard in 1957 entitled "On Nonconformity," along with reproductions of a number of his paintings and drawings.[18] In this text Shahn argued forcefully for the artist's right to experiment, to express new forms and ideas. He also argued that the degree of nonconformity present in a society was an indication of its state of health, and condemned attempts in both the present and the past to censor art. This condemnation would have been particularly timely considering the recent Soviet censorship of Boris Pasternak, the author of *Dr. Zhivago*. Once again, therefore, Shahn emerged as a representative of artistic and political freedom in the United States and of a figurative tradition that allowed for social commentary.

In 1976 the Jewish Museum in New York held an exhibition of Shahn's work. Hilton Kramer, in reviewing the exhibition for the *New York Times*, found that an essential clue to Shahn as an artist and as a cultural phenomenon lay in his audience. While Kramer's review was, on the whole, unfavorable (he preferred a more avant-garde form of art), his description of the show's audience is still revealing and can be read in a more favorable light than Kramer may have intended. While, according to Kramer, Shahn was popular with "people of wealth, privilege and discrimination, who did not share his politics," many of the people who attended the exhibition, particularly in the first few days, did not look like the usual museum crowd. They appeared

> less used to being in a museum than the people one commonly observes at the Whitney or at the Museum of Modern Art. . . . [My impressions] were of people, mainly New Yorkers and mainly Jewish, close to retirement age or beyond it, who were probably members of a labor union during much of their working lives. They struck me as people who had come to this exhibition to relive something that had been important in their lives.[19]

Uppermost among the people at the exhibition was a sense of community and solidarity with causes:

> [Shahn] was adored in his day—and he is adored still—for the way he used his art to give expression to social allegiances and emotions that his admirers already felt, and felt deeply.[20]

Shahn championed many causes throughout his lifetime and encouraged individuals, artists and non-artists alike, to remain involved in campaigns, no matter how limited, for social justice, human rights, and world peace. He also encouraged a critical attitude toward attempts to suppress these campaigns, particularly through the charge of communism. Such encouragement and involvement was especially important in the period 1947 to 1954, when so much of the optimism and idealism of the thirties and early forties had disappeared and when government-sanctioned repression of criticism of government policy was at its height. Shahn was among a number of Americans who consistently pressed for and defended change through social reform. It is out of this social reform tradition that Shahn's work emerged and from which it continues to derive its strength and its meaning.

NOTES

Introduction

1. Milton Brown, "The Forces behind Modern U.S. Painting," *Art News* 46(August 1947):35.

2. Robert Motherwell and Harold Rosenberg, in *Possibilities* 1(Winter 1947–1948).

3. The relationship between abstract expressionism and the Cold War has been investigated by a number of scholars. The most important of these are Max Kozloff, "American Painting during the Cold War," *Artforum* 11(May 1973):43–54; Eva Cockcroft, "Abstract Expressionism, Weapon of the Cold War," *Artforum* 12(June 1974):39–41; David and Cecile Shapiro, "Abstract Expressionism: The Politics of Apolitical Painting," *Prospects* 3(1976):175–214; John Tagg, "American Power and American Painting: The Development of Vanguard Painting in the United States since 1945," *Praxis*, 1976, pp. 59–79; and Serge Guilbaut, *How New York Stole the Idea of Modern Art*, trans. Arthur Goldhammer.

4. The exhibition went to the Institute of Contemporary Art in Boston after it closed in New York on January 4, 1948. A smaller version was sent to Baltimore, Northampton, Minneapolis, Portland, San Francisco, Austin, Beverly Hills, and Philadelphia. See letter from Porter A. McCray, Department of Circulating Exhibitions, MOMA, to Ben Shahn, October 27, 1947, and exhibition checklist and itinerary, Ben Shahn Papers, Archives of American Art, Smithsonian Institution, Washington, D.C., Microfilm Roll D146: 784 and D146:799–801. These papers are henceforth referred to as BSP.

5. James Thrall Soby, *Ben Shahn*. The sixteen paintings illustrated in color had been sent to England earlier in the year in order to be photographed for reproduction in the Penguin book and, while there, were exhibited at the F. H. Mayor Gallery in London (April 9–25). The exhibition was under the sponsorship of the Arts Council of Great Britain, and traveled to Brighton, Cambridge, and Bristol before returning to the United States. A special issue of the *Museum of Modern Art Bulletin* was also issued in the summer of 1947 to accompany the show.

6. Soby, *Ben Shahn*, pp. 3, 5.

7. Ibid., p. 16.

8. Diego Rivera, Foreword to *Ben Shahn: The Mooney Case* (pamphlet), New York, Downtown Gallery, May 2–20, 1933, n.p. According to Rivera, "sophisticated connoisseurs" and workers were the only people who appreciated his own work. People of "middle-class taste" were the ones who objected most strenuously to his emphasis on content (Selden Rodman, *Portrait of the Artist as an American, Ben Shahn: A Biography with Pictures*, p. 104).

9. While Bernarda Bryson Shahn will appear at certain points throughout the following pages, her own story needs to be told separately from her husband's.

10. Ben Shahn Interview, conducted by Saul Benison, October 29, 1956, Oral History Collection, Columbia University, pp. 1–15. This collection is henceforth referred to as OHC.

11. In 1906 approximately 125,000 Russian Jews emigrated to the United States. See Moses Rischin, *The Promised City: New York's Jews, 1870–1914*, p. 270.

12. Soby, *Ben Shahn*, p. 16.

1. The Battle Lines Are Drawn

1. Walter Abell, "Art and Labor," *Magazine of Art* 39(October 1946):262.

2. Rodman, *Portrait of the Artist*, p. 55.

3. Quoted in Kenneth Prescott, *The Complete Graphic Works of Ben Shahn*, p. 97. In 1982 one of these rejected posters finally appeared on the cover of a Steelworkers publication.

4. Norman D. Markowitz, *The Rise and Fall of the People's Century: Henry A. Wallace and American Liberalism, 1941–1948*, p. 97.

5. Maurice Isserman, *Which Side Were You On? The American Communist Party during the Second World War*, p. 209. See also Joseph R. Starobin, *American Communism in Crisis, 1943–1957*.

6. Rodman, *Portrait of the Artist*, p. 56. For more on the anti-semitic attacks leveled at Hillman see Joseph Gaer, *The First Round: The Story of the CIO Political Action Committee*, pp. 169–171.

7. Quoted in Gaer, *The First Round*, p. 60.

8. Ibid., p. 65.

9. Prescott, *Complete Graphic Works*, p. 123.

10. Rodman, *Portrait of the Artist*, pp. 63–64. See Santa Fe East Gallery, *Ben Shahn: Voices and Visions*, Fig. 31, for an illustration of another OWI poster design that was never published. It contains two women viewed from behind, one pulling on a rope, the other on chains, with a Nazi soldier in the distance. The caption reads: "Ask the Farmers of Poland and Denmark, of Czechoslovakia and France, driven to labor by the lash, looted of their livestock, starving while their own crops are stolen from the land whether 'parity' prices are too great a 'sacrifice.'"

11. Rodman, *Portrait of the Artist*, p. 66.

12. Ibid., p. 64.

13. According to Gaer, 20,250 posters were printed (*The First Round*, p. 308). Shahn always signed his posters so that those who saw them would know who the artist was. See also Ben Shahn Interview, conducted by Saul Benison, January 5, 1957, OHC, p. 87, and Abell, "Art and Labor," p. 231. A photo of Shahn's welders poster in a union hall can be found in Abell, "Art and Labor," p. 243.

14. "New Deal Defeatism," *Daily Mirror* (New York), October 16, 1944, p. 17. Earl Browder was the head of the American Communist Party (CPUSA).

15. For a reproduction of the photo on which Shahn based his rendition of the white welder, see Rodman, *Portrait of the Artist*, p. 65.

16. Quoted in Gaer, *The First Round*, p. 71.

17. National Archives, Washington, D.C., Still Pictures Branch, Office of Inter-American Affairs, No. 229-PG-7-5.

18. Quoted in Abell, "Art and Labor," p. 236.

19. Gaer, *The First Round*, pp. 213–221. According to Markowitz, the CIO created NCPAC in order to counter conservative attempts to use the Smith-Connally Act to limit the activities of the CIO-PAC (*Rise and Fall*, p. 127).

20. Gaer, *The First Round*, p. 309. For a photo of the billboard, see Abell, "Art and Labor," p. 235.

21. Prescott, *Complete Graphic Works*, p. 128.

22. Abell, "Art and Labor," p. 256.

23. For example, Shahn sold two paintings in 1945 for $450: *Cherubs and Children* (1944) to the Whitney Museum and *The Red Stairway* (1944) to the St. Louis City Art Museum. One-third of this $900 would have gone to his representative, the Downtown Gallery (BSP, Microfilm Roll D148:687; Edith Halpert, Downtown Gallery, to Mr. Nagel, St. Louis City Art Museum, March 10, 1945, Archives, Saint Louis Art Museum).

24. Abell, "Art and Labor," p. 256.

25. Ibid., p. 260.

26. Daniel Bell, "Interest and Ideology: On the Role of Public Opinion in Industrial Disputes," in his *The End of Ideology: On the Exhaustion of Political Ideas in the Fifties*, p. 202. This essay was originally published in 1954.

27. Markowitz, *Rise and Fall*, pp. 148–150.

28. The Republican Party also contained representatives, like Senator Robert A. Taft, who fought against much of the extreme anti-labor legislation that was introduced by more reactionary party members. See Philip Taft, *Organized Labor in American History*, pp. 579–590, on Senator Taft's efforts to temper the more anti-labor House legislation, and the resulting Taft-Hartley Act of 1947.

29. Alexander Smith to Ben Shahn, June 7, 1946, BSP, Microfilm Roll D147.

30. Markowitz, *Rise and Fall*, p. 153.

31. Quoted in Rodman, *Portrait of the Artist*, p. 73.

32. According to James Grunbaum, two of these CIO officials were David Macdonald and Tillford Dudley (ibid., p. 55).

33. These studies can be found in the Ben Shahn Estate, New York City.

34. For an analysis of Wallace's speech, see Markowitz, *Rise and Fall*, pp. 48–50. A copy of the speech can be found in Russell Lord, ed., *Democracy Reborn*, pp. 191–196. Henry Luce, "The American Century," *Life*, February 17, 1941, pp. 61–63. See also Marty Jezer, *The Dark Ages, Life in the United States, 1945–1960*, pp. 21–22.

35. Eric Sevareid Papers, Box 21, Library of Congress, quoted in Markowitz, *Rise and Fall*, p. 52.

36. See BSP, Microfilm Roll D148:300–336. The drawings for the eight panels were executed by Bernarda Bryson, Shahn's wife.

37. See Kennedy Galleries, 1969, Figure 31.

38. There was a pirated edition of this print that was given the unauthorized title *Les Affaires* (Prescott, *Complete Graphic Works*, p. 10).

39. Jezer, *Dark Ages*, pp. 210–213. See also Taft, *Organized Labor*, pp. 498–503, 584–585. Starobin, *American Communism*, Ch. 5.

40. Robert T. Elson, *Time Inc.: The Intimate History of a Publishing Enterprise, 1923–1941*, p. 130. For further discussion of Shahn's *Fortune* illustrations, see Frances K. Pohl, "Ben Shahn and *Fortune* Magazine: Representations of Labor in 1946," *Labor's Heritage* 1(January 1989):46–55.

41. Dwight Macdonald left *Fortune* in 1936 after an article in a series he was doing on U.S. Steel was rejected because it represented "an interpretative analysis of the whole subject—an editorial," rather than a statement of the facts. A year later Macdonald charged that Luce was the "great mouthpiece" of the ruling business class (ibid., p. 254).

42. Henry Luce, "Directive for the Editorial Development of *Fortune*," 1948, quoted in Robert T. Elson, *The World of Time Inc.: The Intimate History of a Publishing Enterprise, Volume Two, 1941–1960*, p. 199.

43. Rodman, *Portrait of the Artist*, p. 43.

44. Ben Shahn Interview, conducted by Saul Benison and Sandra Otto, March 1, 1957, OHC, p. 97.

45. See quotation from Shahn letter to Chrysler Corporation in Rodman, *Portrait of the Artist*, p. 41.

46. Shahn Interview, March 1, 1957, OHC, p. 97.

47. "Labor Drives South," *Fortune* 34(November 1946):134–141+.

48. Ibid., p. 139.

49. Shahn Interview, March 1, 1957, OHC, p. 99.

50. Ralph G. Martin, "The CIO Takes a Long Lease in the South," *New Republic* 116(January 13, 1947):19–21.

51. "Labor's Cause," *Fortune* 34(November 1946):2–4.

52. Jezer, *Dark Ages*, pp. 208–209.

53. "Labor's Cause," p. 4.

54. For information on Artists Equity Association, see BSP, Microfilm Roll D143. For a discussion of the American Artists' Congress, see Matthew

Baigell and Julia Williams, eds., *Artists against War and Fascism: Papers of the First American Artists' Congress.*

55. Edith Halpert of the Downtown Gallery, Shahn's gallery, was also concerned with artists' economic rights and argued for the payment of full reproduction rights and exhibition rental fees to artists. See letter from Edith Halpert to Ben Shahn, September 30, 1946, BSP, Microfilm Roll D144.

56. Alfred M. Frankfurter, "Vernissage," *Art News* 46(May 1947):13.

57. For a discussion of the causes and nature of this growth in the patronage of American art in the forties, see Guilbaut, *How New York Stole the Idea of Modern Art,* pp. 89–99.

58. Frankfurter, "Vernissage," p. 13.

59. For examples of the countries and individuals requesting the show, see Ralph M. Pearson, "A Modern Viewpoint: State Department Requests," *Art Digest* 22(October 1, 1947):32. For a complete history of the exhibition, see Montgomery Museum of Fine Arts, *Advancing American Art: Politics and Aesthetics in the State Department Exhibition, 1946–48.*

60. Virginia M. Mecklenburg, "Advancing American Art: A Controversy of Style," in Montgomery Museum, *Advancing American Art,* p. 40.

61. Illustrations of a selection of paintings in the show can be found in Alfred M. Frankfurter, "American Art Abroad: The State Department's Collection," *Art News* 45(October 1946):20–31; in "Your Money Bought These Paintings," *Look,* February 18, 1947, pp. 80–81; and in Montgomery Museum, *Advancing American Art.* Seventy-three watercolors were acquired, but thirty-eight were apparently never shown (Margaret Lynne Ausfeld, "Circus Girl Arrested: A History of the 'Advancing American Art' Collection, 1946–48," in Montgomery Museum, *Advancing American Art,* p. 27n.10).

62. Donald Drew Egbert, *Socialism and American Art: In the Light of European Utopianism, Marxism, and Anarchism,* pp. 125–126.

63. A draft of the Program for Political Action and of the PCA's bylaws can be found in the Elizabeth McCausland Papers, Archives of American Art, Smithsonian Institution, Washington, D.C., Microfilm Roll D383:151–161.

64. See Markowitz, *Rise and Fall,* pp. 216–226.

65. A transcript of the minutes of this meeting can be found in McCausland Papers, Microfilm Roll D383:168–169.

66. A.L., "Artists Protest," *Art Digest* 21(May 15, 1947):16. The meeting was also sponsored by the Audubon Society, the New York Society of Women Painters, Artists Equity, the Photo League, the Artists League of America, the Serigraph Society, and the Sculptors Guild.

67. *The State Department and Art,* n.p. A copy of this PCA pamphlet can be found in the Max Weber Papers, Archives of American Art, Smithsonian Institution, Washington, D.C., Microfilm Roll N69/112:295–301.

68. Ausfeld, "Circus Girl Arrested," p. 25.

69. *The State Department and Art,* n.p.

70. Harry S. Truman, quoted in Jane de Hart Mathews, "Art and Politics in Cold War America," *American Historical Review* 81(October 1976):777.

71. William Hauptman, "The Suppression of Art in the McCarthy Decade," *Artforum* 12(October 1973):49. For an example of the use of "vilifying captions," see "It's Striking, But Is It Art or Extravagance?" *Newsweek*, August 25, 1947. It is somewhat ironic that on July 24 Edith Halpert wrote to Shahn informing him that *Town and Country*, a Hearst publication, wanted to do an article on him (Edith Halpert to Ben Shahn, July 24, 1947, BSP, Microfilm Roll D144).

72. De Hart Mathews, "Art and Politics," pp. 780–787. Economic rivalry and status anxiety were also, as de Hart Mathews points out, major factors in the intense opposition of traditional artists to modern art (p. 782).

73. Secretary of State George C. Marshall, *New York Times*, May 6, 1947, quoted in de Hart Mathews, "Art and Politics," p. 778.

74. "Surplus Art Nets $23,000 to the U.S.," *New York Times*, June 25, 1948. While the prices paid for the paintings were low, this was because educational institutions, which bought many of the works, only had to pay ten cents on the dollar. The Hearst press made much of the low prices, ignoring the actual sums that were bid. The artists, on the other hand, made much of the sums bid and said little regarding the final prices paid (Jack Levine Interview, conducted by Louis Starr, November 29, 1956, OHC, pp. 123–124). See also Montgomery Museum, *Advancing American Art*, p. 89.

75. "Shahn Best of 375," *Art Digest* 15(November 15, 1940):8. For more information on the Treasury Department mural program, see Karal Ann Marling, *Wall to Wall America: A Cultural History of Post Office Murals in the Great Depression*, and Marlene Park and Gerald E. Markowitz, *Democratic Vistas: Post Offices and Public Art in the New Deal*.

76. Quoted in Ben Shahn to Edward B. Rowan, November 7, 1940, National Archives, Washington, D.C., Public Buildings Service, Record Group 121/133.

77. Ben Shahn to Edward Bruce, November 6, 1940, National Archives, Washington, D.C., Record Group 121/133.

78. Shahn to Rowan, November 7, 1940.

79. Rodman, *Portrait of the Artist*, p. 74.

80. John D. Morse, "Ben Shahn: An Interview," *Magazine of Art* 37 (April 1944):140–141.

81. Ibid., p. 141.

82. "FSA Ignored in Plea for Removal of Social Security Building Art," *Evening Star* (Washington), June 27, 1947, Sec. I., p. 1.

83. George G. Thorp to Hudson Walker, June 26, 1947, James Thrall Soby Papers, Museum of Modern Art (New York), I.36.13. See also George G. Thorp to Hudson Walker, June 27, 1947, Soby Papers, I.36.13.

84. Alfred H. Barr, Jr., to Francis P. Douglas, *Evening Star*, July 3, 1947, BSP, Microfilm Roll D147:1443. Barr sent a copy of this letter to Shahn.

85. Alan Reitman to Ben Shahn, June 27, 1947, BSP, Microfilm Roll D147:407.

86. James Thrall Soby to Ben Shahn, July 2, 1947, BSP, Microfilm Roll D147:441.

87. Hudson Walker to Ben Shahn, July 24, 1947, BSP, Microfilm Roll D143.

88. Shahn's Social Security Building murals suffered some damage in the sixties during the anti-Vietnam-War demonstrations in Washington. According to Bernarda Bryson Shahn, police had lined up in front of the murals to protect them and were subsequently the targets of stones and bottles, some of which struck the paintings (interview by author, June 2, 1984).

89. Edward Biberman, "The Attack on the American Artist," Edward Biberman Papers, Archives of American Art, Smithsonian Institution, Washington, D.C., Microfilm Roll 106:141–150. Shahn received a personal invitation from Mildred Constantine, a member of the PCA's Art Division, to attend the New York meeting on October 26 at the Barbizon Hotel (Mildred Constantine to Ben Shahn, October 16, 1947, BSP, Microfilm Roll D144).

90. A list of members of the executive committee of the Art Division as well as members active in the initial stages of its organization can be found in the minutes of the Art Division's first executive meeting, January 22, 1947. See McCausland Papers, Microfilm Roll D383:168–169.

91. James Soby to Ben Shahn, January 10, 1948, BSP, Microfilm Roll D147:1436; Alfred Barr, Jr., to Ben Shahn, December 29, 1947, BSP, Microfilm Roll D146:789.

92. For a discussion of the Hollywood Trials, which began in October 1947, see Victor Navasky, *Naming Names.* See also "Leaders in Arts, Sciences Hit Pix Purge," *Daily Worker,* December 1, 1947, p. 3.

93. Interview, Bryson Shahn, June 2, 1984.

94. Typescript of minutes of meeting, BSP, Microfilm Roll D146: 665–667.

95. The term Mugwump was first used in 1884 to describe a group of Republicans who refused to accept the Party's presidential nominee and chose a candidate of their own. See "Mugwump," in *Safire's Political Dictionary* (New York: Random House, 1978 [1st ed., 1968]), pp. 436–437.

96. Prospectus for *Mugwumps,* BSP, Microfilm Roll D146:670.

97. Bryson Shahn could not recall exactly why *Mugwumps* was never published, but Pawley may well have objected to the projected content of the magazine.

98. Dorothy Miller, interview by author, June 5, 1984. The exhibition included fifty-four paintings plus a number of drawings, posters, photographs, and book illustrations. In a letter from Soby to Shahn, dated April 17, 1946, Soby commented on his pleasure at being chosen director of the show (BSP, Microfilm Roll D147:1423). Soby's admiration for Shahn was reflected in the fact that he owned three Shahn paintings at this time: *Liberation* (1945), *Fourth of July Orator* (1943), and *Father and Child* (1946).

99. Russell Lynes, *Good Old Modern: An Intimate Portrait of the Museum of Modern Art,* pp. 70–71.

100. According to Shahn, while the offer was made in the name of Abigail Rockefeller, he believed that she would not knowingly have taken part in such an incident (Ben Shahn, list of suggestions for changes in the manuscript of Selden Rodman's biography, BSP, Microfilm Roll D145). The Sacco and Vanzetti case is discussed further in Chapter 3.

101. Rodman, *Portrait of the Artist*, p. 109. *The Passion of Sacco and Vanzetti* was included in an exhibit of large-scale paintings at MOMA in March 1947, this time without the scandal surrounding the earlier exhibit. The sales price of the painting was listed at $2,500 (BSP, Microfilm Roll D146:766). Shahn finally executed his Sacco and Vanzetti mural in 1967 at Syracuse University, Syracuse, N.Y.

102. For example, in 1938 Shahn's gouache *Six Witnesses Who Bought Eels from Vanzetti* was included in what Conger Goodyear called "the first extensive presentation of the work of American artists ever made in Europe" (letter from Conger Goodyear to Ben Shahn, October 20, 1938, BSP Microfilm Roll D146:726). *Well Known Faces of Politicians* appeared in the museum's "The Artist as Reporter" exhibit in 1940, and *Portrait of Governor Rolph of California* was included in "Twentieth-Century Portraiture," circulated in 1942 and 1943 (Elodie Courter to Ben Shahn, May 10, 1940, BSP, Microfilm Roll D146:728, and Insurance Invoice, MOMA, September 20, 1942, BSP, Microfilm Roll D146:729). Both shows traveled throughout the United States. Four of Shahn's drawings from his Mooney series also appeared in an exhibit of modern drawings at the museum scheduled to take place from February 15 to April 16, 1944. The popularity of the show caused the museum to extend it to May 10 (Loan Receipt, MOMA, January 10, 1944, BSP, Microfilm Roll D146:741).

103. Dorothy C. Miller, "Foreword and Acknowledgement," in Dorothy C. Miller and Alfred H. Barr, Jr., eds., *American Realists and Magic Realists*, p. 5. A reduced version of the show toured the United States after its closing in New York on March 21 (Elodie Courter, MOMA, to Ben Shahn, March 6, 1943, BSP, Microfilm Roll D146:733).

104. Miller, "Foreword and Acknowledgement," p. 6.

105. Quoted in John Charles Carlisle, "A Biographical Study of How the Artist Became a Humanitarian Activist: Ben Shahn, 1938–1946" (Ph.D. dissertation, University of Michigan, 1972), p. 49.

106. Abigail Rockefeller had befriended Shahn in 1930, inviting him to the Rockefeller estate in Cantico to paint her favorite horse, paying him $250 for each canvas (Lynes, *Good Old Modern*, p. 345).

107. A rough draft of Rivera's letter to Rockefeller in Shahn's handwriting is included in the Ben Shahn Papers, Microfilm Roll D147. In a letter to Monroe Wheeler dated October 14, 1947, Nelson Rockefeller claimed that the head of Lenin was a minor factor in the removal of the mural (Soby Papers, Folder 11).

108. James Thrall Soby, Typescript of lecture at the Philadelphia Museum of Art, November 6 and 7, 1961, p. 6 (Soby Papers, Folder 2).

109. Betty Chamberlain, "Ben Shahn," *Art News* 46(October 1947):54.

110. Ibid., p. 56.

111. Ibid.

112. Ibid., p. 55.

113. Bernarda Bryson Shahn, *Ben Shahn*, p. 112.

114. "*Spring* by Ben Shahn," *Gallery Notes* (Buffalo) 12(Spring 1948):26.

115. Ben Shahn, "Biography of a Painting," in his *The Shape of Content*, pp. 45, 47.

116. Robert M. Coates, "The Art Galleries: Contemporary Americans," *New Yorker*, October 11, 1947, pp. 62–63.

117. Ibid.

118. Ralph Pearson, "A Modern Viewpoint: Ben Shahn at the Modern," *Art Digest* 22(December 1, 1947):36.

119. For a complete statement of Pearson's artistic philosophy and examples of the artists he supported see Ralph Pearson, *Modern Renaissance in American Art*.

120. Ann Leonard, "Around the Galleries: Ben Shahn, a People's Artist," *People's World*, December 1, 1948.

121. Maltz's article appeared in the February 12, 1946, issue of the *New Masses*. For a discussion of the Maltz case, see Starobin, *American Communism*, pp. 136–137.

122. Starobin, *American Communism*, pp. 137–138.

123. For an account of Greenberg's "Trotskyist" past, see Guilbaut, *How New York Stole the Idea of Modern Art*, Ch. 1.

124. Clement Greenberg, "Art," *Nation*, November 1, 1947, p. 481.

125. Coates, "The Art Galleries," p. 62.

126. Greenberg, "Art," p. 481.

127. Margaret R. Weiss, ed., *Ben Shahn, Photographer: An Album from the Thirties*, n.p.

128. Morse, "Ben Shahn: An Interview," p. 139.

129. Charles Hagen, "Things Which Should Be Photographed as an American Background," introduction to *American Photographers of the Depression: Farm Security Administration Photographs, 1935–1942*, n.p. See also William Stott, *Documentary Expression and Thirties America*.

130. Allan Sekula, "Dismantling Modernism, Reinventing Documentary (Notes on the Politics of Representation)," in his *Photography against the Grain: Essays and Photo Works, 1973–1983*, p. 67.

131. Shahn, "Biography of a Painting," p. 40.

132. Rodman, *Portrait of the Artist*, pp. 100–101.

133. "Photos for Art," *U.S. Camera*, May 1946, pp. 30–32, 57.

134. James Thrall Soby to Ben Shahn, September 18, 1947, BSP, Microfilm Roll D147:1450.

135. James Thrall Soby to Ben Shahn, December 16, 1946, BSP, Microfilm Roll D147:1433.

136. Soby, *Ben Shahn*, pp. 12–13.

137. This was not the first time Shahn had expressed his opinions on photography. In 1944 he took part in a panel at the MOMA symposium "Photography and the Other Arts" on April 19 along with Paul Strand, Charles Scheeler, and Hyatt Mayor (Willard D. Morgan, MOMA to Ben Shahn, April 14, 1944, BSP, Microfilm Roll D146:752). Shahn's attitude toward photography and its use was undoubtedly influenced by Walker Evans, whom he met in 1925 and with whom he shared a studio in New York City on Bethune Street in 1929.

138. Greenberg, "Art," pp. 481–482.

139. Clement Greenberg, "The Present Prospects of American Painting and Sculpture," *Horizon* 16(October 1947):20–30.

140. Clement Greenberg, "Avant-Garde and Kitsch," *Partisan Review* 6, no. 5 (1939):34–49.

141. For an analysis of the de-Marxization and depoliticization of the artists and critics who formed the abstract expressionist avant-garde see Guilbaut, *How New York Stole the Idea of Modern Art*, Ch. 1.

142. Robert Motherwell, "The Modern Painter's World," *Dyn*, vol. 6 (1944), excerpts in Barbara Rose, *Readings in American Art since 1900*, pp. 134–135.

143. Motherwell and Rosenberg, in *Possibilities* 1(Winter 1947–1948):1.

144. Greenberg, "Present Prospects," p. 28.

145. Clement Greenberg, "Art," *Nation*, March 8, 1947, p. 284.

146. James Thrall Soby, "Ben Shahn and Morris Graves," *Horizon* 16(October 1947):50. The whole of the October issue of *Horizon* was devoted to American culture. Greenberg's article appeared in the first section of the magazine, entitled "The Problem Defined," while Soby's appeared in the second section, entitled "Intimations of Yes."

147. Ibid., p. 57.

2. Wallace, Dondero, and Roosevelt, New Jersey

1. For information on the artists' colony at Woodstock see Vassar College Art Gallery, *Woodstock: An American Art Colony, 1902–1977*, introduction by Karal Ann Marling.

2. Yasuo Kuniyoshi, "What about the Artist?" p. 9, Harold Clurman, "Artist and Public," p. 4, and Mitchell Siporin, "Summation," p. 37, in *The First Woodstock Art Conference* (AEA, August 1947), pamphlet, in BSP, Unmicrofilmed Papers.

3. Clement Greenberg, "The Situation at the Moment," *Partisan Review* 5(January 1948):82.

4. For example, he spoke at a symposium on *Guernica* at MOMA on November 25, 1947, with Stuart Davis, Juan Larrea, Jacques Lipchitz, Jerome Seckler, José Luis Sert, and Alfred H. Barr, Jr., as chair (see Monroe Wheeler to Ben Shahn, November 20, 1947, BSP, Microfilm Roll D146:787). He was also asked to be guest professor of art for the academic year 1946–1947 at the University of Texas, Austin (BSP, Microfilm D148).

5. Markowitz, *Rise and Fall*, p. 274. Shahn also received at least one invitation to speak at a Wallace-related gathering. On April 27 Judith Mogil of Students for Wallace at Smith College, Northampton, requested that Shahn make a presentation at their "convention," which would be part of a mock election they were holding. She noted that it would be appropriate for Shahn to speak on this occasion, as his exhibition from MOMA would be at their gallery through the end of May. Paul Sweezey had also been invited to speak (BSP, Microfilm Roll D147:1369).

6. Mario Casetta, interview with author, July 25, 1986. Casetta was head of the PCA's folk songs for political action program.

7. Helen Fuller, "Dewey's Brisk Young Men Move In," *New Republic*, July 5, 1948, pp. 15–18. Shahn's caricature is on page 17.

8. An illustration of this watercolor can be found in the catalogue of the 1967 Shahn exhibition at the Santa Barbara Museum of Art. Nelson Rockefeller later presented this watercolor as a gift to Truman (Prescott, *Complete Graphic Works*, p. 133).

9. "Truman and Dewey Lampooned," *Minneapolis Star*, July 17, 1948, p. 2.

10. See "Wallace Party Heads Gathering for Meet," *St. Paul Sunday Pioneer Press*, July 18, 1948, p. 17.

11. Henry A. Wallace, "The Progressive Party Is Here to Stay," *Uncensored*, no. 3(September 1948):1–2. The Shakespeare quote also appeared on the back of a postcard version of the painting.

12. See Markowitz, *Rise and Fall*, Ch. 8, pp. 266–303.

13. Carlisle, "A Biographical Study," p. 187. According to Marty Jezer, the CPUSA did not consciously take over the Wallace campaign, but its members were simply among the most committed of Wallace's campaign workers (*Dark Ages*, p. 86).

14. Markowitz, *Rise and Fall*, p. 271. Shahn would elaborate on this position in a 1953 talk entitled "The Artist and the Politician" (discussed in Chapter 3).

15. Henry Wallace, quoted in "We Are for Wallace," *New York Times*, October 20, 1948, p. 32. Shahn was, at this time, co-chair of the Art Division of the New York State Council of the Arts, Sciences and Professions. He was honored as such at a cocktail party on December 16, 1948, where he spoke about his experiences as an artist in the Wallace campaign. A copy of the invitation to this party can be found in the Soby Papers, I.36.14.

16. Ben Shahn, "Responsibility for Standards of Taste in a Democratic Society," Conference of the Committee of Art Education, MOMA, April 24, 1948, typescript in BSP, Unmicrofilmed Papers, p. 2.

17. Markowitz, *Rise and Fall*, p. 277. After the defeat of the Progressive Party in November, the purge of Wallace supporters within the CIO "became a torrent" (ibid., p. 281).

18. Bernarda Bryson, "The Drawings of Ben Shahn," *Image*, no. 2(Autumn 1949):33.

19. See "The Promise of the Shortage," *Fortune* 33(April 1946): 101–103, and George P. Hunt, "Honorable Discharge," *Fortune* 34(September 1947): 69–77+. Shahn also designed the cover of a publicity pamphlet for a radio documentary on juvenile delinquency entitled "The Eagle's Brood" for CBS, as well as a promotional brochure for a program on the problems of the elderly entitled "Fear Begins at Forty." William Golden, the art director for CBS, had been a colleague of Shahn's during the OWI days. See Cipe Pineles Golden, Kurt Weihs, and Robert Strunsky, eds., *The Visual Craft of William Golden*, p. 4, and Shahn's essay on Golden in the same book, "Bill," pp. 126–127. Shahn would also receive many commissions from Cipe Pineles Golden, who became art editor for *Charm* and *Seventeen* magazines in the fifties.

20. John Bartlow Martin, "The Hickman Story," *Harper's* 197(August 1948): 39–52. In a lecture entitled "Biography of a Painting" at Harvard University in 1956, Shahn described in detail the manner in which he approached the *Harper's* commission. The lecture was subsequently published in booklet form by the Fogg Art Museum, Harvard, in December 1956. The complete series of Shahn's talks at Harvard, presented during his tenure as Charles Eliot Norton Professor of Poetry, was published the following year by Harvard University Press under the title *The Shape of Content*. In 1966 Paragraphic Press of New York came out with another version of *Biography of a Painting*, this time in Shahn's own handwriting rather than in type and extensively illustrated by him.

21. Shahn, "Biography of a Painting," in *Shape of Content*, p. 28.

22. For a discussion of the Hickman article and the issue of historical representation in Shahn's work see O. K. Werckmeister, "Ben Shahn's Political Realism," *New Rundschau* 77, no. 3(1966): 476–487.

23. Shahn, "Biography of a Painting," p. 32. Shahn used this same wreath of flames in his illustrations for the article "Guilt by Gossip" by Daniel S. Gillmor, on the threats to individual civil liberties embodied in the current security mania (*New Republic*, May 31, 1948, p. 27). The flames surround a branding iron on which is printed "subversive."

24. John Bartlow Martin, "The Blast in Centralia No. 5," *Harper's* 196 (March 1948): 193–220. For a discussion of Shahn's illustrations for this article, see Carolyn C. Robbins, "Ben Shahn's *Mine Building*: A Symbol of Disaster," forthcoming in *Phoebus V: A Journal of Art History*.

25. Shahn produced almost a hundred drawings for Russell Lynes, editor of *Harper's*, to choose from (Russell Lynes, "Ben Shahn, Compassionate Draftsman," in his *Confessions of a Dilettante*, pp. 110–116). Shahn received $200 for his illustrations (Russell Lynes to Ben Shahn, December 31, 1947, BSP, Unmicrofilmed Papers).

26. Alfred Frankfurter, "The Year's Best: 1947," *Art News* 46(January 1948): 36–37.

27. See "A *Life* Round Table on Modern Art," *Life*, October 11, 1948, pp. 56–68+. See also "Biddle on Modern Art," *American Artist* 12(January 1948): 47; "Boston Goes from 'Modern' to 'Contemporary,'" *College Art Jour-*

nal 7(Spring 1948):230; Lincoln Kirstein, "The State of Modern Painting," *Harper's* 197(October 1948):47–53; René D'Harnoncourt, "Challenge and Promise: Modern Art and Modern Society," *Magazine of Art* 41(November 1948):251–252.

28. "Are These Men the Best Painters in America Today?" *Look*, February 3, 1948, pp. 44–48.

29. Ibid., p. 44.

30. Arthur M. Schlesinger, "Not Left, Not Right, but a Vital Center," *New York Times Magazine*, April 4, 1948, pp. 7, 44–47.

31. Rodman, *Portrait of the Artist*, p. 39.

32. Henry McBride, "The Whitney Museum Show—Has One Picture the Dean of Canterbury Would Just Love," *New York Sun*, 1948; copy in Ben Shahn File, Museum of Modern Art, New York. The Dean of Canterbury, the Very Reverend Dr. Hewlett Johnson, was well known for his support of progressive causes. For example, he attended the All-Union Peace Conference held in Moscow, August 25–27, 1949.

33. See David Caute, *The Great Fear: The Anti-Communist Purge under Truman and Eisenhower*, pp. 58–62.

34. "Gallery on Wheels," *Art Digest* 23(January 15, 1949):16.

35. George Dondero, "Communist Art in Government Hospitals," U.S. *Congressional Record*, 81st Cong., 1st Sess., March 11, 1949, pp. 2317–2318. It is interesting that five of the artists named—Shahn, Kuniyoshi, Levine, Osver, and Weber—appeared in either or both of the ten-best lists published by *Art News* and *Life*. Shahn claimed he was never a member of the John Reed Club (Shahn, list of comments on Rodman's transcript for *Portrait of the Artist*, BSP, Microfilm Roll D145).

36. George Dondero, "Communists Maneuver to Control Art in the United States," U.S. *Congressional Record*, 81st Cong., 1st Sess., March 25, 1949, pp. 3233–3235; George Dondero, "Communism in the Heart of American Art—What to Do About It," ibid., May 17, 1949, pp. 6372–6375.

37. Dondero, "Communism in the Heart," p. 6375.

38. George Dondero, "Modern Art Shackled to Communism," U.S. *Congressional Record*, 81st Cong., 1st Sess., August 16, 1948, pp. 11584–11587.

39. Ibid., p. 11584.

40. Ibid. Another "ism" that was attacked as communistic in the late forties and early fifties was feminism (Jezer, *Dark Ages*, pp. 226–231).

41. Dondero, "Modern Art Shackled to Communism," p. 11585.

42. Ibid., p. 11586.

43. Greenberg, "Art Chronicle: Our Period Style," *Partisan Review* 15(November 1949):1138.

44. Dondero, "Modern Art Shackled to Communism," p. 11585.

45. Charles A. Plumley, "Extension of Remarks of Hon. Charles A. Plumley of Vermont," U.S. *Congressional Record—Appendix*, 81st Cong., 1st Sess., pp. A3980–A3982.

46. James Thrall Soby, "A Going in the Mulberry Trees," *Saturday Review*, July 2, 1949, pp. 30–31.

47. Alfred M. Frankfurter, "Vernissage: Abstract Red Herring," *Art News* 48(Summer 1949):15.

48. Soby, "A Going in the Mulberry Trees," p. 31. For additional responses to Dondero, see Representative Eugene J. McCarthy, "Modern Art," U.S. *Congressional Record*, 81st Cong., 1st Sess., August 18, 1949, p. 11750; Representative Jacob K. Javits, "Modern Art—A Reply to a Colleague," ibid., August 23, 1949, p. 12099.

49. Emily Genauer, "Still Life with Red Herring," *Harper's* 199(September 1949):88–91.

50. Ibid., p. 89.

51. Ibid., p. 91.

52. George A. Dondero, "Is Harper's Magazine Biased?" U.S. *Congressional Record—Appendix*, 81st Cong., 1st Sess., October 13, 1949, pp. A6305–A6306. Dondero submitted to Congress the letter he wrote to *Harper's* protesting Genauer's article.

53. Ibid., p. A6305.

54. Ibid. See "Paintings for Paraplegics," *Look*, April 12, 1949, p. 52.

55. Dondero, "Is Harper's Magazine Biased?" p. A6305.

56. Henry Kissinger again used the phrase when he noted, on September 23, 1984, that "we may be witnessing the preliminaries of a Soviet peace offensive" ("Soviet Signals Are Changing," *Los Angeles Times*, September 23, 1984, Sec. IV, p. 1).

57. Patricia Hills suggests that the headline is the sort one would find in the *Daily Worker* at this time ("Social Realists of the 1930s," typescript of talk at Northwestern University Conference on "The Political Confrontation of the Arts on the Eve of World War II," May 2–3, 1985, p. 22).

58. Caute, *The Great Fear*, pp. 176–177.

59. Ibid.

60. Egbert, *Socialism and American Art*, p. 127.

61. Ibid., p. 126.

62. Joyce and Gabriel Kolko, *The Limits of Power: The World and United States Foreign Policy, 1945–1954*, p. 502. The blockade had, in fact, been prompted by the introduction of the new West German currency into West Berlin. This action was viewed by the Soviet Union as part of an attempt to take over the eastern half of Germany (Jezer, *Dark Ages*, p. 50).

63. Kolko and Kolko, *Limits of Power*, p. 502.

64. For an account of the tactics used by the United States to prevent a communist victory in Italy, see William S. Caldwell, "The Organization and Operation of American Information and Propaganda Activities in Early Postwar Italy" (Ph.D. dissertation, University of Minnesota, 1960).

65. Egbert, *Socialism and American Art*, p. 126. Many of the foreign delegates, such as Siqueiros from Mexico, were unable to attend because the

State Department refused to issue them visas on the grounds that they were active members of a communist party.

66. See "All-American Parley on Peace Called Sept. 5," *Daily Worker*, July 29, 1949, p. 5.

67. Paul J. Kern to Ben Shahn, June 17, 1949, BSP, Microfilm Roll D145. The Civil Rights Congress (CRC) was sponsored by such individuals as Paul Robeson, Vito Marcantonio, Lee Pressman, and the Reverend Harry F. Ward. It was administered on a day-to-day basis by two Communist Party members, William L. Patterson and Aubrey Grossman. The millionaire Frederick V. Field, Dashiell Hammett, and W. Alphaeus Hunton were three of the major trustees of the CRC's bail fund (Caute, *Great Fear*, pp. 178–179). Shahn also received an invitation from Moses Soyer to attend a meeting to form a committee of important artists for the defense of artists' rights (Moses Soyer to Ben Shahn, c. November 1949, BSP, Microfilm Roll D147:1572).

68. Bernard De Voto, "Due Notice to the FBI," *Harper's*, Vol. 199 (October 1949), quoted in Jezer, *Dark Ages*, p. 84.

69. Ben Shahn, "Some Questions," from a symposium at Smith College, Northampton, Massachusetts, 1949, reprinted in John D. Morse, ed., *Ben Shahn*, p. 203.

70. Ibid., pp. 204–205.

71. Ben Shahn, "Ben Shahn," *Magazine of Art* 42(November 1949):266, 269. The theme of the conference was "Focus on World Unity."

72. Balcomb Greene, "Balcomb Greene," *Magazine of Art* 42(November 1949):268. Motherwell did not provide his talk for publication in the *Magazine of Art* issue that published Shahn's and Greene's talks.

73. Thomas B. Hess, "Ben Shahn Paints a Picture," *Art News* 48(May 1949):20–22, 55–56.

74. For more on the history of Roosevelt, N.J., see Edwin Rosskam, *Roosevelt, New Jersey: Big Dreams in a Small Town and What Time Did to Them.*

75. Inter-Office Communication—Adrian J. Dornbush, Director, Special Skills Division, to Grace E. Falke, Executive Assistant, RA, September 1, 1936, p. 1, in National Archives, Washington, D.C., Farm Security Administration Administrator Correspondence, 1935–1938, Record Group 96, AD 986, Entry 1 (henceforward referred to as FSA, RG 96).

76. Katharine A. Kellock to Adrian J. Dornbush, Director, Special Skills Division, October 3, 1935, in FSA, RG 96, AD 994. For a critical examination of the Federal Art Project murals see Jonathan Harris, "State Power and Cultural Discourse: Federal Art Project Murals in New Deal USA," *Block* 13(Winter 1987/1988):28–42. See also Marlene Park and Gerald E. Markowitz, *Democratic Vistas: Post Offices and Public Art in the New Deal.*

77. Inter-Office Communications—Adrian J. Dornbush to Grace E. Falke, April 22, 1936, p. 4, and June 5, 1936, p. 3, in FSA, RG 96, AD 986, Entry 1. For a more complete discussion of Shahn's Roosevelt, N.J., mural, see Fran-

ces Pohl, "Constructing History: A Mural by Ben Shahn," *Arts Magazine* 62(September 1987):36–40.

78. Rosskam, *Roosevelt, New Jersey*, pp. 34–36.

79. Ben Shahn, in Huw Weldon and Humphrey Burton, *Ben Shahn's America*, Monitor Film, British Broadcasting Corporation, 1962.

80. This friendship was noted in "Jews' Struggle Shown in Mural at Homesteads," *New York Herald Tribune*, May 22, 1938, Sec. II, p. 3. Einstein had, in fact, visited David Dubinsky, head of the ILGWU, in an unsuccessful attempt to convince him to support the establishment of the new town. Dubinsky believed that such a community would lead to a runaway shop and ultimately weaken the union (Shahn, in Weldon and Burton, *Ben Shahn's America*).

81. In a photograph of Shahn working on the cartoon for the mural, Einstein is not present, though Sacco and Vanzetti are (see Joe and Emily Lowe Art Gallery, College of Visual and Performing Arts, Syracuse University, *The Mural Art of Ben Shahn*, Fig. 1).

82. Morse, "Ben Shahn: An Interview," p. 140.

83. Rosskam, *Roosevelt, New Jersey*, pp. 61–78, and Rodman, *Portrait of the Artist*, p. 45. Rodman also notes that the co-operative factory site was taken over by the Roosevelt Coat and Suit Company.

84. Hess, "Ben Shahn Paints a Picture," p. 22.

85. Rosskam, *Roosevelt, New Jersey*, p. 74.

86. E. W. Leaver and J. J. Brown, "Machines without Men," *Fortune* 34(November 1946):165. Mechanization decreased the number of workers in manufacturing and industry by 1.5 million between 1948 and 1961, with an increase of approximately the same size during the same period in white-collar jobs (Jezer, *Dark Ages*, p. 215).

87. Quoted in Rosskam, *Roosevelt, New Jersey*, p. 17.

88. Benjamin Appel, "Ben Shahn, Prophet with a Brush," *New Letters* 40(March 1974):6.

89. Rodman, *Portrait of the Artist*, p. 87.

90. Irving Howe, *World of Our Fathers*, pp. 287–343.

91. Ibid., p. 349.

92. Rosskam, *Roosevelt, New Jersey*, Chs. 1–4.

93. Ibid., p. 37.

94. "Veblen College: A Cooperative School to Deal with Problems of Social Change," typescript, n.p., BSP, Unmicrofilmed Papers.

95. Ibid.

96. Rosskam, *Roosevelt, New Jersey*, p. 37.

97. Ibid., p. 76.

98. Quoted in ibid., pp. 77, 78.

99. For information regarding a panel Shahn was doing for the Progressive Party, see Ralph E. Shikes, Public Relations Director, Progressive Party, to Ben Shahn, January 28, 1949 (BSP, Microfilm Roll D147:1262). Rita Newton of Smith College wrote to Shahn on February 28, 1949, regarding

final arrangements for his trip to Northampton for a Student Progressives' event organized to raise money to protest the dismissal of a number of professors in Washington in connection with their work in the field of academic freedom (BSP, Microfilm Roll D147:1367–1368).

100. Rodman, *Portrait of the Artist*, p. 47.

101. Interview, Casetta, July 25, 1986. See also Robbie Lieberman, "People's Songs: American Communism and the Politics of Culture," *Radical History Review*, no. 36(September 1986):63–78.

102. Caute, *The Great Fear*, pp. 164–165, 532–533.

103. Charles Corwin, "Ben Shahn's Rewarding Exhibit at Downtown Gallery," *Daily Worker*, November 4, 1949, p. 12.

104. Ibid.

105. Thomas Hess, "Reviews and Previews: Ben Shahn," *Art News* 48(November 1949):44.

106. "Jackson Pollock," *Life*, August 8, 1949, p. 45.

107. Ibid.

108. Hess, "Ben Shahn Paints a Picture," p. 56.

3. Defending Civil Liberties at Home and the American Image Abroad

1. Emily Genauer, "Shahn's Bitterness Leavened with Wit," *Art Digest* 24(November 1, 1949):12.

2. Shahn received the Art Directors' Club Medal for an illustration for the article "Little Red Jungle" in *Seventeen* magazine and the Art Directors' Award of Distinctive Merit for the drawing for CBS, "The Empty Studio."

3. These exhibitions included: "Juliana Force and American Art" and "The Annual Exhibition of Contemporary American Painting" at the Whitney; "Fifty Years of American Painting" and "American Painting Today" at the Metropolitan; "Recent Acquisitions Exhibition" at MOMA; and "The International Exhibition of Oil Paintings" at the Carnegie Institute.

4. Rodman, *Portrait of the Artist*, p. 119.

5. Alfred Frankfurter, "Vernissage—The Year's Best: 1949," *Art News* 48(January 1950):13, 50. The other four artists were Peter Blume, Balthazar Balthus, Jean Arp, and Lee Gatch.

6. "Ben Shahn," *Look*, July 18, 1950, p. 68.

7. Shahn had appeared on the program "Critic-at-Large" on February 23 to discuss the topic "Does the Camera Lie?" with Edward Steichen and John Mason Brown (BSP, Microfilm Roll D143). Some of the educational institutions at which Shahn spoke in 1950 were Vassar College, Jamesine Franklin School of Professional Arts in New York City, John Herron Art Institute in Indianapolis, and the University of Iowa.

8. Bud Stillman to Ben Shahn, March 11, 1950, BSP, Microfilm Roll D147:1722. Stillman writes movingly of the sense of helplessness that must have overcome so many individuals at this time: ". . . violence toys with us now, and there is something so obscene about our present powerlessness that

I wish (in an irresponsible mood) that somehow the challenges would be given us, that we could better understand our lives . . ." The Communist 11 were eleven leaders of the CPUSA who were convicted in 1949 of advocating the violent overthrow of the U.S. government. Ten received five-year prison sentences while the eleventh, a war veteran, received a three-year sentence. Judith Coplon, the daughter of a wealthy toy manufacturer, was convicted in 1949 of passing secret U.S. government documents to a Soviet agent.

9. Walter LaFeber, *America, Russia, and the Cold War, 1945–1980,* p. 96.

10. After World War II, military spending came to be viewed increasingly by the government and corporations as the key to economic prosperity. NATO created a permanent market for American weapons and the Korean War reversed a downward trend in the economy in 1950, thus feeding into the strength of the military-industrial complex and its drive to maintain a permanent war economy (Jezer, *Dark Ages,* pp. 118–123, and Blanche Wiesen Cook, *Declassified Eisenhower: A Divided Legacy of Peace and Political Warfare*). The results of this policy are evident in the astronomical size of the military budget in the 1980s.

11. Kolko and Kolko, *Limits of Power,* p. 669. In 1985 the number of nuclear weapons in the U.S. arsenal was estimated at 12,000, with 8,000 in the Soviet arsenal. The U.S. government's projected number of nuclear weapons in its own arsenal by 1994 was 17,000 (*L.A. Weekly,* January 18–24, 1985, p. 16).

12. Report, August 4, 1952, p. 4, Ben Shahn File, Federal Bureau of Investigation, Washington, D.C., declassified February–March 1982, obtained through the Freedom of Information Act.

13. James Thrall Soby, *Ben Shahn: Paintings,* p. 22. Shahn used a similar composition of cyclists and acrobats on a flyer produced in the mid-1930s as part of a fund-raising drive for *Art Front.* The two cyclists hold a copy of *Art Front* in each hand.

14. Quoted in Rodman, *Portrait of the Artist,* p. 47. Shahn also included these voting booths in a 1949 painting entitled *Anatomical Man.*

15. In a discussion of *Epoch* published in *Die Zeit,* Karl N. Nicolaus felt the painting should be called "Our Epoch": "Crucified between Yes and No— the new Tower of Babel, a colorful pyramid built on antennas—is there anyone who does not shudder?" ("Crucified Between Yes and No: Report on the Emotional Impact Produced by a Painting," *Die Zeit,* December 4, 1952, translated into English by Hannah C. Kaufman; copy in BSP, Microfilm Roll D135).

16. UNESCO set for itself a threefold program: (1) educational reconstruction and rehabilitation; (2) international understanding; (3) fundamental education (Alfred Frankfurter, "Vernissage," *Art News* 46[April 1947]: 13). The United States withdrew from UNESCO in 1984 after charging it had been taken over by anti-U.S. forces.

17. Grace L. McCann Morley, Director, San Francisco Museum of Art,

to Ben Shahn, February 16, 1950, BSP, Microfilm Roll D146:637. One suggestion that came out of this committee was an exhibition on the subject of human rights (Daniel Catton Rich, Director, Art Institute of Chicago, to Ben Shahn, November 1, 1950, BSP, Microfilm Roll D143).

18. In a February 9, 1950, letter to Shahn, Freda Diamond thanks him for the "stunning cover drawing" he did for the political action manual of the American Labor Party (BSP, Microfilm Roll D144).

19. Ben Shahn, "Just What Is Realism?" *Art Education* 3(December 1950):4.

20. Ben Shahn, "The Future of the Creative Arts," *University of Buffalo Studies* 19(February 1952):127. This talk was presented at a symposium of the same name that took place from December 7 to December 9, 1951, at the University of Buffalo.

21. Carol Seeley, "On the Nature of Abstract Painting in America," *Magazine of Art* 43(May 1950):163, 167.

22. Ibid., p. 168.

23. Ben Shahn to Mrs. Elizabeth S. Navas, March 7, 1955, reprinted in Morse, ed., *Ben Shahn*, p. 63.

24. "Contemporary Documents: Modern Art—1950," *College Art Journal* 9(Spring 1950):339. The statement was also issued in pamphlet form.

25. Ibid.

26. For a discussion of the history of this manifesto, see Serge Guilbaut, "The Frightening Freedom of the Brush: The Boston Institute of Contemporary Art and Modern Art," in Institute of Contemporary Art, Boston, *Dissent: The Issue of Modern Art in Boston.*

27. Henry Varnum Poor, "How This Group Began," *Reality* 1(Spring 1953):6.

28. "Letter to Museum of Modern Art," *Reality* 1(Spring 1953):2. Greta Berman and Jeffrey Wechsler argue that the major modern art museums in New York City, particularly the Whitney and MOMA, "generally seem to have done a very level-handed job" in the early 1950s when it came to the inclusion of both figurative and abstract artists in their exhibitions (*Realism and Realities: The Other Side of American Painting, 1940–1960*, pp. 5–6).

29. Bernarda Bryson Shahn, interview with author, May 20, 1984; Raphael Soyer, interview with author, June 7, 1984.

30. Ben Shahn, "From Paragraphs on Art," *Reality* 1(Spring 1953):6.

31. Dr. Lorin E. Kerr to Ben Shahn, January 3, 1951, BSP, Microfilm Roll D148:230–231.

32. Irving Richter to Ben Shahn, January 16, 1951, BSP, Microfilm Roll D147:448.

33. Ibid.

34. The project was never carried out because Richter did not have enough money to pay Shahn's fee for executing the work (personal communication from Irving Richter, October 1, 1988).

35. Rodman, *Portrait of the Artist*, p. 100.

36. Ibid., pp. 8–9.

37. Selden Rodman to Ben Shahn, March 31, 1951, BSP, Microfilm Roll D145.

38. Ben Shahn, "The Artist and the Politicians," *Art News* 52(September 1953):34–35, 67. The content of this article is discussed later in this chapter.

39. Ben Shahn, "American Painting for the Past Twenty-Five Years: An Unorthodox View," presented at Harvard University, April 12, 1951, typescript, p. 9, BSP, Unmicrofilmed Papers.

40. Ibid., p. 12.

41. Shahn, "The Future of the Creative Arts," pp. 127–128.

42. Kolko and Kolko, *Limits of Power*, p. 614.

43. Major General Emmett O'Donnell, Jr., in Senate Committee on Armed Services, *Military Situation in the Far East* (1951), p. 3075, quoted in ibid., p. 616.

44. Alfred M. Frankfurter, "Vernissage: Freedom to Paint," *Art News* 50(December 1951):17.

45. "Tumult in Los Angeles," *Time*, November 5, 1951, p. 82.

46. *Composition with Clarinets and Tin Horn* was purchased by the Friends of Modern Art of the Detroit Art Institute and presented to the institute as a gift in 1951. That same year John S. Neuberry, Jr., gave the institute six preliminary sketches for the painting. According to these sketches, the figure was originally standing in a thoughtful position (William E. Woolfenden, "A Composition by Ben Shahn," *Detroit Institute of Arts Bulletin* 32[1952–1953]:20–21). A discussion of the *New York Times* ad appears later in this chapter.

47. Cited in Bryson Shahn, *Ben Shahn*, p. 184.

48. Ben Shahn, "Aspects of Realism," delivered at Black Mountain College, July 29, 1951, typescript, p. 5, BSP, Unmicrofilmed Papers.

49. Shahn, "The Future of the Creative Arts," p. 128.

50. Carey McWilliams, "The White House under Surveillance," *Nation*, February 16, 1952, pp. 151–152. See also Elson, *The World of Time Inc.*, pp. 269–280.

51. Dondero was also close to Hoover. According to McWilliams, "in 1946 Dondero told his colleagues in the House that he had spent long hours with J. Edgar Hoover, getting confidential information about spies and such" (McWilliams, "White House," p. 151).

52. Caute, *The Great Fear*, pp. 521–523. Ken Bierly left American Business Consultants in 1952 to "rehabilitate" accused artists—for a fee. See also Jezer, *Dark Ages*, pp. 100–101.

53. See *New York Times*, July 6, 1952, p. 29.

54. *Counterattack*, July 25, 1952, p. 1.

55. Ibid., p. 2.

56. Gwyn Thomas, "As on a Darkling Plain," *Masses and Mainstream* 1(September 1948):50–67; Ben Field, "The Chicken Farmers," *Masses and*

Mainstream 1(November 1948):64–72; Dirk J. Struik, "Public and Private Morals," *Masses and Mainstream* 1(December 1948):58–64; Phillip Bonosky, "Johnny Cucu's Record," *Masses and Mainstream* 2(January 1949):6–16; "Three Drawings by Ben Shahn," *Masses and Mainstream* 1(August 1948): 40–43.

57. Jonathan Shahn, interview with author, May 19, 1984.

58. Prescott, *Complete Graphic Works*, p. 12.

59. *Counterattack*, August 8, 1952, p. 3.

60. Bryson Shahn, interview, May 20, 1984.

61. Caute, *The Great Fear*, p. 529.

62. For examples of work Shahn executed for CBS and Ed Murrow, see Golden, Weihs, and Strunsky, eds., *The Visual Craft of William Golden*. The first work commissioned by Golden after the *Counterattack* fiasco appears to have been a double-page network advertisement in 1955 (after the censure of McCarthy by the Senate). It consisted of a drawing of a wheatfield on one page and a maze of television antennae on the other (see ibid., pp. 64–65). According to Shahn's son, Jonathan Shahn, one of the consequences of Shahn's blacklisting by CBS was that he started doing silkscreen prints in a serious way in order to increase his income (interview, May 19, 1984).

63. Typescript of article on Shahn by Elkan Allen sent to the artist February 9, 1956, BSP, Microfilm Roll D143. Not only did *Fortune* continue to commission Shahn throughout the fifties, but so, too, did *Harper's* and *Charm*. Another Luce publication, *Time*, also commissioned Shahn, for the first time, to do a portrait of Malraux for the cover of the July 18, 1955, issue. Shahn also received a letter from his friend and fellow artist Bob Osborne praising Lionni's action in taking a stand "against this INQUISITION this RANK CALVINISM this *Fear*," and in facing "right up to the issue which confronts all of us" (undated letter, BSP, Microfilm Roll D147:45–47).

64. Elson, *The World of Time Inc.*, p. 273.

65. Shahn File, FBI. Considerable portions of Shahn's file have been deleted, although all deleted material is indicated and remains in chronological order.

66. Carlisle, "A Biographical Study," p. 188; the Reverend Kenneth Ripley Forbes to Ben Shahn, 1952, BSP, Microfilm Roll D144. The petition was organized by Reverend Forbes and signed by 280 people.

67. Aline B. Loucheim, "Ben Shahn Illuminates," *New York Times*, August 30, 1953, p. 8. According to Jezer, "the Broadway theater and the Metropolitan Opera Company, virtually alone, resisted the blacklist without harm to themselves" (*Dark Ages*, p. 101).

68. Lowe Art Gallery, *Mural Art of Ben Shahn*, n.p., and Shahn, in Weldon and Burton, *Ben Shahn's America*.

69. Rodman, *Portrait of the Artist*, p. 63.

70. Thomas D. Mabry to Ben Shahn, June 23, 1942, BSP, Microfilm Roll D146:213.

71. Rodman, *Portrait of the Artist*, p. 63.

72. Cook, *Declassified Eisenhower*, pp. 11–13, 123.

73. Francis E. (Hank) Brennan to Elmer Davis, April 6, 1943, BSP, Microfilm Roll D146:1511–1513. Brennan later became Henry Luce's art advisor.

74. Rodman, *Portrait of the Artist*, p. 66.

75. Ibid.

76. Sydney Weinberg, "What to Tell America: The Writers' Quarrel in the Office of War Information," *Journal of American History* 55(June 1968):85.

77. Elmer Davis to Ben Shahn, July 1, 1943, BSP, Microfilm Roll D146:1517.

78. When Shahn returned from a trip to Europe in the summer of 1963, the Newark office of the FBI requested permission from the director to interview him. Permission was denied because, among other things, the subject was "employed as an artist and writer by profession and might possibly exploit an attempted interview in an effort to embarrass the Bureau" (Shahn File, FBI).

79. Herbert J. Muller, *Adlai Stevenson, A Study in Values*, p. xi. As a highly literate man, Stevenson was seen by many of his opponents as an "egghead" and was constantly contrasted with the more "virile" Republican candidate, General Eisenhower. Stevenson happily accepted this title, declaring: "Eggheads of the world unite! You have nothing to lose but your yolks" (ibid., p. 3).

80. John Bartlow Martin wrote to Shahn on August 2, 1953, telling him that his sketches from the 1952 convention were hanging in the Martin hallway. He also told Shahn that he had bought the Centralia drawings and wanted Shahn to sign them. One of the lawyers on the Hickman case, Leon Depres, had purchased the Hickman drawings (BSP, Microfilm Roll D146:390–392).

81. These sketches can be found in the Ben Shahn Estate, New York City. MacArthur was an unsuccessful contender for the Republican presidential nomination in 1948 and 1952.

82. National Council of the Arts, Sciences and Professions to Ben Shahn, January 3, 1952, BSP, Microfilm Roll D143. Shahn had also designed a pamphlet for the National Federation for Constitutional Liberties in 1946; entitled *Everybody's Business*, it summarized the New York State Anti-Discrimination Laws and how to use them. As with many of the pamphlets on which Shahn worked in the mid-forties, Bernarda Bryson Shahn produced the illustrations.

83. "Harry T. Moore," *Nation*, September 27, 1952, p. 267.

84. Shahn also provided a drawing for the cover of the October 4, 1952, issue of the *Nation* and for an article in the same issue by John Strachey, "The Absolutists," which advocated a reform politics as "the only answer to the absolutists of both the left and the right" (p. 293). In addition, his caricature

of McCarthy accompanied an article by William G. Rice, "The Meaning of McCarthyism," in the August 30, 1952, issue (pp. 164–166).

85. Carey McWilliams to Ben Shahn, May 22, 1952, BSP, Microfilm Roll D146:1060.

86. On the back cover of the August 30, 1952, *Nation*, a miniature reproduction of Shahn's June 28 cover appeared as part of a promotional campaign. New subscribers would receive the special civil liberties issue free of charge. Thus Shahn's image would have reached more than the usual number of *Nation* readers.

87. Daniel J. Boorstin, "Introduction: The Immigrants' Vision," in Hirshhorn Museum and Sculpture Garden, *The Golden Door: Artist-Immigrants of America, 1876–1976*, pp. 16–18.

88. In 1958 Shahn executed two serigraphs using the same drawing, one of which also included the text written in Shahn's "folk alphabet" (see Prescott, *Complete Graphic Works*, pp. 34–35). Also, in an undated letter, Irving Richter, then employed as a publicist for the "outs" at the UAW Ford local in Detroit, asked Shahn if there was a mat or stat available of the Sacco and Vanzetti drawing. He wanted to use it in a tabloid to be distributed to the 15,000 Italian-Americans and other workers at the Rouge plant (Irving Richter to Ben Shahn, undated, BSP, Microfilm Roll D147:446).

89. Arthur Schlesinger, Jr., "History of the Week," *New York Post*, September 2, 1952, quoted in Navasky, *Naming Names*, p. 54.

90. Navasky, *Naming Names*, p. 50.

91. On August 1, 1952, Shahn received an invitation from I. F. Stone to attend C. B. Baldwin's birthday party and fund-raising event. The money would be used by Baldwin "to further the work to which he is devoted as Secretary and Campaign Manager of the Progressive Party" (BSP, Microfilm Roll D143).

92. George S. Counts to Ben Shahn, telegram, January 16, 1953, BSP, Microfilm Roll D144. Irving Kristol of the ACCF also sent similar telegrams to conference organizers, one of whom was Reinhold Niebuhr of the ADA (Navasky, *Naming Names*, p. 56). In March 1952 Kristol had written an article in *Commentary* arguing that liberals should defend the civil rights of communists only after clearly establishing their own anti-communism. For a response to Kristol's article see Alan F. Westin, "Our Freedom—and the Rights of Communists: A Reply to Irving Kristol," *Commentary* 14(July 1952):33–40.

93. In a letter to Shahn dated January 8, 1953, Clark Foreman thanked Shahn for agreeing to do a poster for display outside the ECLC meeting, but no evidence of this poster exists to date (BSP, Microfilm Roll D144). James Thrall Soby was to have joined Shahn in the freedom-of-the-arts session but had to cancel due to thyroid problems (James Thrall Soby to Ben Shahn, February 27, 1953, BSP, Microfilm Roll D147:1461). Other session participants were the writers Matthew Josephson and Merle Miller and the economist J. Raymond Walsh.

94. Shahn, "The Artist and the Politicians," p. 35. (The article had been published earlier in the May 1953 issue of the ECLC publication *Rights* [p. 8] and appeared later in the November 8, 1953, issue of the *Colorado Springs Free Press* [p. 7].)

95. Ibid. Communist participation in liberal causes was undoubtedly the result, in part, of right-wing persecution of organizations and events that were openly communist.

96. Ibid., pp. 35, 67. In Shahn's case, this friend was William Golden.

97. Shahn stated, incorrectly, that the State Department exhibitions were stopped in mid-Atlantic. They had, in fact, been shown in a number of cities before they were recalled. Shahn also stated that the pictures were put together with the expert advice of a number of museum officials. In a letter to Shahn, Hudson Walker pointed out that Lee Davidson of the State Department did not have such advice when selecting the oil paintings but, rather, chose them on his own. When this fact became known at a meeting of the American Federation of Arts, "the State Department men present blanched, because it is very bad policy for one guy to do such a job for the Government, no matter how well qualified." The AFA was then brought in to help with the selection of the watercolors (Hudson D. Walker to Ben Shahn, October 1, 1953, BSP, Microfilm Roll D148).

98. Shahn, "The Artist and the Politicians," p. 67.

99. Ibid.

100. Ben Shahn to Alfred Barr, Jr., February 10, 1953, Alfred Barr, Jr., Papers, Archives of American Art, Smithsonian Institution, Washington, D.C., Unmicrofilmed Papers. Shahn severed his ties with the ECLC in May 1953 because he felt some of his friends, including Paul Lehman of Princeton Theological Seminary and H. H. Wilson of Princeton's Department of Political Science, were being edged out (Clark Foreman to Ben Shahn, May 12, 1953, BSP, Microfilm Roll D144; Ben Shahn to Clark Foreman, May 18, 1953, BSP, Microfilm Roll D144).

101. See Leonard, "Around the Galleries," and Corwin, "Ben Shahn's Rewarding Exhibit."

102. Dondero's objection to the "social protest" in Shahn's paintings would have been less applicable to the artist's work of the late 1940's and the 1950's, which contained few direct references to particular political struggles.

103. William Blake, as quoted in Raymond Williams, *Culture and Society, 1780–1950*, p. 55.

104. Cook, *Declassified Eisenhower*, p. xix.

105. Kolko and Kolko, *Limits of Power*, p. 20.

106. Secretary of State James F. Byrnes, U.S. *Department of State Bulletin*, August 26, 1945, p. 279, quoted in Kolko and Kolko, *Limits of Power*, p. 23.

107. Kolko and Kolko, *Limits of Power*, p. 37.

108. For Italy, see Caldwell, "Organization and Operation."

109. President Harry S. Truman, "Fight False Propaganda with Truth," in Robert E. Summers, ed., *America's Weapons of Psychological Warfare*, p. 28.

110. Propaganda was associated not only with Stalin and Hitler but, in the minds of reactionary Republicans, with Roosevelt's New Deal. See Summers, ed., *America's Weapons;* Charles A. Thomson and Walter H. C. Laves, *Cultural Relations and U.S. Foreign Policy;* Ronald I. Rubin, *The Objectives of the U.S. Information Agency: Controversies and Analysis;* and Gary O. Larson, *The Reluctant Patron: The U.S. Government and the Arts, 1943–1965.*

111. Thomson and Laves, *Cultural Relations*, p. 70.

112. Ibid.

113. Ibid., p. 82.

114. Ibid., p. 86.

115. Ibid., p. 84.

116. Eloise Spaeth, "America's Cultural Responsibilities Abroad," *College Art Journal* 11(Winter 1951–1952): 118.

117. James Thrall Soby, "Does Our Art Impress Europe?" *Saturday Review* 32(August 1949): 147.

118. Quoted in Ben Shahn, "How Can Art Contribute to an Industrial and Scientific Age?" presented at Ohio State University, April 25, 1951, typescript, p. 12, BSP, Unmicrofilmed Papers.

119. Elkan Allen to Ben Shahn, October 19, 1950, BSP, Microfilm Roll D143.

120. Shahn, "How Can Art Contribute," p. 13.

121. Ibid.

122. Stephen Spender, "We Can Win the Battle for the Minds of Europe," *New York Times Magazine*, April 25, 1948, p. 17.

123. Guido Piovene, "Ungrateful Europe," in James Burnham, ed., *What Europe Thinks of America*, pp. 125–126.

124. Lewis Galantiere, ed., *America and the Mind of Europe*, p. 11. This book includes a series of essays originally published in a special issue of the *Saturday Evening Post* earlier in 1951.

125. The involvement of the CIA in supporting and manipulating, through various trust funds and foundations, the promotion of culture during the Cold War is documented in Christopher Lasch, "The Cultural Cold War," *Nation*, September 11, 1967, pp. 198–212.

126. U.S. Information Agency, First *Review of Operations* (August–December 1953): 3.

127. For a discussion of private enterprise's influence on American foreign policy, see G. William Domhoff, "Who Made American Foreign Policy, 1945–1963?" in David Horowitz, ed., *Corporations and the Cold War*, and Gabriel Kolko, *The Roots of American Foreign Policy*. An analysis of MOMA's use of art as a Cold War weapon can be found in Cockcroft, "Abstract Expressionism."

128. Lynes, *Good Old Modern*, p. 384.

129. For a brief history of MOMA's involvement with the Venice Biennial, see ibid., p. 385.

130. Betty Chamberlain to Ben Shahn, February 4, 1950, BSP, Microfilm Roll D144. This talk was later published in MOMA's *Museum Bulletin* 17(Summer 1950):6–9.

131. Alfred H. Barr, Jr., Letter to the Editor, *College Art Journal* 15(Spring 1956):186.

132. Howard Flyn, Chief, International Press and Publications Division, Department of State, to Ben Shahn, October 15, 1951, BSP, Microfilm Roll D147:1654. In a letter dated October 25, 1951, Flyn thanks Shahn for sending the photographs (BSP, Microfilm Roll D147:1654).

133. Barr, Letter to the Editor, p. 187.

134. Egbert, *Socialism and American Art*, p. 127. Shahn had also received a letter from Milton Friedman on February 9, 1951, asking him to support an art sale organized by Rockwell Kent to raise funds for the Robert Raven Rehabilitation Committee. Raven had lost his sight while fighting with the Abraham Lincoln Brigade in Spain (BSP, Microfilm Roll D145).

135. "What Are You Doing Out There?" *New York Times*, January 15, 1951, p. 9. In an interview on June 17, 1984, Raphael Soyer told me that he was unable to travel to Europe in 1954 because his passport and that of his wife had been taken away by the State Department. He was able, however, to go abroad the following year.

136. Shapiro and Shapiro, "Abstract Expressionism," p. 207.

137. Thomas W. Braden, "I'm Glad the C.I.A. Is Immoral," *Saturday Evening Post*, May 20, 1967, pp. 10+.

138. For an analysis of the Congress for Cultural Freedom, see Christopher Lasch, "The Cultural Cold War: A Short History of the Congress for Cultural Freedom," in Barton J. Bernstein, ed., *Towards a New Past: Dissenting Essays in American History*, pp. 322–359.

139. Ibid., p. 332.

140. Shapiro and Shapiro, "Abstract Expressionism," p. 207.

141. Cockcroft, "Abstract Expressionism," p. 40.

142. James Laughlin to Ben Shahn, December 26, 1951, BSP, Microfilm Roll D146:1248.

143. "Proposal for a Quarterly Magazine on American Materials for Distribution Abroad," c. 1951, BSP, Microfilm Roll D145.

144. Ibid.

145. Selden Rodman, "Ben Shahn Speaking," *Perspectives, USA*, pilot issue, January 1952, pp. 59–72.

146. Selden Rodman, "Ben Shahn: Painter of America," *Perspectives, USA* 1(Fall 1952):88.

147. Ibid., p. 94.

4. An American in Venice

1. LaFeber, *America, Russia, and the Cold War*, pp. 147–148.

2. Quoted in Richard H. Rovere, *Senator Joe McCarthy*, pp. 9–10.

3. Ibid., p. 12.

4. Eric F. Goldman, *The Crucial Decade—and After: America, 1945–1960*, pp. 272–273.

5. The ad contained a drawing of chairs and music stands. A copy can be found in the March 2, 1954, issue of the *New York Herald Tribune*, p. 26.

6. Ben Shahn, interview, March 17, 1957, OHC, p. 114.

7. Copies of these drawings can be found in the Downtown Gallery Papers, Archives of American Art, Smithsonian Institution, Washington, D.C., Microfilm Roll ND 37:496–497.

8. The drawings accompanied the article by Edgar Kemler, "Will Joe Bolt the G.O.P.? Ike Would Be Delighted," *Nation*, May 15, 1954, pp. 419–422.

9. LaFeber, *America, Russia, and the Cold War*, p. 141.

10. Piovene, "Ungrateful Europe," p. 132.

11. Burnham, ed., *What Europe Thinks of America*, pp. vii, x, xii.

12. H. Stuart Hughes, *The United States and Italy*, 1st ed., p. 1.

13. "In January 1947 De Gasperi visited the United States, returning with a $100 million loan and advice to eliminate the Communist-Nenni coalition from the Rome government" (Kolko and Kolko, *Limits of Power*, p. 348).

14. Hughes, *The United States and Italy*, 1st ed., p. 144.

15. For an excellent series of essays on the vested interests of certain sectors of American society in the anti-communist campaign, see Robert Griffith and Athan Theoharis, eds., *The Spectre: Original Essays on the Cold War and the Origins of McCarthyism*.

16. Hughes, *The United States and Italy*, 1st ed., pp. 222–230.

17. Hughes, *The United States and Italy*, rev. ed., p. 201. See also "A Premier Goes Skiing: Italy's Pella Quits in the Climax of a Crisis Months in the Making," *Life*, January 18, 1954, p. 38.

18. Amintore Fanfani was Pella's immediate successor, but he remained in power for only two weeks.

19. Hughes, *The United States and Italy*, 1st ed., p. 231.

20. USIA, *First Review*, p. 30.

21. Thomson and Laves, *Cultural Relations*, p. 87.

22. USIA, *First Review*, p. 7.

23. Thomson and Laves, *Cultural Relations*, p. 36.

24. Lawrence Alloway, *The Venice Biennale, 1895–1968: From Salon to Goldfish Bowl*, p. 36.

25. Bernard Denvir, "Mayfair to Manhattan," *Artist* 48(November 1954): 35. These Iron Curtain countries included Bulgaria, Czechoslovakia, Poland, and Rumania.

26. R. H. Hubbard, "Show Window of the Arts—XXVII Venice Biennale," *Canadian Art* 12(Autumn 1954):16.

27. Alloway, *The Venice Biennale*, pp. 139, 141.

28. R. Melville, "The Venice Biennial," *Listener* 52(July 29, 1954):180.

29. Denvir, "Mayfair to Manhattan," p. 35.

30. F. Taubes, "What Is the World Painting Today?" *American Artist* 19(February 1955):59.

31. Alfred H. Barr, Jr., "Gli Stati Uniti alla Biennale: Shahn e De Kooning, Lachaise, Lassaw e Smith," *Biennale di Venezia*, no. 19–20 (April–June 1954):62.

32. Denvir, "Mayfair to Manhattan," p. 35.

33. See Chapter 3, note 133.

34. Clement Greenberg, "Contribution to a Symposium," in his *Art and Culture: Critical Essays*, p. 125.

35. Museum of Modern Art, New York, "Summary of European Press Reaction to the Exhibition 'Two Painters and Three Sculptors from the United States,' Shown at the XXVII Biennale, Venice, June 19–October 17, 1954," October 1, 1956, p. 3. The article in *Spazio* was to be written by the French critic Michel Tapie de Celeyran, but the magazine ceased publication before the article was written. The last three pages of MOMA's press review list the numerous articles written on Shahn. The three sculptors in the show were Gaston Lachaise, Ibram Lassaw, and David Smith. They were represented by one work each.

36. The French would obviously not have taken kindly to American claims of ascendancy over Parisian art. France would also have resented the strong pressure from the American government in the early 1950s to abandon its opposition to the European Defence Community. According to Walter LaFeber, Secretary of State Dulles warned in mid-December 1953 that "France must ratify or face an 'agonizing reappraisal' by Washington of American commitments to Europe" (LaFeber, *America, Russia, and the Cold War*, p. 169).

37. Leon Degand, "La Biennale de Venise," *Art d'Aujourd'hui* 5(September 1954):65, and Alain Jouffroy, from an article in *Beaux-Arts* quoted in MOMA, "Press Reaction," p. 10. The title and date of the article were not given.

38. G. Mario Marini, *Notiziario d'Arte*, nos. 6–7, 1954, quoted in MOMA, "Press Reaction," p. 9. "*Tachisme*" or "*art autre*" was well established in France in the early 1950s, at the same time as the Italian artists Giuseppe Santomaso and Afro were introducing the Italian public to home-grown abstract expressionism. See Dore Ashton, "Avantgardia: Reflections from Rome on the Avant-garde Movements in Italy and America during the Last Decade," *Art Digest* 29(March 15, 1955):16–17, 34.

39. Quoted in MOMA, "Press Reaction," p. 10.

40. Quoted in ibid., p. 9.

41. Ibid.

42. Barr, "Gli Stati Uniti," p. 66.

43. Museum of Modern Art, New York, *2 Pittori: de Kooning, Shahn; 3*

Scultori: Lachaise, Lassaw, Smith; Esposizione organizzatta dal Museum of Modern Art, New York (Venice), and Barr, "Gli Stati Uniti." The original 8,000 copies of the catalogue were such a success that an additional 3,000 were printed (Alloway, *Venice Biennale*, p. 141).

44. Alloway, *Venice Biennale*, pp. 20–21.

45. Carlo Ragghianti, commentary accompanying Ben Shahn, "L'artista e il politicismo," *Sele Arte*, no. 9(November–December 1953):28; my translation.

46. Ibid., pp. 29, 28. *Sele Arte* was a liberal Italian art journal similar to *Art News*.

47. Shahn, "L'artista e il politicismo," p. 26.

48. Carlo Ragghianti, "Lettura Aperta," *Sele Arte*, no. 1(January–February 1953):42. Lists of the senators and artists involved are found on pages 42 and 43 respectively.

49. From statement by Ben Shahn included in MOMA, *2 Pittori*, n.p., and taken from Shahn, "American Painting for the Last Twenty-Five Years."

50. James Thrall Soby, "Ben Shahn," in MOMA, *2 Pittori*, n.p.

51. James Thrall Soby to Ben Shahn, March 17, 1954, BSP, Microfilm Roll D147.

52. Hughes, *The United States and Italy*, 1st ed., p. 197.

53. Vittorio Zincone, "Moral America," in Burnham, ed., *What Europe Thinks of America*, p. 48.

54. Hughes, *The United States and Italy*, 1st ed., pp. 198–199.

55. Ibid., p. 177.

56. Ibid., p. 176. A similar United States–backed purge of labor unions occurred at the same time in France.

57. Soby, "Ben Shahn," in MOMA, *2 Pittori*, n.p.

58. Barr, "Gli Stati Uniti," p. 62.

59. Ibid., p. 65; my translation.

60. See Hughes, *The United States and Italy*.

61. Barr, "Gli Stati Uniti," pp. 64–65; my translation.

62. Ibid., p. 65.

63. Museum of Modern Art, New York, "'Two Painters and Three Sculptors from the United States,' Shown at the XXVII Biennale, Venice, June 19–October 17, 1954," October 1, 1956, p. 3. The museum refused these requests because many of the paintings in the Biennial exhibition had already been traveling in Europe since early 1953 as part of MOMA's exhibition "Twelve Modern American Painters and Sculptors," and the museum felt it would be unreasonable to request the lenders to grant a further extension of these loans (ibid.).

64. H. Lester Cooke to Porter McCray, December 20, 1954, BSP, Microfilm Roll D148. The Italian government did not end up sponsoring a show of Shahn's work. Instead, Rome was included in the schedule of a traveling exhibition of Shahn's work organized by MOMA's International Council in 1962–1963. It was a two-part exhibition—"Ben Shahn" and "Ben Shahn

Graphics." The graphics show traveled to Germany, Yugoslavia, Sweden, and Israel while the larger exhibition was seen in Holland, Belgium, Italy, and Austria.

65. MOMA, "Press Reaction," pp. 11–12.

66. Ibid., p. 13.

67. Lisa Licitra Ponti, "Ben Shahn a Venezia," *Domus*, no. 298(September 1954):37; my translation.

68. Franco Catania, *Corriere di Sicilia*, August 24, 1954, as quoted in MOMA, "Press Reaction," p. 14. MOMA lists this paper as an "independent" daily.

69. Ibid., p. 12.

70. Douglas T. Miller and Marion Nowak, *The Fifties: The Way We Really Were*, p. 406. Roberto Longhi also compared Shahn to Chaplin in "Grossi premi e grosse sorprese," *L'Europeo* (Milan), July 4, 1954.

71. Catania, in MOMA, "Press Release," p. 12.

72. Pilon Ugo to Ben Shahn, September 15, 1954, translated by Leo Lionni, BSP, Microfilm Roll D148.

73. H. Lester Cooke, transcript of Report to Museum of Modern Art on Ben Shahn's exhibition at the 1954 Venice Biennale, pp. 1–2, BSP, Microfilm Roll D148.

74. Ibid., p. 4.

75. MOMA, "Press Reaction," p. 12.

76. Maria Poma, "La XXVII Biennale sul 'leit motiv' del surrealism e dell'astrattismo," *L'Ora* (Palermo), June 24, 1954.

77. Harrison E. Salisbury, "Russia's Art Reflects Trends in Russia," *New York Times Magazine*, September 12, 1954, pp. 8–9.

78. John Berger, "Renato Guttuso," *Apollo* 61(March 1955):70.

79. "Party-Line Painter," *Time*, November 30, 1953, p. 74.

80. Gian Paolo Paoli, "Ben Shahn in Cantina," *Il Contemporaneo* (Rome), September 25, 1954, p. 1. That *Handball* and not one of Shahn's posters accompanied this article was probably due to the fact that the museum only made available to the press reproductions of a limited number of Shahn's works.

81. MOMA, "Press Release," p. 13. The posters were not listed individually in MOMA's catalogue, though they were in the large Biennial catalogue.

82. Paoli, "Ben Shahn," p. 1; my translation.

83. Ibid.

84. Cooke, Report to MOMA, p. 2.

85. MOMA, "Press Reaction," p. 11.

86. Cooke, Report to MOMA, p. 5.

87. Shahn, in Morse, "Ben Shahn: An Interview," p. 138.

88. Ugo, letter to Shahn, trans. Lionni.

89. Marini, in MOMA, "Press Reaction," p. 11.

90. Heinz Keller, "XXVII biennale," *Werk* 41(August 1954):sup. 191; my translation.

91. Quoted in Cooke, Report to MOMA, p. 4.

92. M.W.B., *Corriere Militare*, December 19–25, 1954, as quoted in MOMA, "Press Reaction," p. 11. The *Corriere Militare* was the bulletin of the armed forces in Rome.

93. "Aftermath of War: A Portfolio of Paintings by Ben Shahn," *Fortune* 32(December 1945):169.

94. Ibid.

95. Rodman, *Portrait of the Artist*, p. 58.

96. Cooke, Report to MOMA, p. 3.

97. Barr, "Gli Stati Uniti," p. 64.

98. Ibid., p. 66.

99. Marini, in MOMA, "Press Reaction," p. 11.

100. Quoted in Cooke, Report to MOMA, p. 4.

Conclusion

1. See Prescott, *Complete Graphic Works*, pp. 98–103, 140, 168–169. Shahn also donated both art works and money to such organizations as the South African Defense Fund, the Committee for a Sane Nuclear Policy, and the Bertrand Russell Peace Foundation (Ann Morrisett to Ben Shahn, March 5 and April 7, 1959, BSP, Microfilm Roll D147:1531–1533). Shahn's watercolor *Maximus of Tyre* (1963) was included in the International Exhibition and Sale of Works of Art in aid of the Bertrand Russell Peace Fund, Woburn Abbey, October 27 to November 3, 1963.

2. Grace Davis, MOMA, to Ben Shahn, January 11, 1956, BSP, Microfilm Roll D146:970. The text of the lecture can be found in Morse, ed., *Ben Shahn*, pp. 170–183. According to Mildred Constantine, who worked at MOMA throughout the fifties, the USIA was interested in the museum's international program and helped send both artists and scholars on speaking tours abroad (letter to author, August 7, 1984).

3. Douglas Glass, "Portrait Gallery: Ben Shahn," *London Sunday Times*, February 5, 1956.

4. Ole Henrik Moe, "Ben Shahn," *Kunsten Idag* 35, no. 1(1956):56, 58.

5. U.S. Department of State, "United States and Soviet Union to Exchange National Exhibits," *Department of State Bulletin*, October 13, 1958, p. 577. The text of an additional agreement signed in Washington December 29, 1958, can be found in the *Department of State Bulletin*, January 26, 1959, pp. 132–134.

6. George V. Allen, in U.S. Information Agency, *13th Report to Congress*, July 1–December 31, 1959, inside of front cover.

7. Eugene W. Castle, "Danger Ahead! More Cultural Exchange!" *American Mercury* 89(November 1959):28, 40, 42.

8. U.S. Congress, House Committee on Un-American Activities, "The American National Exhibition, Moscow, July 1959 (The Record of Certain Artists and an Appraisal of Their Works Selected for Display)," 86th Cong., 1st Sess., July 1, 1959, pp. 941–963.

9. Ben Shahn, "Statement of Ben Shahn," typescript, p. 2, BSP, Microfilm Roll D148. A copy of Evergood's paper can be found in Philip Evergood Papers, Archives of American Art, Smithsonian Institution, Washington, D.C., Microfilm Roll 429:820–821.

10. Shahn was also one of the sponsors of an ad in the October 16, 1959, issue of the *New York Times* (page 40) calling for an end to the Cold War and the formation of a new American foreign policy based on détente.

11. For a complete discussion of the U.S.-Soviet exchange, see Cindy Judy Fox, "The Exchange of Easel and Plastic Arts: Soviet-American Cultural Relations, 1945–1976" (Ph.D. dissertation, Fletcher School of Law and Diplomacy, 1977).

12. The full transcript of Eisenhower's press conference can be found in the *New York Times*, July 2, 1959, p. 10.

13. Notes on Legislative Leadership Meeting, June 30, 1959, p. 2, in Dwight D. Eisenhower Papers as President, 1953–1961, Dwight D. Eisenhower Library, Abilene, Kans., Legislative Meetings Series, Box 3, Folder: Legislative Meetings 1959, p. 5.

14. See Cook, *Declassified Eisenhower.*

15. Eisenhower, Press Conference, *New York Times*, p. 10. The jury for the selection of art for the Moscow show was appointed by George V. Allen, director of the USIA, and included the artists Franklin C. Watkins and Theodore Roszak, Lloyd Goodrich of the Whitney, and Henry Radford Hope, chair of the Fine Arts Department at Indiana University.

16. John S. D. Eisenhower, Memorandum of Conference with the President, March 23, 1959, p. 2, Dwight D. Eisenhower Papers as President, DDE Diary Series, Box 40, Folder: Staff Notes March 15–31, 1959.

17. Bryson Shahn, interview, May 20, 1984.

18. Ben Shahn, "Nonconformity," *Amerika*, no. 33(May 1959):16–21. The original text of the lecture was substantially edited in order, in the words of John Jacobs, text editor for *Amerika*, "to bring it within the terms of our charter." What this charter specified was that the magazine and its Soviet counterpart, *USSR*, were to be nonpolitical, which meant, according to Jacobs, that subjects with political ramifications could be discussed as long as there were no specific political comparisons and references. Shahn's lecture did include a specific example of Russian art censorship, which was undoubtedly one of the sections omitted (John Jacobs to Ben Shahn, September 12, 1958, BSP, Microfilm Roll D148:257).

19. Hilton Kramer, "Publicizing Social Causes on Canvas," *New York Times*, November 7, 1976, Sec. II, p. 23.

20. Ibid.

BIBLIOGRAPHY

Archives

Abilene, Kans. Dwight D. Eisenhower Library. Dwight D. Eisenhower
  Papers as President.
Brooklyn, N.Y. Brooklyn Museum. Ben Shahn File.
New York, N.Y. Columbia University. Oral History Collection. Jack Levine
  Interviews.
——. Roy Neuberger Interviews.
——. Ben Shahn Interviews.
New York, N.Y. Museum of Modern Art. Ben Shahn File.
——. James Thrall Soby Papers.
——. "Summary of European Press Reaction to the Exhibition 'Two Paint-
  ers and Three Sculptors from the United States,' Shown at the XXVII Bien-
  nale, Venice, June 19–October 17, 1954." New York, October 1, 1956.
——. "'Two Painters and Three Sculptors from the United States' Shown at
  the XXVII Biennale, Venice, June 19–October 17, 1954." New York, Oc-
  tober 1, 1954.
New York, N.Y. Whitney Museum of American Art. Ben Shahn File.
Rome. National Gallery of Modern Art. Ben Shahn File.
St. Louis, Mo. Saint Louis Art Museum. Archives.
Venice. Archives of the Venice Biennial. Ben Shahn File.
Washington, D.C. Archives of American Art. Smithsonian Institution. Alfred
  Barr, Jr., Papers.
——. Edward Biberman Papers.
——. Black Mountain College Papers.
——. Boston. Institute of Contemporary Art.
——. Downtown Gallery Papers.
——. Philip Evergood Papers.
——. Clement Greenberg Papers.
——. Elizabeth McCausland Papers.
——. Ben Shahn Papers.
——. Raphael Soyer Papers.
——. Max Weber Papers.
Washington, D.C. Federal Bureau of Investigation. Ben Shahn File.

Washington, D.C. National Archives. Farm Security Administration Administrator Correspondence, 1935–1938. Record Group 96, AD 986–987, 994.
————. Public Buildings Service. Record Group 121.

Books, Catalogues, and Dissertations

Allen, James Sloan. *The Romance of Commerce and Culture: Capitalism, Modernism, and the Chicago-Aspen Crusade for Cultural Reform.* Chicago: University of Chicago Press, 1983.

Alloway, Lawrence. *The Venice Biennale, 1895–1968: From Salon to Goldfish Bowl.* Greenwich, Conn.: New York Graphic Society, 1968.

American Photographers of the Depression: Farm Security Administration Photographs, 1935–1942. Introduction by Charles Hagen. New York: Pantheon Books, 1985.

Artists Equity Association. *The First Woodstock Art Conference.* August 1947.

Baigell, Matthew. *The American Scene.* New York: Praeger, 1974.

Baigell, Matthew, and Julia Williams, eds. *Artists against War and Fascism: Papers of the First American Artists' Congress.* New Brunswick, N.J.: Rutgers University Press, 1986.

Barrett, Edward W. *The Truth Is Our Weapon.* New York: Funk and Wagnalls, 1953.

Baur, John I. H. *Revolution and Tradition in Modern American Art.* Cambridge, Mass.: Harvard University Press, 1951.

Bazzoni, Romolo. *60 Anni della Biennale di Venezia.* Venice: Lombroso Editore, 1962.

Bell, Daniel. *The End of Ideology: On the Exhaustion of Political Ideas in the Fifties.* New York: Collier, 1961.

Benson, Leonard G. *National Purpose: Ideology and Ambivalence in America.* Washington, D.C.: Public Affairs Press, 1963.

Bentivoglio, Mirella. *Ben Shahn.* Rome: de Luca Editore, 1963.

Berman, Greta, and Jeffrey Wechsler. *Realism and Realities: The Other Side of American Painting, 1940–1960.* New Brunswick, N.J.: Rutgers University Art Gallery, 1981.

Bernstein, Barton J., ed. *Politics and Policies of the Truman Administration.* Chicago: Quadrangle Books, 1972.

————. *Towards a New Past: Dissenting Essays in American History.* New York: Vintage, 1968.

Bryson Shahn, Bernarda. *Ben Shahn.* New York: H. N. Abrams, 1972.

Burnham, James, ed. *What Europe Thinks of America.* New York: John Day Co., 1953.

Caldwell, William S. "The Organization and Operation of American Information and Propaganda Activities in Early Postwar Italy." Ph.D. dissertation, University of Minnesota, 1960.

Carlisle, John Charles. "A Biographical Study of How the Artist Became a Humanitarian Activist: Ben Shahn, 1938–1946." Ph.D. dissertation, University of Michigan, 1972.

Caute, David. *The Great Fear: The Anti-Communist Purge under Truman and Eisenhower.* New York: Simon and Schuster, 1978.

Contreras, Belisario R. *Tradition and Innovation in New Deal Art.* Lewisburg, Pa.: Bucknell University Press, 1983.

Cook, Blanche Wiesen. *The Declassified Eisenhower: A Divided Legacy of Peace and Political Warfare.* New York: Doubleday, 1981.

Craig, Lois A., and the staff of the Federal Architecture Project. *The Federal Presence: Architecture, Politics, and National Design.* Cambridge, Mass., and London: MIT Press, 1984.

Dallek, Robert. *Franklin D. Roosevelt and American Foreign Policy, 1932–1945.* Oxford: Oxford University Press, 1979.

Egbert, Donald Drew. *Socialism and American Art: In the Light of European Utopianism, Marxism, and Anarchism.* Rev. and exp. ed. Princeton: Princeton University Press, 1967. [1st ed., 1952.]

Elson, Robert T. *Time Inc.: The Intimate History of a Publishing Enterprise, 1923–1941.* New York: Atheneum, 1968.

———. *The World of Time Inc.: The Intimate History of a Publishing Enterprise, Volume Two, 1941–1960.* New York: Atheneum, 1973.

Feingold, Henry L. *The Politics of Rescue: The Roosevelt Administration and the Holocaust.* New Brunswick, N.J.: Rutgers University Press, 1970.

Fox, Cindy Judy. "The Exchange of Easel and Plastic Arts: Soviet-American Cultural Relations, 1945–1976." Ph.D. dissertation, Fletcher School of Law and Diplomacy, 1977.

Freeland, Richard M. *The Truman Doctrine and the Origins of McCarthyism.* New York: Schocken Books, 1974.

Gaer, Joseph. *The First Round: The Story of the CIO Political Action Committee.* New York: Duell, Sloan and Pearce, 1944.

Galantiere, Lewis, ed. *America and the Mind of Europe.* London: Hamish Hamilton, 1951.

Golden, Cipe Pineles, Kurt Weihs, and Robert Strunsky, eds. *The Visual Craft of William Golden.* New York: Braziller, 1962.

Goldman, Eric F. *The Crucial Decade—and After: America, 1945–1960.* New York: Vintage Books, Random House, 1960.

Greenberg, Clement. *Art and Culture: Critical Essays.* Boston: Beacon Press, 1961.

Griffith, Robert, and Athan Theoharis, eds. *The Spectre: Original Essays on the Cold War and the Origins of McCarthyism.* New York: New Viewpoints, 1974.

Grinrod, Muriel. *The Rebuilding of Italy: Politics and Economics, 1945–1955.* London: Royal Institute of International Affairs, 1955.

Guilbaut, Serge. *How New York Stole the Idea of Modern Art.* Translated by Arthur Goldhammer. Chicago: University of Chicago Press, 1983.

Harvard University, Center for International Affairs. *United States Foreign Policy: Ideology and Foreign Affairs.* Washington, D.C.: U.S. Government Printing Office, 1960.

Hills, Patricia. *Social Concern and Urban Realism: American Painting of the 1930s*. With an essay by Raphael Soyer. Boston: Boston University Art Gallery, 1983.

Hirshhorn Museum and Sculpture Garden, Washington, D.C. *The Golden Door: Artist-Immigrants of America, 1876–1976*. May 20–October 20, 1976. Text by Cynthia Jaffee McCabe. Introduction by Daniel J. Boorstin.

Horowitz, David, ed. *Corporations and the Cold War*. New York: Monthly Review Press, 1969.

Howe, Irving. *World of Our Fathers*. New York: Harcourt Brace Jovanovich, 1976.

Hughes, H. Stuart. *The United States and Italy*. Cambridge, Mass.: Harvard University Press, 1953. Rev. ed., 1965.

Institute of Contemporary Art, Boston. *Ben Shahn: A Documentary Exhibition*. April 10–May 31, 1956.

———. *Dissent: The Issue of Modern Art in Boston*. December 5, 1985–February 9, 1986.

Isserman, Maurice. *Which Side Were You On? The American Communist Party during the Second World War*. Middletown, Conn.: Wesleyan University Press, 1982.

Jezer, Marty. *The Dark Ages: Life in the United States, 1945–1960.* Boston: South End Press, 1982.

Judd, Denis. *Posters of World War Two*. New York: St. Martin's Press, 1973.

Kampf, Avram. *Jewish Experience in the Art of the Twentieth Century*. South Hadley, Mass.: Bergin and Garvey, 1984.

Kennedy Galleries, New York. *Ben Shahn*. October 12–November 2, 1968.

———. *Ben Shahn*. November 5–November 29, 1969.

———. *Ben Shahn (1898–1969)*. November 6–November 27, 1971.

———. *Ben Shahn Drawings*. February 21–March 17, 1979.

———. *The Drawings of Ben Shahn*. October 1970.

———. *The Drawings of Ben Shahn*. May 14–June 4, 1976.

Kolko, Gabriel. *The Roots of American Foreign Policy*. Boston: Beacon Press, 1969.

Kolko, Joyce and Gabriel. *The Limits of Power: The World and United States Foreign Policy, 1945–1954*. New York: Harper and Row, 1972.

LaFeber, Walter. *America, Russia, and the Cold War, 1945–1980*. 4th ed. New York: John Wiley and Sons, 1980.

Landau, Ellen G. *Artists for Victory: An Exhibition Catalog*. Washington, D.C.: Library of Congress, 1983.

Larson, Gary O. *The Reluctant Patron: The U.S. Government and the Arts, 1943–1965*. Philadelphia: University of Pennsylvania Press, 1983.

Leicester Galleries, London. *Ben Shahn*. June–July, 1964. London: Shenval Press, 1964.

Levy, Julien. *Memoir of an Art Gallery*. New York: G. P. Putnam's Sons, 1977.

Lord, Russell, ed. *Democracy Reborn.* New York: 1944.

Lowe, Joe and Emily, Art Gallery, College of Visual and Performing Arts, Syracuse University, Syracuse, N.Y. *The Mural Art of Ben Shahn.* September 28–October 30, 1977.

Lynes, Russell. *Confessions of a Dilettante.* New York: Harper and Row, 1966.

———. *Good Old Modern: An Intimate Portrait of the Museum of Modern Art.* New York: Atheneum, 1973.

McAuliffe, Mary. *Crisis on the Left.* Amherst: University of Massachusetts Press, 1978.

Macdonald, Dwight. *Henry Wallace: The Man and the Myth.* New York: Vanguard Press, 1948.

McKinzie, Richard D. *The New Deal for Artists.* Princeton: Princeton University Press, 1973.

Markowitz, Norman D. *The Rise and Fall of the People's Century: Henry A. Wallace and American Liberalism, 1941–1948.* New York: Free Press, 1973.

Marling, Karal Ann. *Wall to Wall America: A Cultural History of Post Office Murals in the Great Depression.* Philadelphia: Temple University Press, 1984.

Martin, John Bartlow. *Adlai Stevenson.* New York: Harper and Bros., 1952.

Miller, Dorothy C., and Alfred H. Barr, Jr., eds. *American Realists and Magic Realists.* New York: Arno Museum Press for the Museum of Modern Art, 1969. [1st ed., 1943.]

Miller, Douglas T., and Marion Nowak. *The Fifties: The Way We Really Were.* Garden City, N.Y.: Doubleday and Co., 1977.

Montgomery Museum of Fine Arts. *Advancing American Art: Politics and Aesthetics in the State Department Exhibition, 1946–48.* January 10–March 4, 1984. Essays by Margaret Lynne Ausfeld and Virginia M. Mecklenburg.

Morse, John D., ed. *Ben Shahn.* New York: Praeger, 1972.

Muller, Herbert J. *Adlai Stevenson: A Study in Values.* New York: Harper and Row, 1967.

Museum of Modern Art, New York. *2 Pittori: de Kooning, Shahn; 3 Scultori: Lachaise, Lassaw, Smith: Espozicione organizzatta dal Museum of Modern Art, New York.* 27th Venice Biennale, June 19–October 17, 1954. New York: Marchbanks Press for the Museum of Modern Art, 1954.

National Museum of American Art, Washington, D.C. *Art, Design, and the Modern Corporation.* October 24, 1985–January 19, 1986. Essay by Neil Harris.

National Museum of Modern Art, Tokyo. *Ben Shahn.* May 21–July 5, 1970.

Navasky, Victor. *Naming Names.* Harmondsworth, England: Penguin Books, 1980.

New Jersey State Museum, Trenton. *Ben Shahn: A Retrospective Exhibition.* September 20–November 16, 1969.

O'Connor, Francis V., ed. *The New Deal Art Projects: An Anthology of Memoirs.* Washington, D.C.: Smithsonian Institution, 1972.

Park, Marlene, and Gerald E. Markowitz. *Democratic Vistas: Post Offices and Public Art in the New Deal.* Philadelphia: Temple University Press, 1984.

Paterson, Thomas G., ed. *Cold War Critics: Alternatives to American Foreign Policy in the Truman Years.* Chicago: Quadrangle Books, 1971.

Pearson, Ralph. *Modern Renaissance in American Art.* Freeport, N.Y.: Books for Libraries Press, 1968. [1st ed., 1954.]

Philadelphia Museum of Art. *The Collected Prints of Ben Shahn.* 1967.

Pratt, Davis, ed. *The Photographic Eye of Ben Shahn.* Cambridge, Mass., and London: Harvard University Press, 1975.

Prescott, Kenneth. *The Complete Graphic Works of Ben Shahn.* New York: Quadrangle/New York Times Book Co., 1973.

————. *Prints and Posters of Ben Shahn.* New York: Dover, 1982.

Presidency of the Council of Ministers, Rome. *Ten Years of Italian Democracy, 1946–1956.* Rome: Apollon, 1957.

Rieselbach, LeRoy N. *The Roots of Isolationism: Congressional Voting and Presidential Leadership in Foreign Policy.* Indianapolis: Bobbs-Merrill, 1966.

Rischin, Moses. *The Promised City: New York's Jews, 1870–1914.* New York: Corinth, 1964.

Rodman, Selden. *The Eye of Man.* New York: Devin-Adair, 1955.

————. *Portrait of the Artist as an American, Ben Shahn: A Biography with Pictures.* New York: Harper and Bros., 1951.

————, ed. *Conversations with Artists.* New York: Devin-Adair, 1957.

Rose, Barbara. *Readings in American Art since 1900.* New York: Praeger, 1967.

Rosskam, Edwin. *Roosevelt, New Jersey: Big Dreams in a Small Town and What Time Did to Them.* New York: Grossman, 1972.

Rovere, Richard H. *Senator Joe McCarthy.* New York: Harper Colophon Books, Harper and Row, 1973. [1st ed., 1959.]

Rubin, Ronald I. *The Objectives of the U.S. Information Agency: Controversies and Analysis.* New York: Praeger, 1966.

Santa Barbara Museum of Art. *Ben Shahn: Paintings and Graphics.* July 30–September 10, 1967.

Santa Fe East Gallery. *Ben Shahn: Voices and Visions.* September 18–October 31, 1981.

Schlesinger, Arthur M., Jr. *The Vital Center.* Boston: Houghton Mifflin, 1962. [1st ed., 1949.]

Schwartz, Barry. *The New Humanism: Art in a Time of Change.* New York: Praeger, 1974.

Sekula, Allan. *Photography against the Grain: Essays and Photo Works, 1973–1983.* Halifax: Press of the Nova Scotia School of Art and Design, 1984.

Shahn, Ben. *Ben Shahn: La Forma e il Contenuto.* Prefazione di Antonio del Guercio. Rome: Editori Riuniti, 1964.

———. *The Biography of a Painting*. Cambridge, Mass.: Fogg Art Museum, 1956. New York: Paragraphic Press, 1966.

———. *Love and Joy about Letters*. London: Cory, Adams and Mackay, 1964.

———. *Paragraphs on Art*. New York: Spiral Press, 1952.

———. *The Shape of Content*. 7th printing. Cambridge, Mass.: Harvard University Press, 1976. [1st ed., 1957.]

Shapiro, David, ed. *Social Realism: Art as a Weapon*. New York: Frederick Ungar, 1973.

Soby, James Thrall. *Ben Shahn*. West Drayton, Middlesex: Penguin Books, 1947.

———. *Ben Shahn: Graphics*. New York: Braziller, 1963 [1st ed., 1957.]

———. *Ben Shahn: Paintings*. New York: Braziller, 1963.

Starobin, Joseph R. *American Communism in Crisis, 1943–1957*. Cambridge, Mass.: Harvard University Press, 1972.

Stevenson, Adlai E. *What I Think*. New York: Harper and Bros., 1956.

Stott, William. *Documentary Expression and Thirties America*. London: Oxford University Press, 1973.

Summers, Robert E., ed. *America's Weapons of Psychological Warfare*. New York, 1951.

Taft, Philip. *Organized Labor in American History*. New York: Harper and Row, 1964.

Thomson, Charles A., and Walter H. C. Laves. *Cultural Relations and U.S. Foreign Policy*. Bloomington: Indiana University Press, 1963.

Tucker, Robert W. *The Radical Left and American Foreign Policy*. Baltimore: Johns Hopkins Press, 1971.

U.S. Information Agency (USIA). *Review of Operations*, First (August–December 1953).

———. *Review of Operations*, Second (January–June 1954).

———. *Review of Operations*, Third (July–December 1954).

———. *13th Report to Congress* (July 1–December 31, 1959).

Vassar College Art Gallery, Poughkeepsie. *Woodstock: An American Art Colony, 1902–1977*. January 23–March 4, 1977. Introduction by Karal Ann Marling.

Venice Biennale d'Arte. *La Biennale di Venezia*. 27th Biennale catalogue. June 19–October 17, 1954.

Von Blum, Paul. *The Art of Social Conscience*. New York: Universe Books, 1976.

———. *The Critical Vision: A History of Social and Political Art in the U.S.* Boston: South End Press, 1982.

Weeks, Robert Percy, ed. *Commonwealth vs. Sacco and Vanzetti*. Englewood Cliffs, N.J.: Prentice-Hall, 1958.

Weiss, Margaret R., ed. *Ben Shahn, Photographer: An Album from the Thirties*. New York: Da Capo Press, 1973.

Williams, Raymond. *Culture and Society, 1780–1950*. Harmondsworth, England: Pelican Book, Penguin, 1976. [1st ed., 1958.]

Zinn, Howard. *The Twentieth Century: A People's History.* New York: Harper Colophon, Harper and Row, 1984.

Articles

Abell, Walter. "Art and Labor." *Magazine of Art* 39(October 1946):231+.

———. "Industry and Painting." *Magazine of Art* 39(March 1946):82–93+.

"Aftermath of War: A Portfolio of Paintings by Ben Shahn." *Fortune* 32(December 1945):169–172.

Alper, M. Victor. "American Mythologies in Painting, Part 2: City Life and Social Idealism." *Arts Magazine* 46(December 1971/January 1972):31–34.

"Angry Eye." *Time,* October 13, 1947, p. 63.

Appel, Benjamin. "Ben Shahn, Prophet with a Brush." *New Letters* 40(March 1974):5–22.

"Are These Men the Best Painters in America Today?" *Look,* February 3, 1948, pp. 44–48.

"Artist Paints for 'Causes,' Eschewing Commercial Work." *Newark Sunday Call,* January 14, 1945.

Ashton, Dore. "Avantgardia: Reflections from Rome on the Avant-garde Movements in Italy and America during the Last Decade." *Arts Digest* 29(March 15, 1955):16–17, 34.

"Baffling Ben." *Time,* November 5, 1951, p. 82.

Barr, Alfred H., Jr. "Gli Stati Uniti alla Biennale: Shahn e de Kooning, Lachaise, Lassaw e Smith." *Biennale di Venezia,* no. 19–20(April–June 1954):62–67.

———. "Is Modern Art Communistic?" *New York Times Magazine,* December 14, 1952, pp. 22+.

———. Letter to the Editor. *College Art Journal* 15(Spring 1956):184–188.

"Ben Shahn." *Life,* October 4, 1954, pp. 96–98.

"Ben Shahn." *Look,* July 18, 1950, p. 68.

"Ben Shahn (1898–1969), Artist of the Exalted and the Common." *Connoisseur* 174(August 1970):310.

"Ben Shahn: Painter of Protest Turns to Reflection." *Life,* October 4, 1954, pp. 96–100.

Benton, James. "The Idea Is First." *Art Digest* 26(December 1, 1951):22.

Berger, John. "Renato Guttuso." *Apollo* 61(March 1955):70.

———. "A Social Realist Painting at the Biennale." *Burlington Magazine* 94 (October 1952):294–297.

"Biddle on Modern Art." *American Artist* 12 (January 1948):47.

"Bikini." *Fortune* 33(December 1946):158.

Bird, Paul. "The Editor's View." *Art Digest* 25(December 1, 1950):5.

"Boston Goes from 'Modern' to 'Contemporary.'" *College Art Journal* 7(Spring 1948):230.

Braden, Thomas W. "I'm Glad the C.I.A. Is Immoral." *Saturday Evening Post,* May 20, 1967, pp. 10+.

Bratt, L. J. P. "A la Biennale de Venise, trois points d'appui." *Arts Plastiques*, special no. (1954):39–46.

Brown, Milton. "The Forces behind Modern U.S. Painting." *Art News* 46(August 1947):16–17, 34–35.

Bryson, Bernarda. "The Drawings of Ben Shahn." *Image*, no. 2(Autumn 1949):31–50.

Calvesi, Maurizio. "Ben Shahn." In *Ben Shahn*, March 31–April 29, 1962, p. 11. Rome: National Gallery of Modern Art.

Castelfranco, G. "La XXVII Biennale." *Bollettino d'Arte* 39(October–December 1954):347–359.

Castle, Eugene W. "Danger Ahead! More Cultural Exchange!" *American Mercury* 89(November 1959):28, 40–42.

Chamberlain, Betty. "Ben Shahn." *Art News* 46(October 1947):41, 54–55.

Chanin, A. L. "Shahn, Sandburg of the Painters." *Sunday Compass*, October 30, 1949, p. 14.

Coates, Robert M. "The Art Galleries: Contemporary Americans." *New Yorker*, October 11, 1947, pp. 62–63.

Cockcroft, Eva. "Abstract Expressionism, Weapon of the Cold War." *Artforum* 12(June 1974):39–41.

"Contemporary Documents: Modern Art—1950." *College Art Journal* 9(Spring 1950):339.

Cooper, D. "Reflections on the Venice Biennale." *Burlington Magazine* 96(October 1954):312–322.

Corwin, Charles. "Ben Shahn's Rewarding Exhibit at Downtown Gallery." *Daily Worker*, November 4, 1949, p. 12.

Degand, Leon. "La Biennale de Venise." *Art d'Aujourd'hui* 5(September 1954):23–25, 65.

de Hart Mathews, Jane. "Art and Politics in Cold War America." *American Historical Review* 81(October 1976):762–787.

del Guercio, Antonio. "Ben Shahn a Roma—America senza belletto." *Vie Nuove* (Rome), April 12, 1962, pp. 32–34.

Denvir, Bernard. "Mayfair to Manhattan." *Artist* 48(November 1954):35.

D'Harnoncourt, René. "Challenge and Promise: Modern Art and Modern Society." *Magazine of Art* 41(November 1948):251–252.

Dondero, George. "Communism in the Heart of American Art—What to Do about It." U.S. *Congressional Record*, 81st Congress, 1st Session, May 17, 1949, pp. 6372–6375.

———. "Communist Art in Government Hospitals." U.S. *Congressional Record*, 81st Congress, 1st Session, March 11, 1949, pp. 2317–2318.

———. "Communists Maneuver to Control Art in the United States." U.S. *Congressional Record*, 81st Congress, 1st Session, March 25, 1949, pp. 3233–3235.

———. "Is Harper's Magazine Biased?" U.S. *Congressional Record—Appendix*, 81st Congress, 1st Session, October 13, 1949, pp. A6305–A6306.

————. "Modern Art Shackled to Communism." U.S. *Congressional Record*, 81st Congress, 1st Session, August 16, 1948, pp. 11584–11587.

F., J. "Ben Shahn." *Art Digest* 26(April 1, 1952):20.

"Five Americans for Biennale." *Arts Digest* 28(April 15, 1954):33.

Flexner, James T. "Behind the Picture Is the Man." *New York Times Book Review*, October 21, 1951, p. 1.

Frankfurter, Alfred M. "American Art Abroad: The State Department's Collection." *Art News* 45(October 1946):20–31.

————. "European Speculation: Modern Art and Marco Polo." *Art News* 53(September 1954):18–23+.

————. "Vernissage." *Art News* 46(May 1947):13.

————. "Vernissage: Abstract Red Herring." *Art News* 48(Summer 1949):15.

————. "Vernissage: Freedom to Paint." *Art News* 50(December 1951):17.

————. "Vernissage: Is There a Gentleman in the House?" *Art News* 48(September 1949):13.

————. "Vernissage—The Year's Best: 1949." *Art News* 48(January 1950):13, 50.

————. "The Year's Best: 1947." *Art News* 46(January 1948):36–37.

Freed, Eleanor. "Artist with a Conscience." *Spotlight* (*Houston Post* Sunday magazine), November 15, 1970, pp. 14, 32.

"FSA Ignored in Plea for Removal of Social Security Building Art." *Evening Star* (Washington), June 27, 1947, Sec. I, p. 1.

Fuller, Helen. "Dewey's Brisk Young Men Move In." *New Republic*, July 5, 1948, pp. 15–18.

"Gallery on Wheels." *Art Digest* 23(January 15, 1949):16.

Genauer, Emily. "Shahn's Bitterness Leavened with Wit." *Art Digest* 24(November 1, 1949):12.

————. "Still Life with Red Herring." *Harper's* 199(September 1949):88–91.

Gillmor, Daniel S. "Guilt by Gossip." *New Republic*, May 31, 1948, pp. 15–27.

Glass, Douglas. "Portrait Gallery: Ben Shahn." *Sunday Times* (London), February 5, 1956.

Glass, Fred. "Ben Shahn in the Age of Abstract Expressionism." *Socialist Review* 17 (March/April 1987):82–111.

Grafly, Dorothy. "What Sells? The Artist's Number One Question." *American Artists* 12(January 1948):26, 44–45.

Greenberg, Clement. "Art." *Nation*, March 8, 1947, p. 284.

————. "Art." *Nation*, November 1, 1947, pp. 481–482.

————. "Art Chronicle: Our Period Style." *Partisan Review* 15(November 1949):1138.

————. "Avant-Garde and Kitsch." *Partisan Review* 6, no. 5(1939):34–49.

————. "The European View of American Art." *Nation*, November 25, 1950, p. 490.

————. "The Present Prospects of American Painting and Sculpture." *Horizon* 16(October 1947):20–30.

——. "The Situation at the Moment." *Partisan Review* 5(January 1948): 81–84.

——. "Symposium: The State of American Art." *Magazine of Art* 42(March 1949):92.

Greene, Balcomb. "Balcomb Greene." *Magazine of Art* 42(November 1949): 267–269.

Guilbaut, Serge. "Creation et développement d'une avant-garde: New York, 1946–1951." *Histoire et Critique des Arts*, July 1978, pp. 29–48.

Gutman, Walter. "The Passion of Sacco-Vanzetti." *Nation*, April 20, 1932, p. 475.

Harris, Jonathan. "State Power and Cultural Discourse: Federal Art Project Murals in New Deal USA." *Block* 13(Winter 1987/1988):28–42.

"Harry T. Moore." *Nation*, September 27, 1952, p. 267.

Hauptman, William. "The Suppression of Art in the McCarthy Decade." *Artforum* 12(October 1973):48–52.

Hess, Thomas B. "Ben Shahn Paints a Picture." *Art News* 48(May 1949): 20–22, 55–56.

——. "Ben Shahn's." *Art News* 51(April 1952):45.

——. "Is Abstraction Un-American?" *Art News* 20(February 1951):38–41.

——. "Reviews and Previews: Ben Shahn." *Art News* 48(November 1949):44.

Hodin, J. P. "Venice Biennale." *Contemporary Review* 186(October 1954): 227–230.

Hubbard, R. H. "Show Window of the Arts—XXVII Venice Biennale." *Canadian Art* 12 (Autumn 1954):14–20.

Hunt, George P. "Honorable Discharge." *Fortune* 34(September 1947): 69–77+.

"Interview: Ben Shahn Talks with Forrest Selvig." *Archives of American Art Journal* 17, no. 3(1977):14–21.

"It's Striking, But Is It Art or Extravaganza?" *Newsweek*, August 25, 1947.

"Jackson Pollock." *Life*, August 8, 1949, pp. 42–43, 45.

Javits, Jacob K. "Modern Art—A Reply to a Colleague." U.S. *Congressional Record*, 81st Congress, 1st Session, August 23, 1949, p. 12099.

"Jews' Struggle Shown in Mural at Homesteads." *New York Herald Tribune*, May 22, 1938, Sec. II, p. 3.

Joughin, Louis. "25 Years since Sacco and Vanzetti." *Nation*, August 23, 1952, p. 152.

Keller, Heinz. "XXVII biennale." *Werk* 41(August 1954):sup. 189–191.

Kemler, Edgar. "Will Joe Bolt the G.O.P.? Ike Would Be Delighted." *Nation*, May 15, 1954, pp. 419–421.

Kern, W. "Anmerkungen zur XXVII Biennale in Venedig." *Werk* 41(August 1954):335–340.

Kirstein, Lincoln. "The State of Modern Painting." *Harper's* 197(October 1948):47–53.

Kozloff, Max. "American Painting during the Cold War." *Artforum* 11(May 1973):43–54.

Kramer, Hilton. "Month in Review." *Arts* 33(April 1959):44–45.

———. "Publicizing Social Causes on Canvas." *New York Times*, November 7, 1976, Sec. II, p. 23.

L., A. "Artists Protest." *Art Digest* 21(May 15, 1947):16.

"Labor Drives South." *Fortune* 34(November 1946):134–141+.

"Labor's Cause." *Fortune* 34(November 1946):2–4.

Lapp, Ralph E. "The Voyage of the Lucky Dragon." *Harper's* 215(December 1957):27–36.

Lasch, Christopher. "The Cultural Cold War." *Nation*, September 11, 1967, pp. 198–212.

Leaver, E. W., and J. J. Brown. "Machines without Men." *Fortune* 34(November 1946):165.

Lenson, Michael. "Shahn Is Biennale Winner." *Newark Sunday News*, September 12, 1954, Sec. III, p. E8.

Leonard, Ann. "Around the Galleries: Ben Shahn, a People's Artist." *People's World*, December 1, 1948.

"Letter to Museum of Modern Art." *Reality* 1(Spring 1953):2.

Leyda, Jay. "Artist's Biography in His Own Terms." *New York Herald Tribune Book Review*, December 23, 1951, p. 3.

Lieberman, Robbie. "People's Songs: American Communism and the Politics of Culture." *Radical History Review*, no. 36(September 1986):63–78.

"A *Life* Round Table on Modern Art." *Life*, October 11, 1948, pp. 56–68+.

Longhi, Roberto. "Grossi premi e grosse sorprese." *L'Europeo* (Milan), July 4, 1954.

Lonzi, Carla, and Marisa Volpi. "Ben Shahn." *Paragone* 69(September 1955): 38–61.

Loucheim, Aline B. "Ben Shahn Illuminates." *New York Times*, August 30, 1953, p. 8.

Luce, Henry. "The American Century." *Life*, February 17, 1941, pp. 61–63.

McCarthy, Eugene J. "Modern Art." U.S. *Congressional Record*, 81st Congress, 1st Session, August 18, 1949, p. 11750.

McWilliams, Carey. "The White House under Surveillance." *Nation*, February 16, 1952, pp. 150–152.

Martin, John Bartlow. "The Blast in Centralia No. 5." *Harper's* 196(March 1948):193–220.

———. "The Hickman Story." *Harper's* 197(August 1948):39–52.

Martin, Ralph G. "The CIO Takes a Long Lease in the South." *New Republic* 116(January 13, 1947):19–21.

Martini, Alberto. "Ben Shahn." *Paragone* 5(September 1954):61–64.

Melville, R. "The Venice Biennale." *Listener* 52(July 29, 1954):180.

Moe, Ole Henrik. "Ben Shahn." *Kunsten Idag* 35, no. 1(1956):30–52; English translation, pp. 56–58.

Monroe, Gerald. "The American Artists' Congress and the Invasion of Finland." *Archives of American Art Journal* 15(1975): 14–20.

Morse, John D. "Ben Shahn: An Interview." *Magazine of Art* 37(April 1944): 136–141.

———. "Henri Cartier-Bresson." *Magazine of Art* 40(May 1947): 189+.

"New Deal Defeatism." *New York Daily Mirror*, October 16, 1944, p. 17.

"Painters Show Woeful Side of Soviet Life." *Life*, May 16, 1955, pp. 147–148.

Paoli, Gian Paolo. "Ben Shahn in Cantina." *Il Contemporaneo* (Rome), September 25, 1954, p. 1.

"Party-Line Painter." *Time*, November 30, 1953, p. 74.

Pearson, Ralph. "A Modern Viewpoint: Ben Shahn at the Modern." *Art Digest* 22(December 1, 1947): 36.

———. "A Modern Viewpoint: State Department Requests." *Art Digest* 22(October 1, 1947): 32.

"Photos for Art." *U.S. Camera*, May 1946, pp. 30–32, 57.

Plumley, Charles A. "Extension of Remarks of Hon. Charles A. Plumley of Vermont." U.S. *Congressional Record*, 81st Congress, 1st Session, pp. A3980–A3982.

Podesta, Attilio. "Italiani e Stranieri all XXVII Biennale." *Emporium* 120 (1954): 113–129.

Pohl, Frances K. "An American in Venice: Ben Shahn and United States Foreign Policy at the 1954 Venice Biennale, or Portrait of the Artist as an American Liberal." *Art History* 4(March 1981): 80–113.

———. "Ben Shahn and *Fortune* Magazine: Representations of Labor in 1946." *Labor's Heritage* 1(January 1989): 46–55.

———. "Constructing History: A Mural by Ben Shahn." *Arts Magazine* 62(September 1987): 36–40.

Pohl, Frances K., and Stephen Lee Taller. "The Cover (*Triple Dip*)." *Journal of the American Medical Association*, July 24–31, p. 420.

Poma, Maria. "La XXVII Biennale sul 'leit motiv' del surrealism e dell-astrattismo." *L'Ora* (Palermo), June 24, 1954.

Ponti, Lisa Licitra. "Ben Shahn a Venezia." *Domus*, no. 298(September 1954): 36–37.

———. "Pittura alla Biennale." *Domus*, no. 298 (September 1954): 28–35.

Poor, Henry Varnum. "How This Group Began." *Reality* 1(Spring 1953): 6.

"A Premier Goes Skiing—Italy's Pella Quits in the Climax of a Crisis Months in the Making." *Life*, January 18, 1954, p. 38.

"The Promise of the Shortage." *Fortune* 33(April 1946): 101–103.

Ragghianti, Carlo. "Lettura Aperta." *Sele Arte*, no. 1(January/February 1953): 42–43.

Reed, Judith Kaye. "New Artists Honored, Abstraction Crowned at Whitney Annual." *Art Digest* 24(January 1, 1950): 7.

Robb, Marilyn. "Chicago." *Art News* 46(January 1948): 39.

Robbins, Carolyn C. "Ben Shahn's *Mine Building*: A Symbol of Disaster."

Forthcoming in *Phoebus V: A Journal of Art History* (Arizona State University).

Rodman, Selden. "Ben Shahn." *Portfolio*, 1951, pp. 6–21.

———. "Ben Shahn: Painter of America." *Perspectives, USA* 1(Fall 1952): 87–96.

———. "Ben Shahn Speaking." *Perspectives, USA*, pilot issue, January 1952, pp. 59–72.

Rosenberg, Harold. "The American Action Painters." *Art News* 51(September 1952):22–23+.

Saarinen, Aline B. "USSR vs Abstract—A Leading Soviet Cultural Organ Attacks International Moderns." *New York Times*, August 22, 1954, Sec. II, p. 8.

Salisbury, Harrison E. "Russia's Art Reflects Trends in Russia." *New York Times Magazine*, September 12, 1954, pp. 8–9.

Schlesinger, Arthur M. "Not Left, Not Right, but a Vital Center." *New York Times Magazine*, April 4, 1948, pp. 7, 44–47.

Seeley, Carol. "On the Nature of Abstract Painting in America." *Magazine of Art* 43(May 1950):163–168.

Seuphor, Michel. "Paris, New-York 1951." *Art d'Aujourd'hui* 2(June 1951): 4–14.

Shahn, Ben. "L'artista e il politicismo." *Sele Arte*, no. 9(November/December 1953):25–29.

———. "The Artist and the Politicians." *Art News* 52(September 1953): 34–35, 67.

———. "An Artist's Credo." *College Art Journal* 9(Fall 1949):43–45.

———. "Ben Shahn." *Magazine of Art* 42(November 1949):266, 269.

———. "From 'Paragraphs on Art.'" *Reality* 1(Spring 1953):6.

———. "The Future of the Creative Arts." *University of Buffalo Studies* 19(February 1952):125–128.

———. "Just What Is Realism?" *Art Education* 3(December 1950):2–4.

———. "Nonconformity." *Amerika*, no. 33(May 1959):16–21.

———. "What Is Realism in Art?" *Look*, January 13, 1953, pp. 44–45.

"Shahn Best of 375." *Art Digest* 15 (November 15, 1940):8.

Shapiro, David and Cecile. "Abstract Expressionism: The Politics of Apolitical Painting." *Prospects* 3(1976):175–214.

Soby, James Thrall. "Ben Shahn." *Graphis* 4, no. 22 (1948):102–107.

———. "Ben Shahn and Morris Graves." *Horizon* 16(October 1947):48–57.

———. "Does Our Art Impress Europe?" *Saturday Review* 32(August 1949): 142–149.

———. "A Going in the Mulberry Trees." *Saturday Review*, July 2, 1949, pp. 30–31.

Spaeth, Eloise. "America's Cultural Responsibilities Abroad." *College Art Journal* 11(Winter 1951–1952):115–120.

———. "Synthesis of Arts in America: 20 Contemporaries." *Hindustan Times Art Supplement*, May 6, 1953.

Spender, Stephen. "We Can Win the Battle for the Minds of Europe." *New York Times Magazine*, April 25, 1948, pp. 15+.

"*Spring* by Ben Shahn." *Gallery Notes* (Buffalo) 12(Spring 1948):26.

Sylvester, David. "Mr. Sylvester Replies." *Nation*, November 25, 1950, pp. 492–493.

"A Symposium on How to Combine Architecture, Painting and Sculpture." *Interiors* 110(May 1951):100–105.

Tagg, John. "American Power and American Painting: The Development of Vanguard Painting in the United States since 1945." *Praxis*, 1976, pp. 59–79.

Taller, Stephen Lee. "The Poster Art of Ben Shahn." *Journal of the Poster Society*, Spring 1987, pp. 9–12.

Taubes, F. "What Is the World Painting Today?" *American Artist* 19(February 1955):34+.

"Tumult in Los Angeles." *Time*, November 5, 1951, p. 82.

"Under the Four Winds." *Time*, June 28, 1954, pp. 74–77.

U.S. Congress. House Committee on Un-American Activities. "The American National Exhibition, Moscow, July 1959 (The Record of Certain Artists and an Appraisal of Their Works Selected for Display)," 86th Congress, 1st Session, July 1, 1959, pp. 941–963.

U.S. Department of State. "United States and Soviet Union to Exchange National Exhibits." *Department of State Bulletin*, October 13, 1958, p. 577.

Vallier, Dora. "La XXVIIe Biennale de Venise." *Cahiers d'Art* 29, no. 1(1954): 109–115.

"XXVIIa Biennale di Venezia." *Sele Arte* 12 (May–June 1954):6–62.

Vishny, Michele. "Ben Shahn, Philip Guston, and Seymour Fogel for the Social Security Building, Washington, D.C." *Arts Magazine* 61(March 1987):40–43.

Vorse, Mary Heaton. "The Pirates' Nest of New York." *Harper's* 204(April 1952):27–37.

Wallace, Henry A. "The Progressive Party Is Here to Stay." *Uncensored*, no. 3(September 1948):1–2.

"Wallace Party Heads Gathering for Meet." *St. Paul Sunday Pioneer Press*, July 18, 1948, p. 17.

"We Are for Wallace." *New York Times*, October 20, 1948, p. 32.

Weinberg, Sydney. "What to Tell America: The Writers' Quarrel in the Office of War Information." *Journal of American History* 55(June 1968):73–89.

Werckmeister, O. K. "Ben Shahn's Political Realism." *Neu Rundschau* 77, no. 3(1966):476–487.

Werner, Alfred. "Ben Shahn: The Artist as Social Critic." *American Artist* 39(December 1975):48–53+.

———. "A Biography of Ben Shahn." *Congress Weekly*, January 14, 1952, pp. 14, 16.

———. "Ghetto Graduates." *American Art Journal* 5(November 1973): 71–82.

Westin, Alan F. "Our Freedom—and the Rights of Communists: A Reply to Irving Kristol." *Commentary* 14(July 1952):33–40.

"What Are You Doing Out There?" *New York Times*, January 15, 1951, p. 9.

Woolfenden, William E. "A Composition by Ben Shahn." *Detroit Institute of Arts Bulletin* 32(1952–1953):20–21.

"Your Money Bought These Paintings." *Look*, February 18, 1947, pp. 80–81.

Films

Kroehling, Richard, and Laura Nathanson. *Roosevelt, New Jersey: Visions of Utopia.* c. 1985.

Weldon, Huw, and Humphrey Burton. *Ben Shahn's America.* Monitor Film. British Broadcasting Corporation, 1962.

Interviews by Author

Bryson Shahn, Bernarda. Roosevelt, N.J., May 20, 1984; June 2, 1984.

Casetta, Mario. Los Angeles, Calif., July 25, 1986.

Miller, Dorothy C. New York, N.Y., June 5, 1984.

Shahn, Jonathan. Roosevelt, N.J., May 19, 1984.

Soyer, Raphael. New York, N.Y., June 7, 1984.

INDEX

(*Works of art by Ben Shahn are indexed by title; works by other artists are indexed under the artists' names.*)

Grateful acknowledgment is made to the following for permission to use archival and previously published materials:

Bernarda Bryson Shahn for excerpts from materials in the Ben Shahn Papers.

Archives of American Art, Smithsonian Institution, for references to and quotes from materials in the Ben Shahn Papers and the Alfred Barr, Jr., Papers, and for references to materials in the Edward Biberman Papers, the Elizabeth McCausland Papers, and the Philip Evergood Papers.

Museum of Modern Art, New York, for references to items in the James Thrall Soby Papers.

Routledge and Kegan Paul and Basil Blackwell for material from "An American in Venice: Ben Shahn and United States Foreign Policy at the 1954 Venice Biennale," originally published in *Art History* 4, no. 1(March 1981)80–113.

Arts Magazine for material from "Constructing History: A Mural by Ben Shahn," originally published in *Arts Magazine* 62(September 1987):36–40.

Labor's Heritage for material from "Ben Shahn and *Fortune* Magazine: Representations of Labor in 1946," originally published in *Labor's Heritage* 1, no. 1(January 1989):46–55.

www.ingramcontent.com/pod-product-compliance
Lightning Source LLC
Chambersburg PA
CBHW020742180526
45163CB00001B/311